M A D N ̄ ̄ ̄

JOSSY CHA

Madness is a story of redemption, faith, and obedience that every Christian needs to read. This is the new face of missions in the 21st century and Jossy Chacko's response to the call of God is already having a profound impact in Asia!
Ps Dan, Living Oaks, California, USA

This is one of the most exciting books I have ever reviewed.
It is challenging as it makes us rethink some of our deeply ingrained ways of life – and of evangelism. It's a must!
Dr Clifford, Melbourne, Australia

Having been a missions pastor in the US for nearly 20 years, I have been exposed to many missions movements around the world. What Jossy describes in his book riveted me both to the pages and my daytimer – I am reordering my life purposes. You will too after reading Madness.
Ps Ron, Atascadero, California, USA

Wow, *Madness* is so inspiring, and so utterly challenging!
John, Perth, Australia

Well done. *Madness* is really well written.
I think it is a terrific book that all Christians should read.
Ps Tim, Tasmania, Australia

I really enjoyed reading your book this weekend. It was amazing to hear the complete story in one package. I am excited to be a small part of this amazing church planting movement. I look forward to sharing copies with others.
Steve, California, USA

It is an amazing story of what God can do when we truly trust and follow Him without counting the cost.
John, Mt Macedon, Australia

It is a God-glorifying story.
Ps George, Wantirna, Australia

Madness is such an enticing read that I have managed to finish it in one day.
Thank you for writing the book. Your book helped me to re-focus and make God my number one priority.
Harry, Geneva, Switzerland

M A D N E S S

Revised Leadership Edition 2016

Copyright © 2008 Jossy Chacko

First Published by Empart
PO Box 980, Croydon VIC 3136 Australia
T +61 3 9723 9989 F +61 3 9723 9969
E info@empart.org
www.empart.org
ABN75118565337

ISBN 978-0-9804710-0-7 (Paperback)

Interviewer: Andy Drewitt
Original Editor: Owen Salter
Leadership Edition Editors: Amy Pierson & Jenni Chacko
Cover photography: Nanci Ricks
Printed by: BethanyPress
Cover and Interior Designers: Tim Walker, DOXA

TO MY GRANDFATHER, K.T. CHACKO

His godly wisdom, generous living and model of leadership enriched my world while he lived and continue to shape my life since he moved into eternity.

CONTENTS

ACKNOWLEDGMENTS

I am so grateful to my family for all the memories, both good and not so good. I'm especially grateful to my grandfather, K.T. Chacko, for his incredible commitment, dedication, wisdom and godliness. And Mum, thanks for your remarkable faithfulness to God. You are a shining example to me and so many others.

To my wife, Jenni: without your love and unending support I would not be where I am. You are truly God's gift to me. I'm so thankful that we are able to serve him together.

To my precious kids, Jemimah, Jacob, Jasmine and Joshua: you are my best cheerleaders! You really are a blessing from the Lord.

To John and Sue Sikkema: your generous friendship, wise counsel and ongoing partnership are a huge blessing to my family and me.

To my Empart family—staff, volunteers, church planters and children: without you this story would not be complete. I look forward to writing new chapters in history with you.

To the Empart board members and other friends who encouraged me to write this book, thank you. I am especially grateful to all of you who believe in the vision and faithfully pray, give and encourage us. May the Lord reward you and bless you.

Above all, to my Heavenly Father: thank you for loving, forgiving and calling me to be a servant of Jesus Christ. May this book increase awareness of the unreached people of the world, and bring glory to the God whose desire is that none of them should perish.

PREFACE

Over the years, many friends and even strangers have asked when I will write this story down. After Empart board members finally demanded a deadline, I knew the time had come.

The biggest personal challenge was how to tell a story of such intimate and personal events without making anyone involved look unduly good or bad. If I have not found the right balance in this, I sincerely hope you will understand. Another challenge has been deciding which stories to keep and which ones to omit. If I had kept all the stories, this book could have ended with well over 500 pages!

As I retraced steps and memories, I found some of them hard to relive. Others brought a renewed sense of joy. Some brought tears and yet others brought to mind the journey still to be traveled—the challenges and opportunities that lie ahead.

While my home is in the West, my heart is in love with the Lord and drawn to serving the hidden and unknown national church planters who are reaching the lost and unreached people of the world.

I pray that this special leadership edition, with the leadership lessons and reflection questions, will stir you in your own journey as a leader. God has positioned you where you are today for His purposes. Seek Him daily and constantly keep an eternal perspective. And, no matter where your leadership takes you, please remember the Lord, the least, the lost and unreached people of our world.

As someone who is living and raising my family in the West, I am deeply concerned about the way our culture is squandering the rich heritage and blessings of God. While the church in Asia may not have grand buildings and facilities, what they do have is passion. I am watching an army of grand leaders—most first generation believers—rise up with audacious dreams and visions. I believe it is time for Christian leaders to enlarge their dreams and visions beyond the walls of their churches to their country, peoples and nations.

God does not hold you to your failures, your past, your cultural background or your experiences. He has a plan for you—and it is a good one! Pursue it. Chase it till you find it. Refuse to settle where you are, no matter how young or old you might be. In eternity you will be so glad you did!

— Jossy Chacko

FOREWORD

For almost thirty years I have devoted most of my time and resources to the development of leaders and healthy churches, specifically to leaders of very large churches throughout the United States. Like Bill Hybels, founder and pastor of Willow Creek Community Church, I believe the church offers the greatest hope to the world. The answers to problems of poverty, disease, racial and ethnic conflict, illiteracy, and the like can't be solved by governments alone—Christian leaders and local churches need to step up to the plate in a strategic and significant way. If the latent energy in Christianity can be released into active, dynamic energy, the church will change the world for the better.

For practical reasons, I initially made a deliberate decision to focus my attention on the church in North America. I was somewhat familiar with the issues facing American church leaders, I had developed relationships with some of these leaders, and the challenge of working alongside the largest churches in America seemed daunting enough for my modest efforts. I also knew that these large churches engaged in various global initiatives, so my efforts would indirectly reach into places like Africa, Asia, Europe and beyond.

Through a series of unlikely events, I became aware of one man's vision to transform 100,000 communities in Asia through the planting of local churches. That number got my attention. My great friend and mentor, the late Peter Drucker, always advised me to aim high when it came to investing my time and efforts because of the potential for greater results. Jossy Chacko not only has set a big, hairy, audacious goal for himself, but he's doing it in one of the most difficult regions of the world. Yet despite the crushing poverty and militant hostility to Christianity, Jossy and his growing cadre of brave church planters are well on their way toward his goal.

I have known Jossy for many years; he was involved with his friend John Sikkema in taking and establishing Half Time from the US to Australia. Like me, Jossy comes from a successful business background. His entrepreneurial approach to the church mirrors my own belief that the best way to help a church become healthy and effective is to develop visionary leaders. And we also share the conviction that the church is an extension of Jesus' ministry to the whole person, caring for the physical needs as well as the spiritual.

Traditionally, Christian churches in places like India have looked to the West for guidance as well as resources. While they still may need our generous sharing from our material wealth, they have much to teach us in the West about what it means to be the church. This is precisely what Jossy does in this book. This is an important book that will challenge you to rethink what it means to be a leader and a follower of Jesus in the twenty-first century.

– Bob Buford
   Founder Halftime Institute,
   Leadership Network and author of *Halftime*

◼ INTRODUCTION

Johnson, our driver, hit the horn and yanked the steering wheel sideways. An auto-rickshaw scraped past our van, inches from the lovely new paintwork. Other horns blared around us, mingling with the shouts of street vendors and the roar of trucks. Johnson crunched the gears as he swung the wheel back again.

Driving in an Indian city is not for the faint-hearted. There's always the chance of clipping a rickshaw or being squashed between a bus and a bullock cart. Bicycles clog the roads like flies while dogs, cows and children wander among the traffic.

But that afternoon, not even running the gauntlet of the Indian roads could dampen our excitement. Just the week before, we had taken delivery of our first Compassion For India (Empart as it is known globally) vehicle, a solid, Indian-made Tata van. It had been a heap of second-hand junk when we first saw it, but after three weeks' work by two mechanics, it had been reborn.

For us the cream-colored eight-seater was a sign of how God was blessing our fledgling efforts to start a church planting ministry in North India. Our vision was as big as half a continent, but that day it was concentrated in the great feeling of being in our own vehicle, driving through Chandigarh, capital of the state of Punjab.

In the best tradition of Indian drivers, who festoon everything from trucks to taxis with bright religious decorations, we had painted a big red cross on both sides of the van and on the windscreen and back window as well.

I looked out at the crowds as we drove past. Women in brightly colored saris haggled with stallholders over piles of fruit and vegetables. A bald-headed man shouldered a watermelon the size of an elephant's foot. Sikh men in yellow, red and green turbans strode purposefully past urchins in brown rags. A group of laughing girls in school uniform inched around a rotting heap of garbage.

We were driving through the dazzling human kaleidoscope of India, the land of my birth: an amazing land of over a billion people, forty per cent of whom had never heard the name of Jesus; the land where God had called me to play a part in reaching those who had never heard the gospel of Christ.

I glanced at Johnson as he concentrated hard on the road. When we'd picked up the van, our Christian mechanic had asked if we needed a driver. "I have just the guy," he offered. "My nephew. He needs to be close to people like you so he can hear the gospel. If you can't afford a wage, I'll even pay him to be with you!"

That nephew was Johnson. He had drug and alcohol issues and was in trouble with the police for various petty crimes. He worked for his uncle as a mechanic and was also a qualified bus driver. Within ten minutes he had packed his bag and was driving us from Delhi to Chandigarh.

Sitting behind Johnson in the back was Thomas, our voluntary representative in Delhi. I'd been in contact with Thomas for two years, ever since I brought a team of Australian Christians to Delhi in 1997. A South Indian by birth, he had worked as a federal police inspector in the north for over two decades. Now he had retired to give himself one hundred per cent to the vision of establishing God's Kingdom in North India.

The van's Mercedes engine purred under the front seat as Johnson piloted it through the streets. We were on our way to visit a pioneer church planter in a village west of the city. We drove through the rich farmland that makes Punjab the breadbasket of India, passing village after village until we came to a town about half an hour from Chandigarh. Less busy than the capital, it still had plenty of people going about their afternoon business and lots of vehicles on the road.

Suddenly a bus appeared from nowhere and pulled straight in front of us. Johnson jammed on the brakes and the van screeched to a halt. We stared in disbelief as the bus's door flew open and young men started tumbling out. There were ten, fifteen, twenty of them. They just seemed to keep on coming.

As they ran towards us, angry and shouting, we realized they were intent on violence.

Our stomachs lurching, we jumped to grab the doors. We were too late. Men reached to yank them open. I pulled back on the passenger door and somehow managed to get it shut again. I rammed the lock down.

Meanwhile, Johnson was wrestling with his door and ducking the punches coming at him through the open window. Thomas was leaning over from the back seat trying to help, but the attackers were snatching at his arms. Men were yelling, pummeling the sides of the van and trying to break the windscreen.

I reached over Johnson and grabbed for the door. Fists hit me on the arm, in the head, in the face. I knew we had to get that door closed because once we were out of the van we were done for. "Don't let go!" I screamed. It was pointless. Both Johnson and Thomas were already halfway out.

Then someone grabbed Thomas' leather jacket and heaved on it, and before I knew it he was tumbling out of the van.

I had no time to think about what might have provoked this extraordinary attack. Perhaps it was antagonism towards the crosses painted on our van—militant Hinduism in northern India was growing stronger by the day. But all I could think of in that moment was this appalling, frantic tug-of-war.

When I saw Thomas sprawl on the ground, for the first time I felt that this may be the end of my life.

Only six months had passed since we'd launched Compassion For India (Empart) in India, the culmination of a remarkable journey full of divine surprises. God had continually caught us unawares, anticipating and exceeding our expectations.

For me, it was a journey stretching back several years that came to a head in 1997. That was the year I founded the organization in Australia with the thought of raising funds to support Christian work in South India. But God shifted my focus to North India to the most densely populated and unreached parts of the subcontinent. By early 1998, when I took a two-month trip through North India, my heart was ready to understand what God wanted us to do.

During that trip I saw things that shocked and astonished me. Although I'd been raised in India, it had been in the relatively sheltered world of the South Indian Christian community. I'd never heard about the unreached people groups of the world. Now I saw them with God's eyes.

Now I saw that everywhere I went people were searching. At countless Hindu shrines, men and women with no food for their bellies put out offerings of rice and fruit before idols, cows, snakes and rats, desperately hoping their gods would bless them. At noon and sunset, Muslims stopped to pray at the roadside, on the train or in the bus. Bearded Sikhs carried swords and spears and bowed before their scriptures, the Guru Granth Sahib. Jains walked around with masks over their mouths, fearful of incurring bad karma by swallowing an insect.

So much spiritual lostness and hunger. It literally made me weep.

I also met Christians whose sacrificial dedication took my breath away. One South Indian man and his wife had given up good jobs and moved north simply because God had told them to. They didn't know the local language and had no one to support them. This man, Pastor John, had an old bicycle tied up with string. He pedaled from village to village, trying to communicate the gospel in struggling Hindi. When we visited them in their tiny shack, they couldn't even offer us chai, the sweet, milky tea basic to Indian hospitality. They hadn't eaten for several days.

I came across a number of pastors like this, all trying to serve God with almost nothing. A North Indian in his fifties, thin and dark, stays vividly in my mind. He was consumed with a burden to preach about Jesus, his motivation being Matthew 24:14: "And this gospel of the kingdom will be preached in the whole world as a testimony to all nations, and then the end will come." He took this as a personal job description. His family ate only one meal a day, saving whatever they could so he could buy or print gospel tracts. He earned extra money by visiting a hospital every month and selling a bottle of his own blood.

I wondered, *When a poor man is prepared to sell his own blood for what God has called him to do, what am I prepared to do for my convictions?*

By the end of my trip, I had reached several conclusions.

First, North India needed a dynamic, effective movement focused on planting churches. Christians were doing excellent work in social development and relief aid, and individual evangelists were making heroic efforts to preach the gospel. But I looked in vain for a movement dedicated to establishing strong, vibrant churches that could nurture new believers. Nothing less than this, I was convinced, could provide the context for truly making disciples as Jesus commanded us.

Second, I saw that someone needed to give moral, spiritual, strategic, emotional and financial support to the national workers already out there doing the work of evangelism. They had unmatched vision, dedication and passion. They were doing their best and more. But often they didn't have the resources or know-how. They were also lonely, there was no one to put an arm around them and pray for them, no one to say, "You're doing great, we're with you." I wanted to be that person.

Third, I realized that North India would never be reached for the gospel by the old model of missions I knew from South India. In that approach you built a mission compound complete with church, school, hospital, orphanage and seminary, then called people into it to benefit. I now realized that in North India, where Christianity is viewed as the religion of colonial invaders, this model would never work. There the gospel had to reach down to where people lived their daily lives. The strategy had to be decentralized and dispersed, creating autonomous, localized bodies of believers and empowering them at the grassroots.

I returned home to Australia with a long list of people I'd met on my trip and started to pray: "Lord, who do you want me to work with?" I reduced the list to thirty-five and then to ten. I talked to none of them but crossed names off according to what I felt when I prayed. Eventually I cut the list to five. Then I went back to India.

I met with those five in Chandigarh. No one would have thought us an impressive bunch. I was a South Indian who lived in Australia and didn't even speak Hindi, the common language of the north. Thomas was a retired policeman and the others had been selling gospel tracts and doing evangelism. No, not particularly impressive. But these were the men I believed God wanted me to connect with.

I shared with them what was in my heart. I spoke about the 500,000-plus villages of North India with 600 million people, most of whom had never heard about Jesus. I described my vision: the birthing of a church planting movement across the most populated, unreached region on earth. Then I challenged them to think and pray about putting their hands to the plough with me to start that movement.

They found it very daunting. None of the five had done anything of great significance before. None of them had experience in running an organization. Yet as we discussed the need, the vision took root. We worked out that if we planted 100,000 village churches, and if each of them reached out to five other villages, we could cover North India with the living gospel. Our excitement grew.

For a week we prayed, shared and sought God. In the end all five wanted to be involved. We put our hands together and agreed to register Compassion For India in India.

Over the next couple of months, backed by a core group of friends in Australia and elsewhere, Thomas and others worked hard to complete all the paperwork. We opened an Indian office by installing a fax machine in the bedroom of his apartment in a congested Delhi slum. When the electricity worked, we could now communicate.

We officially launched the Indian branch of Compassion For India (Empart) in November 1998. Invitations went to everyone we knew, and more than fifty pastors attended the opening ceremony in Chandigarh. Over the next four days we held our first Pastors' Conference with just our five-man team, but we still did it in a big way, with printed notebooks and a banner announcing "Compassion For India Ministries, First Pastors' Conference." It was very exciting.

Anyone seeing us would have thought, *What on earth can these guys do?* Well, not much, but we knew God was doing something.

And that was what led us to that village half an hour from Chandigarh on our way to visit one of our church planters. We were sure that our vision was God's vision, and in both India and Australia enthusiasm was mounting. Plans for a second Pastors' Conference, along with ideas for establishing church planter training centers and other programs, were rapidly developing. We felt God's hand was leading us in even the smallest details.

But it wasn't God's hand that was punching and pulling at us through the van door. At that nightmare moment, it seemed that all our dreams would be destroyed in a torrent of irrational hatred.

I watched horrified as Thomas fell from the van. Remembering his police training, he quickly shrugged off his torn leather jacket. I felt Johnson being pulled from my grasp. And then in an instant the scene changed.

Without warning, a four-wheel-drive lurched to a stop right beside us. Out jumped a bunch of Sikhs. In a flurry they started attacking our attackers. Sikhs carry knives as part of their religious devotion, and when they pulled these, the frenzied group turned tail and sprinted for their bus. The Sikhs were not gentle in helping them on their way.

As the bus took off, one of our turbaned defenders turned to us. "Are you guys okay, sir?"

"Yes, I think so," I said, scarcely able to believe the turn of events. The Sikhs helped us pick up the things that had been scattered on the road in the melee—Thomas's torn jacket, his wallet, money. Then, as quickly as they came, they were gone.

We drove on in a state of shock, our minds swarming with thoughts of what might have been. What if they had set fire to the van? What if…? All the rest of that day I questioned God: Lord, why? Where were you? Finally it dawned on me that perhaps God had sent the Sikhs. He had been there after all.

In the years since that day in 1998, I've discovered that sharing the gospel of Jesus in North India is always fraught with challenge and danger. Reaching the unreached isn't easy. Over and over again I've seen evangelists, church planters and pastors battle against this kind of hostility. And over and over again I've seen deliverances from God every bit as dramatic and surprising as the way he rescued us that day.

Just as we were attacked by anti-Christian forces in a Punjabi village, so these incredible men and women are assailing the kingdom of darkness across North India. And like us half hanging out of our van under a rain of fists, they have learned the one important factor that turns all challenges and dangers into a magnificent adventure: God is our protector.

With his alcohol and drug problems, Johnson, our driver, had already been in jail and still had three court cases pending against him. But after two months on the road he gave his life to the Lord.

Six months later in Punjab, we were on the way home after baptizing ten new village Christians in a river. Abruptly he stopped the van and asked, "What do I need to do to be baptized too?" We explained and promised to organize it later. "No, I want to be baptized today," he said, then turned the van around and headed back to the river. He had no change of clothes but it didn't worry him, he just drove us home dripping wet, joining in our joyous singing.

Creating a team from a South Indian living in Australia who doesn't speak Hindi, a retired police inspector and a drug-addicted ex-jailbird is so typical of God, who delights to do things in ways we would never dream of.

A lot has happened since then. Compassion For India (Empart) is currently working in 21 North Indian states as well as Nepal, Tibet and Bhutan. The vision of planting 100,000 churches is accelerating: at the time of writing, almost eleven new churches are being planted every day. Hundreds of national church planters are being trained. Other village-level programs designed to strengthen the churches' disciple-making ministry—children's homes, tailoring centers and more—are multiplying. So is the opposition, so the adventure of faith and the challenge of persecution are growing side-by-side.

In this book I tell the story of Empart so far. I also tell my personal story and share valuable leadership lessons I've learned along the way. These narratives are woven together like the warp and woof of a beautiful Indian fabric. For me, they can't be separated. Above all, they celebrate who God is and what He is doing to ensure the people of Asia have every opportunity to come to know Him.

It's an amazing tale…my leadership formation started in the tropical jungles of southern India, where wind clatters through the bamboo groves, where elephants roam the thick monsoon forests, and where I learned to catch fish using dynamite and live electric cables.

Note: In 2005, we decided to replace Compassion For India with Empart, restructuring ourselves as a global organization. Compassion For India is who we are on the ground in India. Empart is our global partner name. The name Empart combines the words empowering and partnering, reflecting our core goal of empowering believers to fulfill the Great Commission through partnerships between Christians in the West and in the field.

1 FISHING WITH DYNAMITE

Whoomp! A column of water leapt over thirty feet into the air. When we ran back to check, the fish that had previously escaped our lines were floating on the water like limp lily pads.

I remember well the day one of the tenants on my grandfather's farm showed us how to fish a deep river pool with homemade dynamite. The charge was laid and someone shouted, "Run!" I needed no encouragement.

Fishing was one of my favorite pastimes as a boy. Our farm in Kerala had a wide river running through it, and another river crossed the countryside a little over a mile away. In the tropical climate they were always full of water and fish.

When I was very young, friends and I would hold the ends of a towel and try to scoop fish into it. Then we graduated to lines and hooks. But it was when we discovered electricity that things got really interesting.

It was a simple matter of money and science. We boys would save our pocket money to buy electrical cable (or steal it from our families), twist the lengths together and run the cable about 220 yards from the river to the house. While someone immersed one end in the water, another boy connected the power supply. Then he flipped the switch.

The two-second burst of energy before the fuse blew produced spectacular results. An enormous bang was accompanied by the sight of all the water-life in the vicinity—fish, water snakes, tortoises, frogs—leaping out of the river. They fell back and floated, stunned, on the surface. After disconnecting the wire, we would wade in and pick up whatever we wanted. Five minutes later, the remaining creatures regained consciousness and swam away.

Not exactly the safest way to catch fish, but it had greater success than anything else we tried. At a young age, I learned through this that the greater the risk, the greater the return!

Actually, it was my dad who first showed me this trick. He did all the wiring in our house and none of it was compliant. We boys were thrilled when we discovered we could attach metal to the cable below the water to extend the effect. The whole operation became quite a local attraction among our friends, until my grandfather found out what we were doing and closed it down.

My family—Dad, Mum, my two brothers and I—lived with my father's parents on their farm down an unnamed dirt road in the hills of Kerala. My grandfather, K.T. (Thomas) Chacko, built the original house and my parents added to it so that eventually it had four bedrooms. It was the first brick and tiled house in the region. In this, as in many other things, my grandfather was ahead of his time.

The farm was one of several he owned. Besides the house, it included storehouses for farm equipment, a big cowshed, a chicken house and a row of seven one-bedroom apartments that he rented out.

We grew almost everything we needed. The hills around our house were covered with guava and jackfruit, pepper and cardamom, cassava and yam. The only thing we had to buy was rice. Among the animals we kept were chickens, ducks, cows, goats, parrots, squirrels, mynas, rabbits and bees.

In many ways it was a magical place for a boy to grow up: the hot tropical climate, the waving coconut and palm trees, the brooding mountains. Just two miles away was a forest full of wild animals. All the tigers had been hunted down, but foxes, wild pigs and elephants still lived there. A favorite school holiday treat was to sleep in tree houses at our various plantations, waiting for elephants and monkeys to make nighttime raids. If we heard them coming, we pulled on a string attached to a big metal sheet with rocks on it. The deafening noise sent them packing.

We also contended with snakes. Two local pythons, about ten feet long, used to come after our chickens and goats. Most dangerous were the cobras. One night, my mum was feeding the rabbits when a King Cobra struck at her. Fortunately, without realizing the snake was there, she moved her foot at the same instant and the strike landed just beside her heel.

My grandfather killed that snake and many others. He was an expert. He used a special 6-1/2 foot stick that we called the cobra stick, very old and never to be touched without permission.

We kids had our own methods of dealing with less venomous snakes. When a snake retreated into its hole, we lit a fire outside and dropped chilies on it, then fanned the smoke down into the darkness. It stung the snakes' eyes and drove them out. We used the same technique with squirrels and other things that lived in holes. Being boys, we thought it was great fun.

Kerala, on the southwest coast of India, has a proud and ancient history. Once known as Malabar, it was a kingdom with its own rulers, culture and history totally disconnected from the rest of the subcontinent.

To me its religious history is particularly intriguing. People commonly associate India with Hinduism, but as an Indian I never knew anything except Christianity. Historically St. Thomas, the disciple of Christ, came to Malabar in 52 A.D., sailing on a merchant ship into a port called Muziris. That town, now known as Kodungallur, is only 93 miles from where I grew up.

Many years before Thomas, Jews came to another coastal city, Cochin, and settled there. (A synagogue and some Jewish families remain there to this day.) Thomas lived with this community when he arrived, then moved into the interior villages with the gospel. Many local merchants and others had already heard something about Jesus through their trade links with the Jewish community. Thomas gave historical backing to the stories and gained a substantial following.

The people were more animistic than Hindu and many found the new faith utterly convincing. In the early days, they were known as "Nazaranis"—followers of Jesus of Nazareth—then later became known as "St. Thomas Christians." Over time, Christianity in the region took on a particular quality. With traders and businessmen prominent among the first converts, it became the religion of the upper middle class—unlike elsewhere in India, where it came to be seen as the religion of the poor.

For about 300 years the St. Thomas Christians had no affiliation with any foreign churches. Then in the fourth century a group of several hundred people migrated from Syria. Under their influence various groups became affiliated with the Eastern Orthodox Church in Antioch and became known as "Syrian Christians".

Over the next 1,000 years the church continued to grow and became very influential in Malabar. But everything changed in 1498 with the arrival of the Portuguese explorer Vasco da Gama. He had been sent by the Roman Catholic Church to look for Christians and spices, and in Malabar he found both. He invaded and took control. The Portuguese brought in Catholic clergy and suppressed the local Christian traditions. Many Syrian Christians were jailed and buildings were seized. In 1599, all the Christians in Malabar officially became Catholic by declaration.

After about 50 years, however, the Syrian Christians decided enough was enough. They had been practicing their own form of Christianity for 1,500 years, and they felt as if the Portuguese had attacked their very culture along with their faith. On Friday, January 3, 1653, several thousand gathered at a place called Mattancherry near Cochin and declared themselves independent from the Catholic Church. The event became known as Koonan Kurisu Satyam, the oath of the bent cross, because these Christians vowed on an improvised cross never to submit to papal authority.

This is where our family enters the picture. Among those who rose up against the Portuguese were three of my father's ancestors. Their names were Thomas, Matthew and Oommen. We know little about them except that they had strong convictions and were willing to fight for them.

Their courageous stand placed my father's family firmly in the Syrian Christian Church. Over the next three centuries a number of my ancestors became Syrian Christian priests, some rising high in the church's hierarchy. Then around 1914 my grandfather, K.T. Chacko, did an unheard-of thing. He left the Syrian Christian Church and joined an evangelical group.

Traditionally the Syrian Christian hierarchy exercised strong control over people's lives. By early last century, some Syrian Christians felt they were called out of the church to embrace a new way of thinking. They were an informal, unstructured group. When they began to study the book of Acts and the early church, a revival of sorts broke out. My grandfather's brother, Geverchen, joined this group and went on to become something of a radical figure.

My grandfather was around sixteen when he came into contact with these "called-out ones." This triggered a deep spiritual journey for him—a season of learning and preparation. Not long afterwards he met another group, led by Brethren missionaries from England and New Zealand. They taught similar things to the "called-out ones." The Brethren did not have full-time pastors or leaders; instead they had elders who taught the Bible. They gave great importance to the study of the Word, with everyone contributing their own insights. My grandfather went to these studies and eventually decided to join the group.

His decision was momentous. To break with hundreds of years of history was a huge thing. Although he and his brother were only teenagers, their choice isolated them from the rest of the family, who remained loyal to the Syrian Christian Church. The courage he displayed in the face of this rejection was typical of the way he lived his whole life.

At the time he joined the Brethren, marriages were customarily arranged by parents or even by pastors or other spiritual leaders. Some of the Brethren missionaries, noting my grandfather's passionate involvement in the church, took it on themselves to arrange a marriage for him. They chose a girl from a strong Brethren family named Mariamma ("Mary" in Malayalam, the language of Kerala). She was thirteen years old and my grandfather was eighteen.

Once they were married, my grandfather made another decision that shaped his life. Until then his family had been farmers, but he was attracted to business. So he and another Brethren believer opened a store. It was a kind of grocery, clothing shop, bakery, herbal pharmacy and cafe all rolled into one.

Nothing like it existed for over ten miles. Ninety years ago, the only way to travel in that interior village region was by foot or bullock cart, which made the long weekly trip to the nearest town arduous. The two young businessmen stocked a bit of everything, so people now only had to go to town every three months. The scheme was an instant success, the first sign of my grandfather's flair for business.

But not long after the business took-off, tragedy struck: his business partner's wife ran off with another man. This brought great shame, both to

BE READY TO SACRIFICE: YOUR ABILITY TO ACHIEVE YOUR DREAM IS IN DIRECT PROPORTION TO YOUR WILLINGNESS TO MAKE SACRIFICES.

my grandfather's partner and to their business. Most people in the area were Christians, either Syrian or Brethren, and no one wanted to be associated with such a dreadful sin.

So, when he was about twenty years old, my grandfather immediately offered to buy his partner out. Wanting to make a fresh start, his partner decided to leave the district altogether and sold his house and land to my grandfather as well.

After that my grandfather's energy exploded. His hard work and natural business sense seemed to be met with unbridled favor. As his business generated money, he used every bit of it to diversify.

First he bought a coconut plantation and then built a mill to produce coconut oil. Soon he was milling coconuts from other plantations as well, selling the products in his shop and further afield.

He next expanded from retail into wholesale. Together with a crew of workers, my grandfather would harness up a dozen bullock carts and make the four-day journey south to Cochin. It wasn't a trip for the cowardly—the forests were alive with tigers and elephants, and bandits preyed on unwary travelers. He was an aggressive fighter and armed his men with swords, spears and knives, but sometimes the attackers were too many. He had a lot of harrowing stories to tell, but his drive was undeterred.

Then he ventured into buying farms and acquired all kinds of plantations: pepper and ginger, tea and cocoa, banana and rubber. He bought virtually any local real estate that came on the market, often virgin bush he could develop. For one who was only able to attend school for three years, his business acumen was extraordinary.

My grandfather's skill at reading market trends became legendary. Once, when the value of pepper dropped low and farmers abandoned pepper production, he leased a huge farm and planted it completely with pepper. Within a year, a pepper shortage sent the price skyrocketing 500%. Another time he ordered his workers to chop down an entire cocoa plantation and plant rubber trees. Everyone thought he was crazy, but within a couple of years there was a cocoa glut and prices plummeted.

All this reached its zenith after my father was born. He was the youngest of my grandparents' seven children, and his birth heralded what our family came to call "the golden age." Over the next fifteen years they accumulated so much wealth they didn't know what to do with it all. Part of the "shine" of these years highlighted more than his professional skill; grandfather K.T.'s character was a beacon for his family and those who worked for him.

At his professional peak, my grandfather employed perhaps 200 people. A great team builder, he treated his workers with respect and kindness. Some actually lived on his land more as caretakers than mere workers. Six or so families were involved—husband, wife, children, sons-in-law, daughters-in-law—and everybody had a job. If anyone fell sick, my grandfather took care of them.

Generosity was a theme in many areas of his life. One time, a neighbor mortgaged his house and land to borrow money but then died unexpectedly. This left his wife and four children at the mercy of the mortgagees. When they decided to throw the family out, my grandfather was so incensed he walked straight into his bedroom, opened his safe and took out enough money to pay off the loan and redeem the land deeds. He gave them straight back to the dead man's wife.

Another facet of my grandfather's generosity was the way he embraced people. He never practiced discrimination on the basis of caste—a rare thing, especially for someone with his influence. He appreciated hard-working people whatever their background. One family of Dalits (untouchables) that worked for him had six children who simply ran around all day, so he sponsored them to go to school and later university. Through this, the whole family became Christians, and all the children went on to occupy influential positions.

When it came to Christian causes, he was also extremely generous. He financed missionaries, funded Christian schools and built numerous church buildings. Sometimes he heard about a young man who had graduated from Bible school and was looking for a ministry opportunity. So he bought land (or allocated a portion of his own), put up a church building and home, and gave the keys to the young pastor. Many of those churches are still thriving today.

That was the kind of man my grandfather was. Whenever he heard of a genuine need and had the ability to respond, he always would.

Of all the people my grandfather's largesse embraced, however, his own family benefited most of all. For reasons I will explain later, my father was not able to raise me as a father normally would, so my grandfather filled that role. He influenced me profoundly, and I count it as one of the greatest honors of my life to have been raised by him.

Five-foot nothing and skinny as a bamboo pole, he nonetheless had boundless energy. He walked extremely fast and did everything with one 100% effort. He hated wasting time. He was always focused, always purposeful.

> PRACTICE GENERATIONAL DECISION-MAKING. TO ENSURE YOUR VISION IS SUSTAINABLE, WEIGH HOW YOUR DECISIONS WILL IMPACT THOSE WHO COME AFTER YOU.

By the time I woke around 7 a.m. each morning he had already been up for two hours. First he went out to organize the day with his workers. When he came back, he ate breakfast and sat in a big easy chair for half an hour, reading the newspaper. No one was allowed to disturb him. Then he would be on the move again, and often I would go with him.

As he went about his work he shared his life experience with me. He was a purposeful and practical teacher. Though I didn't take much notice at the time, now I can recall those conversations and I'm living the principles he taught me.

Here's how he taught me about financial management: whenever I asked for money, he always gave me more than I requested. The next time I asked he would say, "Last time you wanted five and I gave you ten. What did you do with the other five?" If I'd spent it rather than saved it, he would give me a lecture. Thus he taught me to manage money by maximizing what he gave me so that I had to decide what to do with the surplus. Even today, I can have $765 (USD) in my wallet but not feel I have to spend it.

When it came to self-esteem, what I learned from him was foundational, too. "Work hard, do your day's work and you'll feel fine," he said. He spoke about being proud of who you are, proud of the way God made you. He also showed me the importance of self-confidence, of backing your own judgment and taking risks. Today we call it "gut instinct."

With the help of a stick and a guava tree, grandfather K.T. taught me another important principle. At the time, we were working on the farm and I was telling him about my future dreams.

"Many people have big dreams but they never achieve them," he said. "Do you know why?"

I didn't.

"It's not just about having a big dream; it's being willing to pay the price to achieve it." He bent down and picked up a stick. "Put this under your arm," he said. "Now, I want you to climb that guava tree over there and pick the fruit at the top—but without dropping the stick!"

Easy, I thought. But as soon as I started to climb, the stick clattered to the ground. "I can't do it," I said.

"Exactly," he nodded. "If you want to achieve your dreams, you have to be willing to let go of things you want to hang on to."

Reflecting on this idea later in life, I learned for myself that my grandfather was right: your ability to achieve your dream is in direct proportion to your willingness to make sacrifices.

Loud and clear, another principle I learned from him is that people matter. My grandfather never valued material possessions above people, whether family, workers or even strangers. In his decisions, people came first, even if it wasn't to his advantage. I remember he would sometimes send his laborers to work on a struggling farmer's property for a week or so and pay their wages himself. He expected nothing in return.

He also taught me to be generous with time and to value wisdom. People from across the district searched him out for advice. No matter who they were or how sticky their situation, he gave his time and counsel freely. The reverse was also true: he knew the power of seeking counsel himself. He believed that "in a multitude of counselors there is safety" (Proverbs 24:6, KJV). He often went to people and said, "If you were in my situation, what would you do?" His final decision was not always what others advised, but he accepted their input. That taught me that if we take time to listen to others, we can make wise decisions.

My grandfather personally practiced this in a robust manner. When he needed wisdom, he sought counsel at three levels: from someone older, from a peer and from someone younger (often one of his sons). This was totally contrary to Indian culture. A father never consults his children. Why, sometimes he even consulted his workers! Today management experts call this "360 feedback" and teach it in business seminars. My grandfather lived it.

In all these things, he was living out the faith he had chosen in his teenage years. The Lord used grandfather K.T.'s faithfulness and self-discipline to establish his solid character. This character served as both a beacon and a heritage to those near him. The depth of his mature Christian commitment is typified for me by an event that took place one night after the tapioca harvest.

Tapioca is a root vegetable harvested twice a year, and after each harvest we held a big bonfire. The kids played games while the adults sat around in the firelight telling stories. On this particular night, I listened to my grandfather tell my grandmother about the Bible story he'd read that morning. It was the story of the servant forgiven an enormous debt who then beat up another servant who couldn't repay a small debt.

"I felt the Lord was convicting me about my own life," my grandfather said. "I started with nothing and God has blessed me. Now I feel that I should forgive everyone who owes me money."

I caught my breath. He was very wealthy and loaned people money constantly. In his bedroom he kept five or six big books, filled with the names and addresses of people he'd loaned money to. Hundreds of names. Decades worth of loans.

That night I watched as he brought the books from the house and tossed them into the bonfire. "That's it, it's all forgiven," he said.

Somehow my grandfather's example in turn generated in me a strong desire to forgive people. And when I think of the power of God's forgiveness today, the flames of that fire dance brightly in my memory.

My grandmother influenced me too, but in a completely different way. Where my grandfather was brisk and action-oriented, she was meditative and oriented to prayer. I never saw her angry or upset. She was always soft, patient and warm.

She showed no interest in business but had absolute confidence in my grandfather to make wise decisions. Her home was very much her castle. One reason my grandfather was so fruitful was that he had her behind him.

Prayer was her life, and her life was prayer. It flowed through all aspects of her being and doing. Whatever she was doing—walking, cooking, cleaning—she whispered away, talking to God. As a boy I would hide behind the door or under the bed, listening to her pray for my brothers and me: "Lord, I pray that Jossy will grow up to be a godly man and have a good life, that he will serve you, Lord." Sometimes I'd jump out and yell, "It's never going to happen, Grandma! I'm never going to serve God!" She would smile and rub my head and say, "God still loves you. He'll still use you."

She was always thankful. She could literally sit for two hours thanking the Lord—for the day, the weather, the house, the family, the roof. The list went on and on. If she cut her finger chopping vegetables she would say, "Praise the Lord! Thank you, Lord!" I told her, "Grandma, you should be cursing God because he didn't protect you!" She'd smile again and say, "Son, I'm thanking God because I've still got a finger."

With this went an extraordinary contentment. My grandmother had few possessions of her own. She was content as she was—knowing that God was in control. One of her favorite sayings was, "All things work together for good because we love Jesus." If there were a problem—if a business deal went wrong, say, or someone fell sick—she would simply say, "God's in control. The steps of a righteous man are ordered by the Lord."

Thanks to her, I've come to accept that. All I need to do is make sure that my relationship with God is right and he will organize my steps.

Occasionally, people would spread rumors about our family or try to damage my grandfather's businesses. But if we criticized them she would rebuke us. "Those people have something good about them," she would say. "You should bless those who curse you." In doing so, my grandmother taught me to never speak evil about anybody.

Her life was soaked in God's Word; quoting scripture was absolutely natural to her. It was as if she had programmed her mind with it. Whatever the situation, she constantly spoke out God's truth rather than voiced what she thought. Many of the scriptures I know today are those I heard her use over and over again.

My grandmother's life with God was neatly integrated into all aspects of who she was and what she did. This woman's amazing loyalty and commitment to godliness made her a quiet but powerful force of influence in my leadership and in the lives of others around her.

Today, I can say without a doubt that the best of my character is a direct result of my grandparents' influence. I see now just how God carefully orchestrated their presence in my life. I believe this is true for all of us. Even when we don't realize it, God is preparing and training us through our experiences and the people we live among.

My grandfather died in 1991 at the age of 93, which was very old for an Indian. His death was as remarkable as his life. One morning he performed his normal duties—he still worked eight to ten hours a day—and then came home and asked for a glass of milk. That in itself was unusual because he normally preferred tea. Then he gathered the family together and said, "I think everything is under control. I've done my job. It's time for me to go." He climbed into bed, said goodbye, closed his eyes and was gone.

I took the phone call that he'd passed away while I was at college in

Melbourne. I hadn't seen him for several years and the news was devastating. I was just 21 years old, but I had to deal with it alone; no family or friends were near who understood the depth of my relationship with him. He was my mentor, my hero. While he was still alive I didn't fully appreciate all he'd done for me. Since that time, I've grown to see that an enormous part of who I am is the result of his investment in my life.

To understand why my father's parents—especially my grandfather—played such a pivotal role in my upbringing, I must tell you about my own parents. And a good place to start is the arrangement of their marriage.

CHAPTER 1 LEADERSHIP LESSONS

+ Be what you believe. Live and lead from your convictions.

+ Practice generational decision-making. To ensure your vision is sustainable, weigh how your decisions will impact those who come after you.

+ Live generously. Generosity is a way of living, not just a way of giving.

+ Never confuse your self-worth with what you have or don't have. Materialism is a tragedy and a trap!

+ Be ready to sacrifice. Your ability to achieve your dream is in direct proportion to your willingness to make sacrifices.

+ Prioritize people over profit—*always!* People matter most.

+ Value wisdom. Wisdom is about making right choices, not simply acquiring information and knowledge.

+ Forgiveness is power. In all your relationships, demonstrate the truth of the grace you have received.

+ Live prayerfully. Make prayer a lifestyle—not an occasional ritual.

+ Exercise gratitude. Live gratefully—thankful for all that you receive and all that you haven't lost.

CHAPTER 1 REFLECTION QUESTIONS

1 Who are the people who intentionally invested in you to shape your character? Have you shared with them how they influenced you? If they are still alive, take time now to let them know.

2 Are you just passing information to those around you or are you shaping their character? Whose character are you intentionally shaping today?

3 Write down one thing you are going to change or modify because of what you've read in this chapter?

2 MEMORIES AND MADNESS

One day a man named Joseph Thomas went to visit his sister and on the way met an old friend K.T. Chacko—my grandfather. They had not seen one another for a long time and were excited to renew their friendship.

"So what's happening in your life now?" Joseph asked.

"Well," said grandfather K.T., "I'm looking for a good wife for my youngest son, K.C. He's twenty-one years old."

Joseph's ears pricked up. "That's interesting. My youngest daughter, Chinnamma, is nineteen. She'd make a good wife for your son. But," he added wistfully, "she's already engaged. To a schoolteacher."

The young man in question was not just any schoolteacher. He and my mother had grown up together, and the marriage had been arranged carefully, taking into account their similar spiritual journeys. Moreover, they liked each other very much.

After thinking for a few moments, however, grandfather Joseph decided that marriage to K.T.'s son would be very desirable. Perhaps he thought K.T.'s business success meant Chinnamma's future would be more secure, or perhaps he simply wanted to renew a close relationship with his old friend. Breaking an engagement in India risks family honor and reputation, but Joseph made his decision. The deal was done, right there on the road.

Chinnamma was devastated. She tried everything to talk her father out of it, even enlisting the help of her mother, brothers and older sister—all to no avail.

KC and Chinnamma met only once before the wedding. My father and one of his brothers visited my mother's house, where she served them tea and biscuits. They didn't speak. She took him a cup of tea on a tray and had a good look at him; he picked up the cup and had a good look at her. That was it. The wedding date was set for September 30, 1966.

There was only one potential hiccup. Ever since high school, where my father had excelled in both studies and sport, he had become very moody. He spent a lot of time in his bedroom alone. The family consulted a doctor, who advised them to get him married and everything would be fine. Grandfather K.T. wasn't sure, and he discussed this with grandfather Joseph. But Joseph was confident all would be well. God wouldn't let anything harm his daughter. In typical Indian fashion, the wedding was held at my father's family home and celebrations lasted a full week.

Thus began my mother and father's life together.

Everybody thought that now my father was married he would be back to his old self, active and energetic. When this didn't happen immediately, they comforted themselves with the thought that it was just a matter of time. People continued to pray for his healing.

Soon after the wedding my mum got pregnant. In those days, custom dictated that the wife should move back to her parents' home from three months before the birth until three months after. This was so her mother could care for her. During this time her husband would make only brief visits.

At the appropriate stage my mother moved back to her parents' home, but about a week later my father became very distressed. He was convinced something terrible was going to happen to his wife and baby. He started to accuse his father-in-law and brothers-in-law of taking Chinnamma from him and demanded her back. He became aggressive.

After some weeks of this, my father's family decided to bring my mother back to the family house. My mother's family felt this as an insult, and it created tensions between the two families.

Two weeks later my mother gave birth to a baby son, James. But now my father didn't want to see him. My dad was still very withdrawn, spending time in his bedroom or on long walks alone. He refused to eat, living on little more than liquids.

By this stage, grandfather Joseph was filled with remorse at having arranged such a sorry marriage for his daughter. Mum's brothers were also worried—their little sister had become precious to them since their mother died. She was only twenty, and the thought of her spending a lifetime married to a crazy man was more than they could bear. Divorce was unheard of among South Indian Christians and the stigma would cling to the family for generations, but they made the agonizing choice. There was no other way to save Chinnamma.

My father's family was naturally angry at this suggestion at first, but finally they too came to see the situation was not fair to my mother. The two families negotiated and agreed—the marriage would be dissolved.

Then someone went to tell my mother.

Mum had not been involved in the discussions at all, any more than she had been involved in the marriage arrangement in the first place. So she was shocked when one of her brothers appeared on the doorstep and told her to pack her belongings. She refused, saying she wanted to stay with her husband. Her brother stormed out.

A week later, her father and all eight brothers returned, determined to take her home. My mother faced them down.

"I appreciate your concern for my well-being," she told them, "but I made a commitment that, in sickness and in health, until death do us part, I would remain faithful to this man. And I made that promise not to him or to you, but to God. I don't want to break that promise to the Lord. Please let me stay."

They were livid with rage. "Okay, we'll leave you here," they shouted as they stormed out. "But don't bother coming to us for help. If you die here, it's your decision."

From that moment, they cut my mother off completely. It was many months before she was able to break the deadlock and resume contact with her family. Their relationship remained fragile, and for many years her decision not to leave my father came back to haunt her. During this time, though she suffered much, she was never able to go to her family for support.

About two months after James was born, something quite unexpected happened. My dad woke up one morning bright and chirpy, as if nothing had ever been wrong.

Grandfather K.T. watched him carefully and concluded he had turned a corner. Wanting now to set his son up in business so that he could provide for his family, K.T. converted one of his farm buildings into a bakery and handed the keys to my father. Mum and Dad worked in it together, and the business grew until it was operating as both a retailer and wholesaler. My grandfather was pleased and proud.

After a year, however, my father became moody again. He started to drink and smoke, and took money from the business without repaying it. He went on trips without telling anyone. Months went by and the mismanagement grew worse. Debts mounted. My twenty-two year old mother kept the bakery going as best she could, but then she became pregnant again. Finally, in early 1969, my grandfather stepped in and closed the bakery down, taking all its debts on himself.

Once again my father lost the plot. Losing the business was like having his baby taken away. He raged and fumed. Doctors were called in, and this time their verdict was different: "He has a mental illness; you need to take him to a mental hospital." A week or so after the business closed, my father was committed to a mental hospital about five hours from home.

By this stage my mother was nearly ready to have her second baby. After the trouble with Dad during her first pregnancy, she had not gone to stay with her own family as the birth approached. On the day she went into labor, she was at home alone with two-year-old James. She delivered the baby on the bed by herself, trying simultaneously to comfort little James who was screaming hysterically.

And that's how, in July 1969, I arrived in the world.

To this day my mother says it's a miracle that I'm alive.

Over the next several years, our lives were like the proverbial roller coaster. A week after I was born they brought my father home from hospital to show him his second son. He was still depressed, so my grandfather invited a group of pastors to the house for a week of fasting prayer for his deliverance. Even my mother joined in though she was recovering from childbirth. Much to their joy, my father improved noticeably. They concluded that the problem must have been spiritual.

LET STRUGGLE REFINE YOU. CHARACTER IS RARELY DEVELOPED IN COMFORT; IT IS TESTED AND REFINED BY STRUGGLES. HARDSHIP AND TRIALS ARE THE MOST FERTILE GROUND FOR CHARACTER FORMATION AND LEADERSHIP DEVELOPMENT.

Gradually my father took responsibility for his family and home again. Soon my grandfather made him overseer of one of his tea plantations. My father did a fine job—when he was well he had the energy of four men. Encouraged by his progress, my grandfather set him up in business once more. With the surrounding district gradually developing, he decided to build a three-room shop for my father on the dirt road near the farm.

As the building was nearing completion, however, one of my grandfather's nephews, his wife and six children were evicted from their house. Thinking my father had plenty to occupy him with farm management, my grandfather handed the shop over to his nephew.

Once again this tipped my father over the edge. He grabbed all the cash he could find—my grandfather's money—and disappeared. It was ten days before someone found him 90 miles away, staying at a cousin's house. They convinced him to return home, where he lapsed back into an uneasy moodiness.

After this episode my father changed even more. He became restless at night and prowled around the house. He lost his temper easily and smashed and threw things. If my grandfather did anything to help someone else—gave them money, say, or built them a house—it only fueled my father's rage.

One memory is particularly vivid although I was only a toddler when it occurred. For some reason my father became incredibly violent. At the time he had been working on a tapioca plantation for some months and had planted hundreds of dollars worth of plants, but in a rampage he ripped them all up and piled them in a huge mountain. Then he came home with sticks and beat my mother. I can still hear her screams as she ran through the house.

Sometimes in his violent fits I yelled at him, trying to stop him. Once, when I was four, I grabbed him, looked him in the eye and said, "Stop, Dad, don't do this!" The effect was amazing. He lay down on the grass, sat me on his chest and pulled out a cigarette. "You need to learn how to smoke," he said.

His attitude to me was always like that. Although he would hurt my mum, he never harmed me once.

During this time, family and friends undertook more prayer and fasting, believing for healing. Many pastors came to pray, and seven times our family held forty-day fasts, taking only liquids. My grandparents and mother always participated, sometimes my father, and occasionally even my brothers and I joined in to some extent. But little changed.

Finally the family returned my father to the mental hospital. Doctors prescribed electric shock therapy and placed him on heavy medication.

When I was around four years old, my younger brother Biju was born, and once again my father's mental state improved. For the next six years, he was a great husband, fantastic father, good businessman, great farmer. My mum calls these the golden years of her marriage.

I have lots of good memories of that time. My father was the best person to be around when he was well. He was a bit of a clown and loved to crack jokes. One of his goals at church was to find the most serious people and make them laugh. Sometimes he would preach, and he had a remarkably sharp memory for the slightest details.

But it didn't last. One morning in 1979, when I was ten, he woke up and wouldn't talk to anyone. He was sick again.

From that point on a pattern evolved. My father swung between periods of relative normality and periods of madness. Every few months he would break down again.

The anger and violence returned, worse than ever. Some nights he kept a knife under his pillow, and then no one could sleep, listening in terror for the slightest sound. Numerous times my mother took us three young children outside to sleep under a tree and sat up watching over us all night. It had to be a different tree each time in case he discovered what we were doing. Around four or five o'clock, she would wake us to sneak back to our beds.

Violent rampages could occur at any moment, day or night. The only way to control him was to tie him up. This took twenty or more men because my father was very strong. My brothers and I had the job of running and calling our uncles and neighbors. Secrecy was paramount; otherwise he would lock himself in a bedroom or run away. Catching him required planning and strategy. The men would hide in the bushes and behind the house, waiting to pounce. It could take several hours, and people were frequently hurt.

When they caught him, they usually strapped his whole body with ropes and tied him to a bed. Sometimes his hands and feet bled with the strain of the cords. He would scream and weep and plead with us to let him go. I remember having to feed him because his hands were tied.

Once he had been subdued and medicated, he would become like a little baby. It broke my heart to see him. His entreaties got the better of me on one occasion and I took a knife and cut him loose. For a day or two he was fine, but then he refused to take his medication. Three days later he ran amok again.

After each rampage the family had to decide what to do. If there was enough medication in the house, we usually waited for several days to see what difference it made. If there was no improvement, we took him back to the mental institution.

The institution was a violent, flea-ridden place—more like a jail than a hospital. My grandfather didn't want his son to live there, so he always rented private accommodation nearby. From there my father attended the hospital daily. This arrangement was horrendously expensive because treatment could stretch over several months. Apart from medication, the bills included travel, food and accommodation—not just for my father, but for two or three people to look after him as well. Eventually this consumed most of my grandfather's wealth.

From this time onwards grandfather K.T. wound back his business affairs so that he could focus on the family. Apart from attending to my father's needs, he made sure my mother was financially secure and acted like a father to us boys.

I was never angry with my father. I knew he was sick. When he was well, there wasn't a better dad in the world. He never remembered anything he'd done. Numerous times I talked to him and tried to explain, but he was always adamant he would never do such things.

Why wasn't my father healed? I don't know. However, I firmly believe that God answers prayer. At the same time, I know God is sovereign. I believe that God is good, His plans are good and no matter what you are going through, He will bring ALL things together for good. We don't know how or when. Our job is not to question God, rather trust Him. Over time I would see that even this sad chapter of my life helped prepare me for the bigger plans God had in store for me. Many times I asked myself, would I be the same person if I had a different childhood? I doubt it!

Not having had a strong connection to my father, I don't know what a loving relationship with a human father is like. God is the only loving, caring, protecting Father I've ever known. When I say "My Father in heaven," it has huge meaning and a personal connection in my life.

After 1979, my father never went back to being the man he once was. His medication kept his energy levels low. But he retained many practical skills and attended to odd jobs. He still liked to do things on a grand scale. He converted one of the farm storehouses into a gigantic hutch for two hundred rabbits. He kept beehives and had many pets, including birds he taught to talk and squirrels that ran around the house. Once some friends and I brought home three parrots we'd caught in the forest, and Dad got straight in and built them a big cage. Those are good memories.

And of course there was the time he taught me to fish using a live electric cable. Which brings back memories of other events in my childhood—some of which I was fortunate to survive.

CHAPTER 2 LEADERSHIP LESSONS

+ Commit. Never allow people or circumstances beyond your control to break your promises and commitments to the Lord.

+ Trust God. He is good and His plans are good. No matter what you are going through, God will bring ALL things together for good at the end (Romans 8:28). It is not our job to know how or when He will accomplish his will, to question His methods, or to hold Him accountable. Our job is to trust God.

+ Walk confidently. If your relationship with Jesus is right, then your steps are organized by the Lord. Keep walking confidently even when things don't work out as you planned and hoped.

+ Let struggle refine you. Character is rarely developed in comfort; it is tested and refined by struggles. Hardship and trials are the most fertile ground for character formation and leadership development.

CHAPTER 2 REFLECTION QUESTIONS

1 As you look back on your life, are there negative things for which you hold God responsible? What are they? Take some time to release them to the greater wisdom of God and allow Him to bring good from them in His time?

2 Of the things that are beyond your control, what erodes your confidence?

3 What specific experiences in your past have shaped your character and made you a better leader today?

3 WILD SIDE

By just about anyone's standards—Asian or Western—I wasn't exactly the kind of kid who seemed destined for much good. But my Grandfather K.T., ever the visionary, realized that I needed every possible help so he paid for me to attend private Christian schools.

The first thing my Christian education taught me was not to bite my tongue off. The kindergarten class was held on an open-air platform without walls, about seven feet above the ground. One day I copied a boy doing somersaults and tumbled over the edge. When I hit the ground, my top and bottom teeth were locked together with my tongue in between.

The teacher rushed me back to the farm, blood streaming from my mouth. No one was home, so one of our field workers, Pachu, lifted me onto his shoulders and took off for the small local hospital. It was more than three miles but he ran the whole way. The staff held my arms and legs down and pried my mouth open, then stitched my tongue without an anesthetic. I can still feel the needle going in.

I wasn't actually supposed to be in school—I wasn't old enough. But a local Christian institute was in danger of losing government funding because it didn't have enough students, so the staff went house-to-house recruiting. I was a month too young to qualify, but the teachers were so worried about losing their jobs that they adjusted my birth date to get me in.

44

> LIVE IN THE LIGHT OF KNOWLEDGE. TRY TO LIVE IN THE LIGHT
> OF THE KNOWLEDGE YOU HAVE NOW. DON'T LET HINDSIGHT
> HOLD YOU RESPONSIBLE OR ACCOUNTABLE FOR WHAT YOU
> DID NOT KNOW AT THAT TIME.

Schooling in Kerala thirty years ago focused on what were considered practical subjects like languages, math and science. The curriculum had no room for anything like art, music or dance. Even sport was very basic. We learned three languages: Malayalam, our mother tongue; Hindi, the national language; and English. Malayalam and English were okay, but I found Hindi impossible.

Primary school lasted just four years, until I was eight. During that time I came under the influence of a wild boy named Onni Krishnan. He did crazy things like crushing glass and eating it. We all tried to copy him, but no matter how small I ground it, I couldn't get the glass down. The school's water supply came from a deep well, and one day during recess Onni ran to the edge and jumped down. The other kids screamed, the teachers came running and somehow they pulled him out. He was suspended.

I enjoyed school because my friends were there, but I was never a great student. I preferred the outdoors. Walking to school with a bunch of other guys was my favorite time—trekking through the forest, wading the river, chasing dogs and rabbits.

In secondary school, biology became my favorite subject when the teacher took a personal interest in us and showed us her own garden. Our math teacher was also excellent—he allowed struggling students like me to come to his home for extra tutoring, free of charge. My grandfather particularly wanted us to master math. He himself was remarkable at mental arithmetic, doing all his calculations in his head up to the hundreds of thousands.

I passed everything except Hindi. One day my Hindi teacher grew so frustrated she made me stand on the teacher's table at the front of the class and ridiculed me as a hopeless failure. She said I would never achieve anything in life. Then she made me sit under the table for the rest of the class.

How wrong she was. The Bible says that God has a plan and purpose for each one of us. It's not the words of a teacher or anyone else that creates your future, but it is God who holds your future.

Thankfully, however much I struggled at school, I always felt my grandfather was behind me. He organized extra tutoring for us at home, and any time a parent was required to attend the school it was he who came. I went straight to him the day another teacher stood me on a desk and hit my leg with a ruler until the flesh broke. A group of us boys had been playing desktop cricket with a wad of paper and a pencil at the back of the classroom, and the other boys had pointed me out as the ringleader. I don't recall if I was or not, but I told my grandfather I was innocent. He immediately transferred me to another school and got the teacher fired.

I had plenty of friends as a boy, but I did my share of fighting too. With my father's unstable mental condition, anyone at school who wanted to rile me simply had to say, "You're crazy like your dad." Once a classmate called me "crazy mad boy," I challenged him to a fight in a rubber plantation after school. There he tried to stab me with a pencil, but I split his head open with a metal lunchbox filled with rocks. Panicking at all the blood, I made a deal with him: if he said he'd slipped on rocks while we were playing in the river, I'd give him two rabbits. I stole these from our farm. The plan went well until his father came to thank my father for the rabbits.

My brothers and I also used to fight, sometimes violently. Once at a family bonfire I poked a burning stick into James's eye. Another time he and I disagreed over the best way to catch grasshoppers, so while I was bent over looking for one he crept up behind me with a machete. My head needed eight or nine stitches after that.

At the age of nine, I came close to death again when I contracted typhoid fever. I remember curling up trying to get warm, then having ice put all over me because I was so hot. I spent two months in hospital, and at one point the doctor told my mother to prepare herself for the worst. Somehow, by God's grace, I pulled through. But wracked by hallucinations from the fever, I babbled incoherently, and rumors spread that I'd contracted my father's disease. When I finally went back to school, I was no longer the madman's son—I was the mad boy.

In addition to my life on the farm and at school, another important context of my childhood was the Brethren church. My grandfather had a passionate faith and never missed the Sunday meetings, Bible studies or prayer meetings. Neither did we: if we didn't attend Sunday school and church, there was no lunch or dinner.

Each night, my grandfather also gathered us for a family prayer meeting. Woe to you, if you weren't there at 9:30 pm sharp. One evening I decided to go to bed instead, so he marched into my room and poured a bucket of cold water over me. After the prayer meeting, when my mum came to change the bed, he said, "No, he needs to sleep in it." That one night in a cold, soggy bed did wonders for my punctuality.

The Brethren church we attended was extremely conservative. Our meeting hall stood inside a compound behind ten-foot high walls and a padlocked gate. Most of the members were solidly middle- to upper-class. The men sat on one side and the women on the other, in age order—the oldest at the front down to children and untouchables at the rear. We sat (never stood) to sing old hymns and listen to the elders preach and pray. There was no music. Women never spoke and had to wear head covering. Communion was held every week, but only members approved by the church could take part. Any non-Christian who came to a meeting was politely encouraged to leave.

Beyond a handful of songs and Sunday school stories, I have few specific memories of what I was taught there. Sadly, my main recollections are of a rigid legalism, along with integrity problems with some of the elders. They were quick to condemn so many things, yet we young people sometimes hid at night and saw them behaving in ways they shouldn't, like smoking or chewing tobacco. Their hypocrisy desensitized us to the truth.

Sometimes it seemed to me that religion was just a game. Being a Christian simply meant going through particular rituals, just as the Hindus and Muslims went through their rituals. Good Christians studied the Bible, prayed and worshipped—that was all. Do this and you would go to heaven.

One thing I now realize was missing was any idea that the gospel needed to be shared with our non-Christian neighbors. The attitude was "live and let live." I never saw anybody saved in our church. Growing up I had many Hindu friends, but the thought of telling them about Jesus never once crossed my mind. I regret that now. What would have happened if I had told them about Jesus? That lost opportunity motivates me to this day. I now believe that, if a person knows Jesus, there should be no one in his or her life who hasn't heard about him. It is not our responsibility to make them believe, but it is our responsibility to share with them.

Another part of my childhood that I now see very differently was the caste system. The caste system was officially outlawed in India in 1950, but it still dominates social structures and behavior everywhere.

Among the tenant workers on our farm were families from about four different caste groups. I never questioned the unspoken rules by which they related. All the children played together, but their parents would never visit one another's houses or even share the same dishes.

These rules seemed to encompass our family too, although Christians were technically not part of the caste system. Each day our cooks provided all meals for the workers except the evening one, but our family always ate at the dining table while the workers ate in a room outside, sitting on the floor. Their plates and ours were never mixed up. Even the cooking pots used for them were separate, and their food often lacked the nice ingredients we enjoyed.

All this I took for granted, just as everyone else did. The workers themselves never complained. Working for our family was their life. My grandfather looked after them well by the standards of the day—they had homes, food, health care, security and a job for life. They were content.

I never thought twice when I left for school and the workers' children stayed back at the farm. Now looking back, I wonder if some of them could have been doctors, engineers or lawyers. They had as much right to an education as I did. My family did its very best in the light of the knowledge we had, but I now understand the world differently.

I never heard anyone teach a biblical perspective on the caste system. Even in our church, people from a low-caste background could not take communion from the same cups as others. They were consigned to benches at the back of the hall. Since then I've learned that when untouchable families come to Christ, they often start their own churches rather than be treated as third- or fourth-class citizens in established churches. Yet Jesus died for all. If we can't live for sixty years on earth as brothers in the love of Christ, how are we going to share eternity together?

After my brother James struck me with a machete, I wanted to learn to fight properly. I joined a karate club. It was a secret, of course—my family would never have approved. South Indian Christians don't do things like that! I'd already joined the voluntary army cadet program at school, so I invented fictitious cadet training sessions to cover my after-school absences. I stole money from home to pay the fees.

I attended karate classes for over three years. Together with the cadet training that I thoroughly enjoyed, I felt invincible. Unfortunately, that led to a lot of fighting. I fell into bad company and began drinking, smoking, stealing and damaging other people's property.

But then, another brush with death occurred that pulled me up short.

My father had been in one of his frenzies all afternoon, and a crowd of relatives and neighbors had assembled to try to subdue him. Evening came and they hid outside the house, waiting. Eventually Dad sat down in the living room to drink a cup of tea and they decided the moment had come. Everyone rushed into the room and tried to grab him.

Suddenly, without warning, the lights went out, plunging the room into pitch-blackness. Nobody knew who was grabbing whom. A voice shouted, "He's got a knife!" Everybody panicked.

I don't know why there was a fifteen-pound hammer in the room, but someone picked it up, probably for self-defense. I was in the thick of the scuffle, and when they swung the hammer in the darkness it landed slap bang in the middle of my head. I didn't even scream. I simply crumpled unconscious to the floor.

I was hospitalized for about a month. Altogether I had twenty-eight stitches, and once again the doctors thought I might not survive. Severe headaches plagued me for a long time, and I have a permanent tender lump on the top of my head as a legacy.

Fortunately, this was the last of my list of childhood traumas. A difficult birth, typhoid, a machete wound, a hammer blow—on several occasions I could have lost my life. Somehow God had protected me each time. Thankfully, Scripture promises: "He who began a good work in you will carry it on to completion until the day of Christ Jesus" (Philippians 1:6). He wasn't done with me. God used my boyhood experiences as part of his ways and means—positioning me for bigger purposes and plans.

My future was before me. Now I was fifteen years old and my grandfather K.T. encouraged me to think about my future, saying, "There is not much point in staying around here. You should learn English and go to a Western country where you will have lots of opportunities."

It was time to move on with my life. Plans were put in place for me to leave school and travel to Andhra Pradesh where my uncle ran a large Bible college. I was to study there. As I set off alone on the nearly three-day-long rail journey across southern India, I had no idea that I was saying goodbye to all that was known to me. I would never again return to live at my childhood home.

CHAPTER 3 LEADERSHIP LESSONS

+ Don't let appearances fool you. When searching for leadership talent, don't miss the package because of the packaging. Wise people may not come to you dressed nicely, smelling good or with fancy degrees—so be careful not to overlook them! Keep in mind that God loves to use the weak and foolish things of the world (1 Cor. 1:26-31).

+ Live in the light of knowledge. Try to live in the light of the knowledge you have now. Don't let hindsight hold you responsible or accountable for what you did not know at that time.

+ Celebrate how God made you. God did not make a mistake in any aspect of how he made you or where he placed you. Don't insult Him, celebrate His work—you! You are His masterpiece.

+ To whom much is given, much is expected. This truth includes our knowledge and experience of Jesus. If we know him, we have been given much. If we know him, much is required of us—never miss an opportunity to generously share what you have been given, including Jesus and his grace.

CHAPTER 3 REFLECTION QUESTIONS

1 Are there people around you who don't have the right leadership package or appearance but may be worth investing in? Ask the Lord to show you who you may be overlooking because of your own bias.

2 Do you carry shame from things in your past? Is the devil trying to confuse or torment you with things that have already been forgiven by the Lord?

3 Are there people in your life who do not know who Jesus is and how much he loves them? If so, ask the Lord to inspire you with an intentional and meaningful strategy to share your faith. Write it down and act on it.

4 EAST MEETS WEST

As my train pulled into Visakhapatnam, a port city in northern Andhra Pradesh overlooking the Bay of Bengal, I stretched to get the stiffness out of my limbs. Three days in a railway carriage with strangers who did not speak my language seemed an eternity and I was excited to arrive. Vizag (as the city is commonly known) was the location of my uncle's college; this was my first big step into a wider world.

My main goal for attending Bible college was to improve my English. At this point, my faith was very much an inherited belief rather than a deep personal conviction. My uncle had a large ministry with a number of Christian institutions. People expected that in the future I would be involved in ministry as well. More than anything, I wanted to go into business. For that I needed to improve my English skills. Vizag was a good place to do so because no one spoke my mother tongue. It forced me to learn English . . . quick!

My grandfather's influence, of course, had pointed me to business and I made no secret of my desires. While I studied over the next twelve months, my uncle and I discussed various ways to link my passion for business with Christian ministry. The offset printing industry seemed a promising possibility. I could establish a business and print Christian literature in order to channel financial resources to various ministries. We started to look at training options, both in India and overseas.

My Uncle had many foreigners from Western countries visit him. Most of them stayed in expensive hotels, traveled in air-conditioned cars and ate at expensive restaurants. But one guy from a church in Western Australia, whom I'll call Steve, was different. Steve mixed with the students and shared meals with us, eating local food. He even ate with his hands, Indian-style! He was laid-back, down-to-earth and friendly.

I knew nothing about Australia except that they played cricket there and had a lot of kangaroos and sheep. But I was instantly drawn to the easy-going Aussie style.

I talked with Steve about my dreams and was surprised to learn that a business guy in printing attended his church in Perth. This man might be interested in helping me, Steve said, and he promised to make inquiries when he returned home.

While I waited to hear, I did a little research. I discovered that Australia was twice the size of India but had a population of just 17 million people (in 1986). Kerala alone had twice that number! Then somebody told me about a gold rush there when anyone could go out and dig up gold. Lots of space, few people, easy-going lifestyle, gold for the taking—that was the place for me!

After a few months Steve wrote to say his printer friend was willing to take me on as an apprentice and teach me both printing and business skills. I was over the moon. Here at last was the opportunity I was hungry for. My grandfather had passed on to me his can-do attitude and his must-do spirit; from a young age I'd been determined to do something with my life. Anything was possible—I just had to make it happen.

My number-one drive was to succeed, especially financially. I noticed that family members who were involved in ministry activities usually didn't have much money, but business was an area of abundant resources. To me

FAITH OVER FACTS. WHEN YOU ARE TAKING STEPS OF FAITH, SOMETIMES IT IS BETTER NOT TO INSIST ON HAVING ALL THE FACTS. IF YOU KNOW TOO MUCH, YOU MAY NOT TAKE THOSE LIFE-CHANGING STEPS OF FAITH.

as a seventeen-year-old, the future seemed simple: go to Australia, learn the printing business, make my fortune, and then return to India with the latest Western technology and blow every other printer out of the water.

The arrangements were made. My grandfather bought me a one-way ticket to Perth and one of my aunties gave me twenty dollars. I had some nice new shirts and trousers made by a tailor and arrived at the airport with my one suitcase, which weighed just thirty-seven pounds. I figured I didn't need to take more because I was going to make it big time.

A couple of hours into the flight, I got my first surprise. The airplane meal came with cutlery wrapped in a little plastic bag. I'd never used a knife and fork in my life. A couple of people gave me funny looks when I started to eat with my fingers. Then a kind stewardess tore open the plastic and tried to help me. But I couldn't do it.

Interesting, I thought. I'm going to have to make some adjustments.

When I arrived in Perth I got my second surprise—more of a shock, really. I came out into the arrival lounge and saw a sea of white-skinned faces. It hit me: I'm in a strange place and I'm different. I'd never experienced that emotion before. It was a sick kind of feeling and made me nervous.

Steve had arranged for two students from his church to pick me up, an Indonesian named Usuk and a Kenyan named Paul. They drove me to Steve's apartment where I was going to stay until I made permanent arrangements. On the way I watched for kangaroos to hop across the road, just as cows roam the streets in India. I was disappointed not to see any.

The next day was Sunday, so Steve took me to church. It was one of the largest charismatic churches in Australia and I'd never seen anything like it. I'd grown up in a conservative Brethren church where we didn't even stand up to sing. But here a thousand people were standing, clapping, swaying and raising their hands. In my church we used no musical instruments, but here guitars, keyboards and drums led the worship.

Wow!

Then it was time to take the offering. Someone gave a long, impassioned teaching about faith and giving—how important it was to sow generously so that you would reap blessing. Well, I certainly wanted to be blessed. I noticed people were putting notes in the offering bags, not coins, and remembered the twenty dollars my aunty had given me. It was the only money I had, but I thought, Well, I'm in Australia now and I'm going to be rich. I stuffed the note in the bag as it went past.

I expected people to come up to me after the service and start giving me money. I was in for a big disappointment, and not just because no one filled my pockets with cash. No one did much for me at all. Only a few people said a quick "hi" before they ran out the door. After a church meeting in India people stay and talk, drink chai (tea) and eat a meal. But here there was only a coffee shop and you had to buy what you wanted. That really shocked me. I had no money to get a drink and no one offered me one.

It was a huge let down. When missionaries came to India we looked after them and gave our very best. We took them around and fed them and provided whatever they needed. I wasn't ready for the feeling of being neglected. My glowing expectations of Australia took a nosedive.

Within days my other dreams were unraveling as well. I started my apprenticeship program, but the owner of the business didn't work on site. I was put to work as a kind of general factory boy, carrying boxes and sweeping floors. At home we had servants to do this kind of work! Then after about three weeks the manager called me into his office and dropped a bombshell. The business was bankrupt and had been taken over by liquidators. My apprenticeship was over.

To me this wasn't the end of the company. It was the end of me.

I'd been discussing with Usuk and Paul the idea of moving in with them, along with another Indonesian, Edwin, and a Thai, Assa. They were all struggling Bible school students and would welcome an extra contributor to the rent. Now I had no income—in fact, I hadn't even been paid for the work I'd done. But these marvelous brothers took me in anyway. I slept on the floor in the living room of their two-bedroom apartment and shared their food.

Soon I was running out of everything I'd brought from India: toothpaste, soap, shampoo. My roommates knew I had very little, but whenever they asked if I needed anything, I always said no. In Indian culture, you're expected to refuse an offer two or three times before reluctantly accepting. I was actually desperate! If they had asked three times I would have told them the truth, but they never did!

For the next three months I got up every morning and went job hunting. Nothing. I went on brushing my teeth with my finger and showering with water only. I was too proud to ask anyone back in India for help because I wanted to prove myself. Instead I became more and more despondent. I started to take some classes at the church's Bible college each morning, but underneath I was resentful towards the church for not showing the love and care I expected and wondered if there was a God.

Then one morning I washed my clothes and hung them out on the line behind the block of flats. That evening I went to collect them. Every one of them had been stolen—even the socks and underpants. All the clothing I owned, except what I was wearing, had been on that line. In India, I had never had anything like this happen. If I had known what was ahead, I would have never left home. Since then, I've learned that when you are taking steps of faith, sometimes it is better not to insist on all the facts. If you know too much, sometimes you may not take those life-changing steps of faith.

Now I was in a real crisis. One afternoon about a week later, I climbed up to the flat roof of the apartments. I was depressed and wanted to end my life.

I stayed up there through the evening and into the night. Lying on the roof and looking up at the stars, I thought about everything. Finally I prayed.

"Look, God, if you're out there somewhere, you need to help me. I haven't got anybody else."

The words went out into the darkness, hanging in the silence. And then, to my complete astonishment, I felt a voice answer: "Now you are mine."

I wasn't sure who it was that had spoken or what was going on, but a response spontaneously rushed out of my mouth: "Well, you can have me. Nobody else wants me. I'm an absolute failure, but sure, you can have me." It was a total, white flag surrender. If it was all or nothing that God wanted, I was all in. For the first time in my seventeen years, I handed everything over to God, including all my shattered ambitions and dreams. I didn't think he could do much with me, but from then on I would be his to command. Later I learned that the level to which God can use you is directly proportional to the level of your surrender to him.

After that prayer I fell into a deep sleep and didn't stir until morning. Immediately, I knew something was different. In place of my crushing sense of anxiety, I felt a new positivity—an amazing clarity and purposefulness. The hopeless and depressive feeling was gone, replaced by a profound sense of peace. It's hard to explain the strength of that feeling. It was the complete opposite of the thoughts tormenting me before. Somehow I knew everything was going to be all right.

Without that rooftop encounter and the circumstances that led to it, I wouldn't be where I am now. Looking back, I believe that my early

Australian experiences were part of God's plan to bring me to a place of utter surrender. The heart of compassion I have now—the love for people, the desire to help others—was all created in those three months.

It was just as my grandmother used to say: *The steps of a righteous man are organized by the Lord* (Psalm 37:23).

I came straight down off the roof, showered and went out job-hunting again. Around eleven o'clock I knocked on the door of a big warehouse. The sign above the entrance read "Cleland Cold Stores."

I was taken to meet a short Italian man named Claude. He looked at me over his big moustache.

"What do you want?" he asked.

"I need a job."

"What can you do?"

"Anything."

"When do you want to start?"

"Today."

"No!" he said. "You can start tomorrow."

After three months, it happened that easily.

The Cleland's business was to blast-freeze processed food and store it. They dressed me in overalls, jacket, hat and gloves, gave me a pick and shovel, and showed me into one of their gigantic glass storerooms. It was about 21,000 square feet. My responsibility was to chip ice from the floor so the forklifts didn't skid and overturn.

It was a challenging job for a South Indian. In Kerala the average maximum temperature is over 86°F (30°C); in the cool store the temperature was –11°F (-24°C)! Big noisy fans constantly blew out frigid air. Every five minutes I had to step outside the room to thaw out. My ears, lips, nose and fingers ached continually. I would put my head under the hand-dryer in the toilet to get dry.

But it was wonderful to be working at last. I'd discovered what it does to you to be unable to contribute—how it shatters your confidence and self-respect. My first pay packet was a big event. I went to the supermarket and bought toothpaste, soap, shampoo and deodorant, then took my roommates out for dinner at an Indian restaurant. Now I could contribute to the rent and put gas in their cars. I felt back in control.

God gave me favor at Cleland. I did a good enough job to bring the accident rate down. As the months went by I was promoted, first to picking and packing orders for supermarkets, then to the chiller

SUCCESS IN GOD IS NOT ABOUT YOUR ACHIEVEMENTS.
SUCCESS IN GOD IS MEASURED BY THE LEVEL OF YOUR
SURRENDER TO HIM, NOT BY YOUR ACHIEVEMENTS.

(positively hot at 40°F or 4°C), then to forklift driving. My confidence and optimism returned.

I got along well with Claude and my workmates, the first working-class Aussies I'd met. At first I couldn't understand half of what they were saying, but over time I figured things out and felt more at home.

I must admit, though, that some aspects of Australian culture were pretty puzzling. I remember being invited to dinner by a well-to-do family in the church. As I walked through their beautiful house, I noticed the antique dining table and chairs, the chandelier, the sideboard full of exquisite china and elegant glasses. I grew excited at the thought of dining in such an opulent setting. Then my host said, "Come out the back. We're having a barbie." I didn't know what a barbie was, but I soon found out when they handed me a disposable cup, a paper plate and a plastic knife and fork. With flies buzzing around my head and smoke in my eyes, I hacked my way through burnt meat. Barbecues were a big letdown. I couldn't understand why anyone would choose to suffer through all this when there was a beautiful dining room inside the house!

Another time some friends invited me to go camping. *What's camping?* I wondered. We ended up in the bush in a tent with ants crawling over us. I couldn't understand it. In India we never went away for vacations. Our home was our resting place. My Aussie friends worked overtime to pay for their dream homes, with air conditioning, heating, carpets, mattresses, pillows, comforters, indoor plumbing—all of which they locked up and left two hours away. Instead, we slept on the grass and froze in the rain like people in the Indian slums just to get some rest and recover from the rat race. It took me ages to get the hang of Aussie vacations.

I couldn't work out lawns either. Although I'd grown up on a farm, I'd never seen a lawn. Grass was for cows and goats. In Australia people paid real money to rip the natural grass out of their yard, lay new soil, sow other

57

grass, fertilize it and water it to make it grow. Then they paid more money to buy a lawnmower and gas so they could cut it down again. Everyone always said they had no time, yet they mowed their lawn every Saturday, then watered it on Monday to make it grow so they could mow it again the next Saturday.

I thought, *These people are crazy!*

Sometimes I was glad to escape home to my apartment with my non-Australian roommates. At least we could be confused together. But gradually I started to see the funny side of these experiences. Perhaps I was becoming an Aussie!

During all this time I was still going to the Bible college. I went to morning classes and then worked afternoon and night shifts. I thrived on the busy regime, handling it with the work ethic I learned from my grandfather.

Since my rooftop surrender to God, my faith had also entered an entirely new dimension. For the first time in my life I had directly experienced God's goodness for myself. I had surrendered to God and the very next day got a job. God was real! Before, I had head knowledge; now, I had a personal relationship. As a result, studying the Word and prayer took on new meaning.

The more I studied, the more I wanted to learn. After a year-and-a-half I looked for another Bible college where I could go even more deeply into the Scriptures. I found what I wanted in the Bible College of Victoria in Melbourne. I applied and was accepted for the Bachelor of Theology and Diploma in Ministry.

I handed in my resignation letter to Claude, along with a thank you card for everything he and the company had done. "Look, Jossy," he said, "I don't think you need to resign. You're a great worker, and Cleland has a Melbourne branch. I'll organize a transfer for you."

At the end of 1989, I flew to Melbourne to take up my new work position and to learn more about God and his work. But the Lord had much more in store for me in my new city than the things I went there for.

CHAPTER 4 LEADERSHIP LESSONS

+ Faith over facts. When you are taking steps of faith, sometimes it is better not to insist on having all the facts. If you know too much, you may not take those life-changing steps of faith.

+ Say "Yes, Lord!" When God speaks to us, our response should be "Yes, Lord" not "How, Lord?"

+ Surrender all. The level to which God can use you is directly proportional to the level of your surrender to him.

+ Success in God is not about your achievements. Success in God is measured by the level of your surrender to him, not by your achievements.

CHAPTER 4 REFLECTION QUESTIONS

1 Does a desire to have all the facts and the details prevent you from pursuing your dreams and goals? What do you need to do to increase your capacity to take steps of faith?

2 If success in God requires a total surrender to Him, how successful are you? What are the areas that you need to work on?

3 What are the areas of your life where you need to stop asking "How, Lord?" and start saying, "Yes, Lord!"?

5 TWO WORLDS

The leafy rural campus of the Bible College of Victoria (BCV) perches on a hill overlooking the beautiful Dandenong Ranges. I didn't expect to find a Christian melting pot there, but that's what I got. My fellow students came from a host of backgrounds—Anglican, Brethren, Churches of Christ, Presbyterian, United Methodist Church, Baptist, Salvation Army, and Assemblies of God. I felt that if I lived on campus with such a community I would learn and grow more, so I signed up and moved in.

More than formal classroom teaching, it was living and interacting with this wonderfully varied group of Christians over the next three years that shaped my thinking and answered many of my questions.

Until then my thinking had been very black-and-white. I wanted to know what was right and what was wrong. Now I learned that the Kingdom of God isn't about being right or wrong as much as loving and living as brothers and sisters in Christ. We can have passionate debates about various issues (and we did), but our relationships with God and with people are what really matter.

I discovered that love covers a multitude of doctrinal misunderstandings as well as sins.

I also learned that perhaps God is less interested in getting doctrines right than in getting hearts right. He wants to shape our characters to the stage where we love each other unconditionally.

The twelve disciples all had different personalities and perspectives. For example, Peter was eager and impetuous; Thomas, skeptical and questioning; John, sensitive and feeling. But Jesus related to them all, and they lived as a community.

Similarly, though the Apostle Paul founded many of the New Testament churches, we don't find two churches the same.

Opportunities abounded at BCV to live this out. With a couple of hundred people living on campus, I was constantly interacting with young people, older people, singles, marrieds and families. Chapel times, prayer times, daily devotions, lectures and work duties all provided an excellent climate for spiritual development.

One of my biggest lessons at college was the importance of teams. We did almost everything in teams, from kitchen duties to cleaning and gardening. On weekends, the cooks were off-duty so the students had to make the meals. Helping plan a menu and then order, prepare and serve the food was a steep learning curve for me. It all helped me grow up enormously as a person and to become, practically speaking, more rounded.

I also discovered the reverse side of good teamwork. If one person failed to pull their weight everybody suffered, and the outcome was less than it should have been.

Jesus was the ultimate team leader. When Jesus invited the disciples to follow him, he meant for them to be with him, not a mile behind! He didn't keep them at a distance, but right alongside of him.

Alongside college life, I got involved with a small group trying to plant a new church in the nearby suburb. We gathered each week at the elderly citizens' hall, putting out the chairs ourselves and worshipping with just one guy on a guitar. Coming to this from a mega church of 1,500+ gave me a new appreciation of what the church really is. It's not buildings or programs, it's a community of people with a passionate love for each other, for the lost and for God.

I learned a lot about church planting during this time. The Lord blessed us in many ways. A young migrant family started to come along to our little church with two small boys; one of them later became the first Australian Idol winner—Guy Sebastian. I learned that you don't necessarily have to be large to have big and strategic impact.

From the moment I started at BCV, I also began work at Cleland. Each day I attended classes in the morning then drove twenty miles through heavy suburban traffic to work. After putting in ten or eleven hours there,

I would get home around midnight and settle down to study. I usually managed two or three hours sleep before the first lecture of the new day kicked off at 8:30 a.m.

I'd lived this way for two years in Perth and thrived on it, but no one else at college seemed to understand what this strange Indian was doing!

The combination of the worlds of study and work excited me. In the morning I sat in the classroom, grappling with profound theological ideas. In the afternoon I was in the office dealing with real people. Most of them were warehouse workers or truck drivers—blue-collar workers whose world (and language!) was very colorful indeed. The management team was equally diverse, and almost all of us had come up through the company system. It was a fascinating world to relate to.

I was learning at Cleland, too. Everyday when I arrived at work I would see Percy, one of the directors, walking around the factory talking to people and encouraging them. I used to think, he's wasting a lot of time talking to staff on the floor. He needs to do something more strategic! One day I asked him, "Don't you have anything better to do? If not, you can help me with some of my work!"

He responded with a smile, "Jossy, talking to the team on the floor is one of the most strategic things I can do for our business." He saw my puzzled expression. "It prevents little things from becoming big problems that we will have to spend more time and money to solve. Happy workers make better profits for the company. The more money we make, the happier the stakeholders."

Percy intuitively recognized that people are created for community and relationship. In fact, they crave it! By investing in their unique value, he affirmed each person's significance, built authentic loyalty, reduced conflicts and increased the profit.

Again God gave me favor at Cleland and I moved up through the ranks, all along learning and growing as a leader. Each morning was spent working through deep theological issues at college. Then in the afternoon I would be looking at productivity and the bottom line, working hard to keep abreast of industry trends and ensure customer satisfaction.

Although I enjoyed both parts of my life, I remained fundamentally business-oriented. So when our company decided to list on the stock exchange, I made the most of the learning opportunity. Transitioning from a family-oriented business into the corporate world of the stock market was exhilarating and addictive for me. Working with various consultants and watching how 'the big boys' did business was much more exciting for me than thinking through the nature of the Trinity or the theology of Paul's letter to the Romans.

After my encounter with God on the apartment roof in Perth, my spiritual walk had been healthy, and I definitely wanted to serve him. But I saw this in terms of working in business so I could contribute financially to God's work, with some kind of spare-time ministry involvement in a local church. The drive to be financially secure still motivated me, and I didn't think full-time ministry was for me.

This was especially true of missions. Each week at BCV a different mission agency gave a presentation. I was not interested in missions because I thought that was only applicable for white people because all the missionaries I knew where white! I thought people of other races were exempted from this work. I was grateful that I was brown! But the more I saw and heard, the more frustrated I became. Missionaries on furlough gave such gloomy reports. Few people had come to the Lord. Few were being discipled. Few churches had been planted. Mission organizations were struggling to survive. The whole story seemed rather sad.

This raised a lot of questions in my mind. If God was behind the Great Commission, shouldn't it be the most successful enterprise in the world? If preaching the gospel was the whole purpose of our existence as Christians, as BCV taught, shouldn't we see everyone rushing to get involved?

I was very productivity-oriented, but in missions I saw no productivity. I saw little strategy, little accountability for progress and no set goals, no ongoing revision, and no set indicators for failures or success.

What a contrast to the ministry of Jesus! Wherever he went he was fruitful, and he expected fruitfulness from his disciples. He gave clear instructions—for example, telling the Twelve to go out and preach, heal the sick, raise the dead, cleanse lepers and drive out demons (Matthew 10:7–8). That was strategy. Then when the Seventy came back from a mission, they reported, "Lord, even the demons submit to us in your name" (Luke 10:17). That was accountability. And when the disciples failed to cast out a demon, Jesus explored with them what had gone wrong (Matthew 17:14–20). That was evaluation.

Jesus' teaching backed this up. He not only commanded his disciples to go into the world, he also said, "If people do not welcome you, shake the dust off your feet when you leave their town, as a testimony against them" (Luke 9:5). In other words, Jesus said to move on to where you are received, where

> LEAD ALONGSIDE. YOUR LEGACY WILL TESTIFY AS TO
> WHETHER YOUR FOLLOWERS WERE BEHIND YOU OR WITH YOU.
> LEADERS WHO HAVE THEIR FOLLOWERS RIGHT ALONGSIDE
> THEM BUILD LASTING LEGACIES.

there is a response. Elsewhere he compared the world to fields that were ripe for harvesting. He was sending his followers out, he said, not as sowers, but as reapers to bring in the crop for eternal life (John 4:35–38). Harvest is a time of abundant fruit, not barrenness.

A lot of missions thinking seemed to hold that outcomes weren't as important as being faithful. As I saw it, faithfulness was directly linked to being fruitful. In the story of the talents (Matthew 25:14–29), the master asked his servants what they had done with the resources he gave them. It was the ones who had been productive who received the master's commendation: "Well done, good and faithful servant." The non-productive servant had been "faithful" in a sense—at least he hadn't lost his talent. A fear of losing what he had kept him from using what he had. But clearly, from God's perspective, faithfulness involves multiplying what you have been given. Faithfulness and fruitfulness are two sides of the same coin. In God's eyes, you cannot be faithful without being fruitful.

In the end I concluded that mission work was for people who couldn't quite make it at home or didn't fit in anywhere, and so were sent overseas. The way they were (or weren't) supported and celebrated affirmed this message in my mind. It never captured my imagination.

One of the more interesting aspects of my early days at BCV was that I was able to further my personal cross-cultural education. In Perth I'd lived with other overseas students, but now Aussies surrounded me day and night. I was met with even more of their peculiar ways.

In India, when a man becomes good buddies with another man, it's common to hold his hand or put your arm around his shoulder—even to sit on his lap or lie on his bed. It's just a way of saying, "You're my best friend." So when I started to build friendships with guys at college, I naturally put my arm around them or sat holding their hands. I wondered why people started to become a bit unfriendly towards me.

Fortunately one of the guys confronted the issue head on. "Are you gay?" he asked.

I had no idea what he meant, even in Perth I hadn't come across the term. "What do you mean, 'gay'?"

"Well, are you interested in men?"

"Oh yes!"

"I mean are you sexually interested in men?"

"Oh no!"

I had to change my expressions of friendship significantly after that.

Another thing I found both strange and intriguing was the Western approach to relationships between men and women. In India it's pretty straightforward: a guy just keeps living his life until someone in the family taps him on the shoulder and says, "Okay, it's time to think about getting married." Usually his parents arrange everything, including his bride.

The college scene was completely different. Before, I'd never seen a guy trying to get the attention of a girl, or several guys, all interested in the same girl! There was competition and emotion and people getting hurt. Families seemed to have zero involvement, which I found disrespectful. At the very least, I thought, parents who had sacrificed everything to raise a child deserved to have their guidance and wisdom valued. But here people did whatever they felt was right. And where was God in it all?

To me it all seemed undignified and uncivilized.

These puzzles notwithstanding, on the whole I found Australian culture very appealing. It gave me a new perspective on Indian culture, too, especially some of its more negative aspects. For the first time I understood India's shame culture, which dictates that you live for what other people think about you. I also realized how inward-focused the Christianity I'd grown up with had been. With these and other revelations, any thought of returning to my homeland faded more and more into the background.

My first year in college passed in a satisfying blur of activity. As I entered the second year, life was working pretty well for me.

One day it occurred to me that the time had come to let my grandfather know how well things were going. We had been in regular contact by mail throughout my time in Australia, but I had never expressed my appreciation for everything he'd done to make this possible. I sat down at my desk and poured out my heart in a letter. I described how well I was doing and thanked him for his incredible investment in my life. I sealed the envelope and set it down on my desk to mail later.

Unfortunately, in the busyness of life, the letter lay there until the day I got a phone call from India to tell me my grandfather had died.

I learned the awfulness of regret that day. Not only was the person closest to me gone, I had failed to communicate my gratitude to him by my own tardiness. This event changed my life. From that point on I became even more of a doer. That day, as my good intentions choked at the hand of my own procrastination, I learned an important lesson: Good intentions are a good beginning but a bad ending. It's always better to do what you feel led to do, whether it's wise or foolish, and to face the consequences than not to do it and live with regret.

The following year I got another unexpected call from home. My father had suddenly died of a heart attack. This news came as a huge shock. Apart from his mental illness, my dad had always been as fit as a bull. He was in hospital at the time, staying in a special room arranged for him after my grandfather's death the year before. My father's passing naturally saddened me, though I was relieved that my mum would no longer have to endure a living hell. But my strongest feelings came a month or so later. That was when it hit me that the two most significant men in my life were gone. I was now alone, and life was up to me.

In my third year I was elected student body president. My responsibilities included leading the college community in various events and managing daily duty rosters. I also represented students to the BCV management and faculty. Difficult behavioral issues and fervent doctrinal conflicts between students were big challenges. The year provided great practical training in leadership skills.

One flashpoint of student discontent was in the area that so perplexed me when I first entered college: relationships between the sexes. The college had some very strict rules. One was that any student interested in a member of the opposite sex had to talk to a faculty member before starting a relationship. No doubt the idea was to ensure accountability and enable an older person to give guidance, but the stipulation was not always appreciated.

Students also weren't allowed to enter the rooms of the opposite sex. One part of your body had to be outside the other person's room at all times. This was a challenging exercise during Melbourne's cold and wet winter months. It led to some ludicrous situations. Sometimes when you walked past particular rooms, all you would see was the tip of a toe hanging out the door.

This all seemed little more than an oddity to me until I started to become more aware of one particular young lady.

Jenni Ussher was the daughter of missionaries, raised in Irian Jaya, Malaysia and Papua New Guinea where her father served as a pilot with Missionary Aviation Fellowship. A nurse, Jenni started at BCV the same year I did, though in a different course. Within a short time of moving into college, about a dozen of us clicked and formed a strong friendship, and Jenni was one of those.

Over the next eighteen months I got to know her better, as I did others in the group. She had lots of energy, a great sense of humor and plenty of initiative. She emerged as the kind of person others looked up to—in fact, she was elected student body president the year before I was. Above all, she had a fantastic heart for the Lord.

For me, though, she was simply one friend in a larger group of friends.

Then one Sunday night, arriving back from a church service, I got out of the car and saw Jenni saying goodbye to another girl in the BCV car park. I went up to say hello and noticed that Jenni looked upset. When the girl left, I asked Jenni if she was okay. She burst into tears. So I did what to me was the most natural thing—I put my arm around her shoulders, lifted my other hand to heaven and prayed for her.

I found out later that Jenni, who was upset over some personal issues, walked back to her room praying, "Lord, that's the kind of husband I want, someone who will put you first and be willing to bring me before you at any stage."

ACT ON INTENTIONS. PROCRASTINATION IS THE CERTAIN ASSASSIN OF GOOD INTENTIONS. GOOD INTENTIONS ARE A GOOD BEGINNING BUT A BAD ENDING. GOOD INTENTIONS DON'T MAKE GREAT PEOPLE: ONLY THOSE WHO ACT UPON THEIR INTENTIONS WILL BECOME GREAT.

Over the next few months, Jenni seemed to get progressively more interested in me. I admit I didn't know how to handle it at first. The thought of finding a wife at college had never crossed my mind. In my family there had been a few cross-cultural marriages that hadn't worked out. I simply assumed I would marry someone from India when my family arranged it. I had wondered how I would cope with marrying an Indian girl because I'd become quite Australianized—or rather, how an Indian girl would cope with me! But generally I was so flat out with study, work and the church plant that the idea of developing a relationship had never been on the agenda.

Slowly we began to explore the possibility that we were meant to be together. I had a lot of doubts. I didn't feel ready for the weight of responsibility that my Indian upbringing told me a husband had to bear. And I felt very alone without my grandfather to discuss the decision with. Jenni and I spent a lot of time together as close friends, but I always held back from making a commitment I wasn't sure I could follow through on.

Midway through her course, Jenni had to do a three-month cross-cultural component for her diploma, and she chose to go to South India. For her it was also an exploratory trip: she felt that if she was to marry me, she had to understand my culture. God did something special in her heart on that journey—she later said that visiting South India was like coming home. She returned to Australia even more confident that this was God's call on her life.

Finally, after a night of prayer that left me just as uncertain, I decided to fast and pray until I had clarity. It was a tough time. I still had to fulfill all my commitments at college and work. On the twenty-eighth day I had my answer. I didn't hear a distinct "yes" from the Lord. I simply felt more at peace and confident in myself. My doubts about my own competency to be a husband were gone.

My immediate family was happy with our decision to marry. My mother had met Jenni on her trip to India and was delighted, and an uncle to whom I was quite close approved. On the other hand, we did face some skepticism in my extended family. Indians generally have a perception that Westerners lack the commitment necessary to make a marriage work.

At first Jenni's parents, Winston and Ruth weren't confident either. Having lived in other cultures, they were aware of the challenges a cross-cultural marriage can bring. This was difficult for Jenni, and even more so when I told her we would not get married without the full endorsement of all our parents. But eventually they gave us their blessing.

Jenni had trained and worked as a nurse, and at times she shared with me how much she would love to do something with her gifts mission-wise. However, I think she understood my deep reservations about missions. I certainly admired people like her parents for the sacrifices they made for God, but I could never see that for my life. Jenni never forced the issue with me.

We decided to have two weddings, one in South India and one in Australia. Little did we realize that behind our plans, God was preparing to ambush me and turn my heart upside-down.

CHAPTER 5 LEADERSHIP LESSONS

+ Think as a team. A leader is only as fast as his/her slowest team member.

+ Lead alongside. Your legacy will testify as to whether your followers were behind you or with you. Leaders who have their followers right alongside them build lasting legacies.

+ Create community. People are created for community and relationship; leaders who facilitate genuine community and multi-level relationships will have greater influence and success.

+ Guard relationships. It is more important to love people and have relationship with them than to be right and lose the relationship.

+ Be faithful and fruitful. Faithfulness and fruitfulness are two sides of the same coin: you can't have one without the other.

+ Gain with God. Don't allow the fear of losing what you have keep you from gaining what God has for you.

+ Act on intentions. Procrastination is the certain assassin of good intentions. Good intentions are a good beginning but a bad ending. Good intentions don't make great people: only those who act upon their intentions will become great.

CHAPTER 5 REFLECTION QUESTIONS

1 Where are your followers? Are you keeping them at a distance or with you? What do you need to do to bridge the gap?

2 Are you a faithful and fruitful leader? What are the good things that you may be holding too tight at the expense of the great things God may have for you?

3 Write down one thing that you have been procrastinating about. Then, commit to a date by which you will complete it. Put someone in place to hold you accountable.

6 | AMBUSHED BY A SLUMDOG

Finally, the big day for our Indian wedding arrived: February 15, 1995.

Just about everything that could interfere with our plans had happened. There was plane trouble when an engine died mid-flight. My luggage was lost, including my wedding suit. Visa problems almost kept Jenni from attending her own wedding. And then there was an eye full of lime juice.

On the big day I received a special visitor, my barber, Chinna Rao. He, his father and his brother ran their business in a fish market under a big shade tree, their mirrors nailed to the trunk. I had gone to Chinna Rao during my college years for my haircuts. During my business success I had helped him to build a modern air-conditioned shop with all modern equipment (first of its kind in town). He heard I was getting married and he wanted to bless me by preparing me for my big occasion with a haircut and a soothing head massage.

His attentions were very welcome. Getting to this day had been a whirlwind ride—almost literally.

I'd flown to Mumbai a week before with Jenni's grandmother, and then caught a domestic flight for Vizag. But an hour into the flight we hit bone-jarring, rollercoaster turbulence. One of the plane's engines had failed. As we were tossed up and down, we sat terrified, squeezing each other's hands and praying desperately. For a while we thought we wouldn't make it to the wedding.

The plane limped back to Mumbai and a new engine was fitted while we sat on the plane for four hours. At that point, half the passengers refused to fly on because the engine hadn't been tested, so their luggage was unloaded. Finally we landed in Vizag, only to discover that our bags had been unloaded in Mumbai as well, including the suitcase with all my wedding clothes. It took a week for them to arrive—the day before the wedding.

Jenni and her family also had a rough time getting to India. Her parents, Winston and Ruth, were now working in Cambodia with MAF, so Jenni and her youngest sister Lynelle stopped there on the way. No visa was required for Australians to enter the country, but during their week in Phnom Penh the law changed. Now, when they tried to leave without visas in their passports, the authorities wouldn't let them. Ruth literally stood on the boarding steps of the plane, refusing to let it take off, while Winston ran around sorting out the problem.

Somehow, in the end, we all got to Vizag. I sat back and closed my eyes while Chinna Rao's gentle fingers pressed and kneaded my scalp. Everything was ready now. I had my stylish wedding suit and Jenni had her wedding sari with its curious Western-style veil. Twelve hundred guests were coming from across India for our Indo-Australian hybrid wedding service, along with the five hundred students from my uncle's Bible college. Soon we would be husband and wife.

Chinna Rao patted my head to signal the massage was over. His eyes twinkled.

"There's something special we do for men on their wedding day," he said.

I asked him what it was. "You must be joking," I said.

"No, no, it's fantastic. It takes all the heat out of your head and cools you down so you feel great all day."

I was dubious, but he was a good friend and I trusted him. I told him to go ahead.

He took out a lime and cut it in half, then told me to put my head back. Grabbing one of my eyelids with his fingers, he started to squeeze lime juice into my eye. He held the lid open for a while to let the juice wash around. Then he did the same with the other eye.

He may as well have poured chili onto my eyeballs. They blazed like fire! I couldn't stop crying for fifteen minutes. But when the burning finally died down, I felt surprisingly invigorated!

The wedding service was very short by Indian standards—only about two hours. It was conducted in English and translated into Malayalam. Afterwards we stayed for three nights in a city hotel, traveling each day to either the railway station or the airport to say goodbye to guests from other parts of India and from Australia. Then we set off on the main part of the honeymoon: a four-week visit to North India.

I had never been to northern India. It was like a foreign country to me. Many people don't realize that the various parts of India are as diverse as the countries of Europe, with different languages, cultures, customs and foods. Jenni was particularly keen to visit the Taj Mahal. Soon we discovered that none of my immediate family had ever seen it either, so we decided to take them along too. And of course we wanted to include Winston and Ruth.

Just a small honeymoon party of eight! Unorthodox perhaps, but it would be enormous fun, and a great chance for the two families to get to know each other.

We arrived at Vizag railway station and found our train, an old diesel engine that sat like a big bull elephant waiting to be prodded into work. With its dozen or so carriages it was a grimy but proud part of the largest transport system in the world. Over twelve million people are traveling on the Indian rail network at any given moment—around half the population of Australia. It's total organized chaos, but somehow it works.

Beside our train the platform was a flurry of travelers, porters and vendors. We pushed through the crowd towards a door and climbed aboard.

Train travel is one of the defining experiences of India. The vast majority of Indians who travel long-distance go in "Unreserved 2nd Class" (not much different from cattle trucks) or the slightly less uncomfortable "Sleeper Class" (carriages like dormitories). In these you have to jostle with hundreds of other passengers to get a seat or bunk. We, however, had booked our own room in business class, complete with air-conditioning and the greatest luxury of all on Indian trains—space.

Our journey to Delhi took three full days. As we rattled northwards we looked out on the kind of countryside that is home to nearly three-quarters of India's massive population. Hundreds of miles of farmland stretched on and on, dotted with thousands of villages. People live here much as they have for centuries, plowing their fields with oxen, carrying their water on their heads. It reminded us of what life must have been like in Bible times.

Most memorable were the stations. Every time the train stopped and the doors opened, we were assaulted by the furor of India.

Indian stations are not just transit points. They are centers of life, crammed with small businesses, travelers, beggars, even criminals. Men walk back and forth wheeling small mobile shrines on trolleys so that people can pray without finding a temple. Prostitutes eye potential customers, drug pushers do deals and pickpockets work the crowds. Every time we stopped, large numbers of hawkers thronged the windows or marched through the train, touting tea and coffee, soft drinks, food, jewelry and watches. They wouldn't take no for an answer. My rule for dealing with them was ironclad: pretend they are not there until they go away. Many were children as young as six or seven.

Often when we pulled to a halt we saw large slums nearby, spilling right up to the rails. Many people in India congregate near railway stations because they can get work there as porters or hawkers. Or they can scavenge food tossed from the carriages. Water is available and the platforms provide shelter, especially during the rainy season when flimsy slum huts become unbearable. Made mostly from black plastic, these hovels are about nine-by-nine square feet, with whole families squeezed into them. It's an unimaginable sight. If you saw the movie, *Slumdog Millionaire*, its depiction of poverty was not an exaggeration.

We arrived at New Delhi station and stepped out into a sea of humanity. Everyone seemed to be pushing and shoving. "Hang on to your bags!" I shouted as a dozen laborers grabbed for them. They chattered away in Hindi, impervious to our English commands not to touch anything. One man heaved a piece of our luggage onto his head and started disappearing into the crowd. I jumped after him and retrieved the bag.

BE PASSIONATELY CURIOUS. THE DAY A LEADER STOPS BEING CURIOUS, HIS OR HER CREATIVITY AND SENSE OF ADVENTURE DIES. ALBERT EINSTEIN SAID, "I HAVE NO SPECIAL TALENTS. I AM ONLY PASSIONATELY CURIOUS."

We had pre-booked a hotel but getting to it was a challenge. Trying desperately to keep together, we pushed past mountain ranges of cardboard boxes and trolleys piled high with mail sacks into the main entrance hall. All of India appeared to have chosen this day to come to New Delhi, and half of them were trying to sell us something.

"Taxi! Taxi!"

"I have nice hotel for you!"

"Rolex, sir? You like Rolex?"

"Do you want a leather belt? Handkerchief? Scarf?"

Around us groups of people squatted on their haunches or slept, waiting for trains. Homeless people laughed raucously together, exposing brown teeth. Hindu ascetics draped in saffron colored robes jostled at ticket windows with men dressed in business suits. Beggars held out their hands for money and urchins tugged at our sleeves.

Even for me as an Indian, New Delhi station was an intimidating introduction to North India. Eventually we escaped the uproar and made our way by taxi to our hotel.

We spent the next few days sightseeing in the Indian capital, then made our way back to the station to take the train to Agra, home of the Taj Mahal. After running the gauntlet of the platforms once more, we found our business-class compartment and sank gratefully into our seats.

The trip this time was only four hours or so. Hawkers came and went through the carriage after various stops, and as usual I ignored them. Then I noticed a small dark boy, perhaps seven or eight years old, dressed in grubby shorts and a torn T-shirt no better than rags. Under it I could see his distended stomach and gaunt ribs. He was barefoot and carried a small grass broom.

The boy obviously saw it as his job to sweep the carriage. Sitting on the floor, he moved slowly along, lifting bags and passenger's legs to brush beneath them. He guided the growing pile of refuse with his broom and his bare hand. It was filthy work, Indians carry all sorts of things into trains on their shoes, but he did it well. Then he came back through the carriage asking for money.

The lad intrigued me. He was so young yet so diligent. Rather than give him money, we handed him a banana and an apple. He smiled broadly.

I wanted to ask him about himself but I didn't know any Hindi. I tried English but he looked blank, then Malayalam, again without success. Next

I tried Telugu, the language of Andhra Pradesh, which I'd picked up while studying in Vizag. To my astonishment he responded. He told me he had learned it traveling on the trains. Long ago, my grandfather had taught me that the best way to discover things is to learn the art of asking questions, so that's where we began. My curiosity took over.

As we talked, I discovered amazing things about this small boy.

His name was Raju. He had no idea how old he was or where he came from. He had no family or relatives. His knowledge of his background was zero.

His earliest memories were of New Delhi railway station, where he had lived all his life. He had scrounged a few bits of cardboard and metal in a nearby slum to make a small cubby house among the other huts. There he kept his few possessions, things he found that interested him, and the grass brooms he made, all in a small box.

Sometimes, he said, he returned after a day working on the trains and found his makeshift home gone. Then he had to start all over again.

"What do you do with the money you earn?" I asked.

"I try to save it," he said. "I put it in a plastic bag and hide it under the railway tracks at night. But when the men come along to repair the tracks, they take it. Or sometimes gangs beat me until I give it to them."

I couldn't contain my curiosity, so I continued chatting with Raju, translating from time to time for Jenni beside me. He told us about some of his troubles, including abuse by coolies at the station and run-ins with the railway police. More than once he had been caught without a ticket and literally thrown from moving trains. He showed us scars from cuts and broken bones that had never properly healed.

His story had a remarkable effect on me. For the first time in my life, someone was showing me the real world of the poor. I'd grown up in a Christian home on a nice farm, attended private schools and always enjoyed an abundance of material things. Never for a second had I stopped to imagine the suffering of people like Raju.

Jenni was also profoundly moved. Although I didn't translate the more sordid details of Raju's experience for her, she found what she heard heart wrenching.

After a couple more hours our journey was nearing its end. Normally Raju would go back to Delhi on the train, trying to earn more money, but a thought occurred to me: Why not ask him to come with us? We were planning to travel around for another three weeks. It would perhaps be a chance to do something to help him. It was a bit risky, but something prompted our willingness.

Jenni and I talked it over quickly and agreed. I asked Raju if he would like to travel with us.

He thought for a minute, and then answered seriously. "Normally I would never do this, but I think I'd be safe with you."

Something about his answer puzzled me. "What do you mean?"

"Bad things happen to kids who go off with strangers," he said. "They say, 'We'll give you clothes, we'll buy you toys,' but some of my friends have done it, and they've ended up next day dumped at the side of the road with their stomachs stitched up. These people take the parts out of children's bodies. Some of my friends have disappeared and never come back."

It was the first time I had heard of India's illegal street trade in human body parts, especially kidneys for transplants. It naturally shocked me, but what shocked me even more was Raju's matter-of-fact way of describing it. He was a little boy who spoke like a fifty-year-old.

As we got to know Raju over the next three weeks, we discovered there were few things he hadn't seen. He knew far too much for his age.

He had been constantly sexually abused by railway station workers and even by train conductors, some of whom let him travel on the trains in return for sexual favors. He had faced violence from drunks and gangsters in the stations. Once he came across two men fighting over drugs in the slum and watched as one of them stabbed the other several times. Raju looked at the man screaming and dying, then simply walked away.

He had seen a lot of other deaths in the slums too, especially when the summer temperatures rose to 118°F (48°C) and the little black plastic huts became ovens. With no cooling or water, many older people simply died. In winter, the temperatures plummeted below 32°F (0°C). Sometimes, desperate parents left little children at home while they went to find work, only to return at night to find them dead.

In Agra, we took Raju to a local shop and bought him some new clothes and shoes, then got him a haircut. Next we went to our hotel where he took his first-ever bath with soap and shampoo. His reactions were fascinating— the only parts of a hotel he'd seen before were the rubbish bins outside the kitchens where he scavenged for food. After his first night in an air-conditioned room, he gave us an extended description of sleeping in a bed for the first time—and why he'd ended up on the floor because the mattress was too soft.

In the hotel restaurant, the waiters didn't know how to react to him. He gobbled the food straight down, getting it all over his face and dribbling and grunting. He had no manners at all. When we went to other restaurants—nice restaurants, too, since this was our honeymoon—he tried to order everything on the menu. "Slow down!" we said. "You can eat again tomorrow!"

All the time he kept up a running commentary about what he was experiencing. "I used to stand outside restaurants like this and look through the window. I saw well-dressed people sitting eating their dinner, and I felt so angry at them because they could pay so much money and not even finish their food."

He explained how he used to hang around street stalls that sold tandoori chicken, hoping somebody would drop a piece on the ground so he could just taste it. Once he tried to steal a bird and got caught—he showed me the marks on his back from the beating he'd received. Now he ordered the spicy dish whenever he could and would eat a whole chicken.

I have always been curious and aware of what is around me. That is why Raju first caught my attention. The more he talked, the more he amazed me. His eloquence captivated me. Despite his young age, his thoughts and opinions were well-processed. His fierce experience of survival against the odds had taught him a kind of raw wisdom.

Had I not been paying attention, I could have missed this priceless boy and the insight he traveled with. Most of the time we are so self-focused that we miss the things that God put around us. Jesus was less aware of himself and his own needs, and more aware of the people around him and their needs. He walked through pressing crowds that I imagine to be somewhat like those of an Indian train station. Teeming with people of extraordinary appeal, Jesus never failed to find the one with essential need: the woman with the issue of blood, Zaccheus up in the tree, the woman at the well, to name a few. The disciples were too busy with other things, but the lives of these people and others were transformed because of Jesus' awareness about the people who were around him. To be less self-aware and more others-aware is to become like Jesus.

Turning my attention back to Raju, what struck me most was that he had dreams. When he grew up, he said, he wanted to get married and have

DON'T MISS OUT BECAUSE OF YOUR BIAS. GOD MAY HAVE
WRAPPED UP YOUR DESTINY INSIDE PEOPLE THAT YOU
DON'T EXPECT. YOUR WILLINGNESS TO EMBRACE THEM WILL
DETERMINE YOUR FUTURE.

a family. He wanted to send his children to school. He wanted to build a house in the slums out of brick and asbestos sheeting with a little kitchen on the side. To do all this, he planned to start a shoe business, with a small push-trolley from which he could polish and repair shoes, and sell cheap footwear like thongs and slippers. This was what he was trying to save money for.

Listening to Raju began to do something in my heart. His story reminded me of my own childhood. I too had been a boy with dreams. I realized something monumental: this scraggy, uneducated, uncouth street urchin was just like me. I had always thought people lived in poverty because they made bad choices—that it was their fault. This meant it wasn't my responsibility to fix their problems. I'd never had any real understanding of their world. Raju opened my eyes to see they were people just like me. They had emotions, just like me. They had desires and aspirations, just like me.

This raised several disturbing questions: Why had Raju ended up the way he had? He hadn't chosen to be born in a slum; he had done nothing wrong. And what about me? Why had I been born into such a privileged position? I, too, had had nothing to do with the process. It was beyond both our choosing.

Jenni's parents returned to Australia after Agra, and we went on to travel with Raju and my family for nearly three weeks. Eventually we took him back with us to my mother's home in Kerala. Mum was eager to keep him with her after we returned to Australia, but the language gap was too big an obstacle.

Then one day the contents of her cashbox went missing. I confronted Raju. He admitted that he had found the key. My heart was moved as he spoke again about his desire to set up a shoe business, about his useless attempts to save money by hiding it under the train tracks, about having his pitiful earnings stolen by thugs.

I decided then and there to give him the money to start the business. It was equivalent to about 200 Australian dollars. When I handed it to him he knelt down, grabbed my legs and wept uncontrollably for 15 minutes. For the rest of the day he said very little—it was as if something had happened inside him.

The next morning we went to visit another of my relatives. On the way Raju told me, "Beginning today, my life is going to start. I will be a businessman. You will never see me on the streets. I will get married and have children, and they will learn English so they will be like you, Jossy."

He asked me to bless him. I thought he was being funny and didn't take it seriously, but he grabbed my hand and put it on his head, and smiled.

Later that day he was gone. We were concerned for him as he did not speak Malayalam and was more than 2,100 miles from Delhi railway station. But we knew he was street smart and would be okay.

Since that day I've thought a great deal about Raju. Sometimes when I walk along the streets in Delhi, I catch myself looking at faces, wondering if I would recognize him now. Over the years I've met almost no one else in North India who speaks Telugu. He was unique.

We've since invited hundreds of boys to come with us as Raju did, but not one of them has taken up my offer. Why was he different? I even wonder sometimes whether he was an angel.

Whatever Raju's time with us meant for him, it planted the seed that would change the trajectory of our lives. As I look back, I would now say that Raju impacted my life more than anyone other than Jesus and my grandfather. He changed the way I see the world. God ambushed me on my honeymoon through an eight-year-old slumdog.

CHAPTER 6 LEADERSHIP LESSONS

+ Learn to ask good questions. The art of learning to ask good questions could open up a new destiny for you.

+ Be passionately curious. The day a leader stops being curious, his or her creativity and sense of adventure dies. Albert Einstein said, "I have no special talents. I am only passionately curious."

+ Be aware of others. Your greatness as a leader greatly increases when you become less self-aware and become more other-aware; then, you are truly able to focus on their needs. To be more other-aware and less self-aware is to be like Jesus.

+ Don't miss out because of your bias. God may have wrapped up your destiny inside people that you don't expect. Your willingness to embrace them will determine your future.

CHAPTER 6 REFLECTION QUESTIONS

1 How would you rate your level of curiosity? Write down specific things you can do to increase and improve your curiosity.

2 How good are you in asking questions—especially of strangers? How can you change to improve this skill?

3 On a scale of 1-10 (1=Low, 10=High), how would you rate your self-awareness? Now, rate your other-awareness? How do these compare? What specific things you can do be more like Jesus in this area?

7 YOU ARE THREE MONTHS LATE

Jenni and I returned to Australia and settled into married life. We had both finished our studies, so Jenni went back to nursing and started midwifery training. I continued working at Cleland.

Soon after our return, we held our second wedding service at BCV. I had the same suit and tie but thankfully not the same lime juice! We showed the video of our Indian service up to the point where, in Western custom, rings were normally exchanged. Then we switched the video off and exchanged rings. Guests laid hands on us and prayed. It was a wonderful celebration.

On the surface, then, life rolled on. But beneath the veneer of normality, something was happening to me.

Even on the plane flight back from India I felt I'd crossed some sort of divide. My perspective seemed to be in the middle of a seismic shift. Up until that point, all I'd wanted was to live a "successful" life and be a good Christian contributing to my local church. My goal was to be a millionaire by the age of thirty and then retire to a beautiful farm in the country. Now I asked myself a troubling question: *Why?* Was it simply to prove I could be the kind of self-made man my grandfather had been? Perhaps that wasn't such a high aspiration after all.

I was on track to achieve all my goals until I met Raju. Now more questions plagued me. In the light of everything he said, how should I be living? Why had God rescued and blessed me? If the Bible was really true, what should I be doing? Why had God given me all the opportunities and privileges I'd enjoyed? What was my responsibility with the things I'd been entrusted with?

One particular Bible verse kept going around and around in my mind: "From everyone who has been given much, much will be required" (Luke 12:48). *What was required of me? And in the face of such overwhelming need, what could one person actually do?*

It was all extremely perplexing. My attitude had always been, "I have a life and I'll do whatever I want with it." I'd never wondered what I was supposed to do with it.

But life must go on, even if your whole understanding of its direction and meaning is in upheaval. I filled my time with long work hours, earning enough to enable us to buy a house outright before our first anniversary. I also took up part-time lecturing opportunities at a couple of Bible colleges, teaching world religions and New Testament theology.

None of this did anything to resolve my questions, but at least being busy helped me to ignore them. God had to do something more pointed to get my attention.

At this time, Jenni and I were financially supporting some of my relatives in South India who were involved in ministry. They were doing good work—running orphanages, medical programs and the like—and I felt a sense of obligation to help them. Through these family contacts, I came to know a man named Evangelist Philip, a South Indian who occasionally traveled to North India. From time to time, he would write and challenge me about the needs of the north, especially the millions there who had never heard the gospel.

I admit I largely ignored him. The idea that there were people in the world who had never heard the gospel seemed strange to me. Even the Hindus I'd grown up with in Kerala and the hard-drinking workers at Cleland knew the name "Jesus." So I had little sympathy for his entreaties.

But he kept nibbling away. In one letter he urged me to consider Moses, who had been put in a basket in the Nile but ended up in the Pharaoh's palace. God had organized that for a purpose, Philip said. And God had blessed me for a purpose too.

That at least made some sense. But I still had no idea what that purpose might be.

Early in 1996 I planned to visit my family in South India, so I finally wrote to Philip and told him I would go to North India with him. "If you can introduce me to people who have really never heard the gospel, I'll think about what you're saying," I wrote.

Secretly, I doubted that such people existed. How wrong I was.

A couple of months later I landed at Delhi airport and was met by an energetic young man named Sam. A South Indian Christian in his late twenties, he was based in Delhi and drove a van filled with Christian literature, which he sold to make a living. Evangelist Philip had been unable to come, so he had asked Sam to look after me.

He bundled me into a taxi and we set off.

Over the next couple of days we visited several villages. At each one, Sam, who spoke Hindi, told the people we were Christians and asked them if they had heard about Jesus. In every case the answer was yes.

Then we drove into a village much like the others. Mud-plastered huts lined the narrow streets. Water buffaloes and dogs wandered about where children played. Being winter, well rugged-up men and women were gathered in separate groups around small fires.

We climbed out of the taxi and approached a group of men sitting on beds outside a hut. After Sam introduced us, he asked his usual question: "Do people in this village know about Jesus?"

The men looked blank. "No, we've never heard of 'Jesus,'" one of them said. "What is it? Something you buy in a shop?"

I caught my breath.

"If it's a person, we've never heard of him," another added. "People in Delhi might know him. Perhaps they could tell you where to find him."

I could hardly believe what I was hearing. These people literally had no concept of who or what Jesus was. Evangelist Philip had been right!

I quickly joined the conversation. "No, Jesus isn't some product you buy in a shop," I said while Sam rapidly translated. "He's a person. In fact, he's the Son of God." With mounting excitement I explained the gospel, telling these men, for the first time in their lives, about the God who loved them enough to send his Son to die for them.

As I spoke I watched people's reactions. One man in his early twenties named Rakesh seemed to be listening particularly intently. Soon his eyes flared with anger.

"Stop! Stop!" he shouted.

I stopped.

"Are you trying to tell us that this Jesus is the only way to God?"
I was pleased that he understood so clearly. "That's right. That's what the Bible says. There is no other way to God except through Jesus."

"So you really believe this?"

"Yes, we do."

Rakesh fixed his eyes on me. "Then where have you been?"
I didn't understand. "I've been in Australia," I said naively.

"We've been traveling here and there around different villages," Sam added.

"Well, how many others believe this?" Rakesh asked.

"Lots of people."

"Then why hasn't anyone come to tell us before?"
I thought I was starting to grasp his point, but his next words really shook me.

"Now you're too late."

"What do you mean, 'too late?'"

"My father died three months ago and he never heard this truth. Where have you been?"
I was too stunned to reply. I had no idea whether he accepted what we were saying or was simply questioning our conviction, but it didn't matter. His angry questions penetrated my heart and I had no answer.

Suddenly I wanted to be anywhere but in that village. I was completely undone. We stammered out some kind of apology for the fact that no one had come to tell them about Jesus before. Then Sam took their details, offering to send them literature that would tell them more.

"Let's go!" I urged him as we walked to the car. I couldn't get away quickly enough.

We canceled any further village visits and I flew back to Australia. All the way, Rakesh's words kept ringing in my ears: "Do you really believe this? Where have you been all this time? How many of you believe this? Why hasn't anyone told us before?"

All the questions I'd struggled with since meeting Raju came back with renewed force. And now another joined them—a question of such significance it took my breath away. Was Jesus really the only way to God? Logically speaking, I believed that Christianity was by far the best religion in terms of its social and personal benefits. I even taught this in my Bible college lectures. But the only way…?

Relentless doubts pressed in. It was a nightmare—a nightmare that became a crisis.

The real issue was not intellectual, but personal. Deep down I was terrified. If Jesus was the only way to God, and if I really believed this, then my life would have to be different. I would have to do what Rakesh was asking. I would have to tell everybody.

But I didn't want my life to be different. I still wanted my business career and all the material rewards it brought. I wanted to serve God on my terms. I was not prepared to leave my comfort zone.

As the weeks and months went by, the crisis deepened. I began to wonder whether the Bible was really the truth. Its teachings were good and I'd chosen to live my life by them. But other people chose differently. Were their choices any worse than mine?

With these doubts I found it hard to pray the way I used to. Where once I played worship CDs in the car and sang along, praising God and talking to him, now I drove in silence. What was the point? My intimacy with God faded.

Gradually I was hardening my heart. Outwardly, I continued to live as I had been, very active in our church, lecturing at Bible college and even preaching in other churches. But it was activity without strong conviction.

Something had to give, and as so often in God's dealings with me, it happened when I least expected it.

In mid-1996, when Jenni and I had been married about eighteen months, I was invited to go to the United States to visit relatives and do some preaching there. The trip was scheduled for October. While Jenni stayed home with work commitments, I jetted off to Los Angeles. After that, I was due to visit Indiana, Texas and New York. The northern autumn would be cool but the welcome would be warm, and I set myself for a thoroughly pleasant three-week stay.

CAST A BIG-ENOUGH VISION. A BIG-ENOUGH VISION IS ONE THAT MAKES YOU WONDER, "IS THIS TOO BIG?!" IT'S ONE THAT KEEPS YOU AWAKE AT NIGHT AND ENERGIZED DURING THE DAY. A BIG-ENOUGH VISION HAS AMPLE SPACE FOR OTHERS TO JOIN YOU AND IT REQUIRES ONGOING MIRACLES TO CONTINUE.

> LEAVE YOUR COMFORT ZONE. COMFORT ZONES DO NOT EQUATE WITH SUCCESS. A LEADER NEEDS TO CONTINUALLY MOVE OUT OF HIS/HER COMFORT ZONE; YOU CANNOT TAKE STEPS OF FAITH INSIDE YOUR COMFORT ZONE. BREAK OUT!

A week after I arrived, I spoke at a Sunday evening meeting in a hotel in Indiana. Around a hundred people from a larger church had come to a special meeting to hear me. As always, I set out to challenge them to love God with all their might and serve him with all their strength. At the end, I called them to respond, and many came to the front.

Some knelt, some wept quietly, others lifted their hands. I started to move around praying for them.

Suddenly a thought struck me like a lightning bolt. You hypocrite! You need to surrender *your* life. You need to serve God with all *your* strength. You need to love Him with all *your* heart.

The inaudible words crashed into my mind and went straight to my heart. I felt physically shaken. In a flash, I saw what I was doing and was appalled. It was so wrong! Who was I to tell these people to serve God with everything when I wasn't living that way myself? I didn't believe half of what I was preaching!

Conviction swept through my body, and right there beside the others I fell to my knees. With everything I had, I prayed, "I offer myself to you, Lord—I dedicate my life to you—and I will love you with all my heart."

Instantly, an unshakable clarity gripped me: Jesus is the only way to God. There is no other name than his by which people can be saved. There was no argument or debate. I just knew.

I also knew what accepting this fact meant. It meant *everything in my life was now for God. It meant I needed to use every opportunity to share the gospel. It meant the separation between my spiritual life and work life was over. And it meant all my finances and time belonged to God—not just 10% and an hour or two on Sunday morning.*

Since our encounter with Raju, I'd thought this scenario through many times. *This was what I had been resisting for so long,* but it was what I accepted wholeheartedly now.

Without stopping to analyze what had happened, I rose to my feet and finished the service. Then I walked straight outside, found a pay phone and slid some coins into the slot.

Half a world away, Jenni answered. It was mid-morning in Australia and she was rather surprised.

"Jen, I can't go into all the details, but something's happened and everything has changed," I said. "From now on, we're only going to do the things God wants us to do." I marveled that everything was suddenly so clear, the conviction so strong. "I'm resigning my job. We'll be serving God now!"

Silence greeted my announcement. *Well, she's not jumping up and down about it,* I thought, *but she's not arguing either!* As far as I knew, she was largely unaware of the turmoil I had been going through for two years. I had kept the details to myself, being a person who processes things internally rather than talks about them with others. Now I'd dropped a bombshell and I was in no mood for negotiation. All I knew was that I was ready to step out of my comfort zone and keen to get going.

But negotiation wasn't necessary. Jenni, who all her life had wanted to do something special for God's Kingdom, took it magnificently in her stride.

The following day I waited until 9 a.m. Melbourne time and then called one of the managers at Cleland. I told her I was resigning and would not be coming in again. She was stunned. When she finally spoke, she was obviously trying to keep her voice gentle.

"Look, Jossy, I know you've been under a lot of stress lately, with your heavy workload and lots of pressure. Why don't you go and see a psychologist? The company will sort everything out; just do whatever you need to do. We'll talk things over when you get back."

I assured her I wasn't going crazy but she seemed unconvinced. When I arrived back in Melbourne, I immediately took in my resignation letter. For two years I'd been bottling everything up and now the cork had popped. Those few intense moments in the church in Indiana had been an explosion of enlightenment, truth and reality. I surrendered not just my life, but my life purpose as well.

And then, I wondered: *What do I do now?*

CHAPTER 7 LEADERSHIP LESSONS

+ Demonstrate your commitment. It needs to be 100%—don't hold anything back.

+ Leave your comfort zone. Comfort zones do not equate with success. A leader needs to continually move out of his/her comfort zone; you cannot take steps of faith inside your comfort zone. Break out!

+ Cast a big-enough vision. A big-enough vision is one that makes you wonder, "Is this too big?!" It's one that keeps you awake at night and energized during the day. A big-enough vision has ample space for others to join you and it requires ongoing miracles to continue.

CHAPTER 7 REFLECTION QUESTIONS

1 Have you ever asked God what he requires of your life (Luke 12:48)? Explain.

2 Do you agree with this statement: "Big visions come outside of our comfort zones, out where we have to be solely reliant and dependent on God"? Why or why not?

3 What comfort zone/s do you need to break out of?

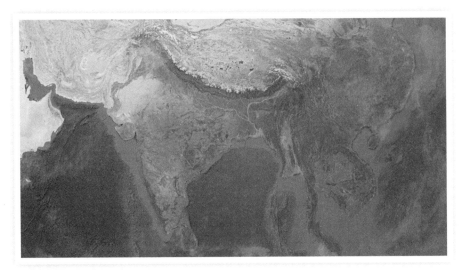

8 THE ADVENTURE BEGINS

Less than a week after I returned from America, the phone rang in our kitchen. John's familiar voice greeted me. He and his wife Diane were friends from our church plant days.

"Hey, Jossy! We'd like to catch up with you now you're back from the US. Can we get together?"

"Sure," I said, "come round for a coffee."

I hung up the phone, wondering what they would make of the abrupt changes in our life. I had just handed my formal resignation letter to Cleland without any idea of what lay ahead. It had happened so quickly that no one besides Jenni and I knew anything about it.

When John and Diane arrived, we sat around our kitchen table sipping coffee and nibbling biscuits. Before I had a chance to explain recent events, however, John caught us by surprise.

"Jossy," he said, "We have something to say to you. We feel God is challenging us to support you guys financially."

His words came out of the blue. As far as John and Diane knew, both Jenni and I were working and had no financial needs. At that time, in fact, by God's grace we were free from debt and had savings in the bank. Money was not yet a concern. In the natural, this does not make any sense as we were in a far better financial position than they were.

Quickly, I filled John and Diane in on recent developments. Their offer seemed an incredible confirmation that God's hand was on our new direction. It was also an affirmation that he would provide for us. Clearly God wasn't just working in my heart; he was challenging other people's hearts as well. This gave us an enormous spiritual and emotional boost.

The big question was what to do next. By now I had two deep convictions: First, the only reason for anyone to exist as a Christian in this world is to fulfill the Great Commission. If God's only objective was to take us to heaven, he should have and could have taken us home a long time back. He could make us disappear when we say "the sinner's prayer" or when we are water baptized, but he doesn't. God allows us to continue to live in this world even after we are saved. Why? Because he has a given us a clear mission to fulfill.

Sharing Jesus with the world and caring for the poor and needy are the only two things in life that we won't be able to do in heaven. Everything else that we currently do in our Christian life, we will do bigger and better in heaven. So while we are on earth, shouldn't we be more focused on doing what we can't do in heaven?

Second, the greatest injustice in the world is that you and I can choose to hear about Jesus anytime we want to, while others don't have that option even if they want it. This is the greatest of all injustices because the consequences carry over into eternity. It's not about making people Christians. It's about giving them the choice. If they reject the good news, then they have to answer for it; if we fail to share that good news, we will have to answer for it.

With these guiding convictions I started to read, study and research. Now I had time. Here's what I learned:

North India was home to 80% of the country's population yet only 5% of its Christians. 95% per cent of Indian Christians lived in South India and in a small group of eastern states such as Nagaland, yet 95% of mission work was concentrated in these areas. In the north, where only 5% of the mission work took place, an estimated 500 million people had never heard the gospel even once.

I learned that North India had the world's highest number of unreached people groups within a single country. It was the heartland of Hinduism and the world's third largest Muslim region. Untold millions lived in social deprivation and economic inequality, suffering unimaginably.

Some further calculations told me that up to half the world's population was influenced by religious or philosophical beliefs born in North India.

> JUMP THE HURDLES. THE LEADERSHIP RACE IS LIKE RUNNING HURDLES—UNLESS YOU JUMP OVER THE OBSTACLES ALONG THE WAY, YOU WON'T REACH THE FINISH LINE.

These ranged from Hinduism, Buddhism and Sikhism to the New Age movement flourishing in the West. What if we could take the gospel to North India and break that spiritual stronghold? What if the North Indian genius for propagating religion could be transformed and enlisted in the service of God's Kingdom? Imagine the untold numbers of Western New Agers who visit India every year encountering the gospel.

North India, then, was absolutely strategic from a global religious viewpoint. A quote from missiologist Patrick Johnson summed it up for me: "North India will probably be the touchstone of our success or failure in completing world evangelization in our generation."

Ideas that had once flickered vaguely at the back of my mind now sprang into full flame. My old Bible College dissatisfaction with traditional mission strategies was one of them. Rather than sending people from the West to Asia, I reasoned, wouldn't it be better to train and empower national Christians?

I knew this flew in the face of traditional strategies favored by the so-called "modern missionary movement," but those strategies were "modern" more than 200 years ago in a colonial world. Missionaries like William Carey and Hudson Taylor were pioneering radicals in their day, but they would be shocked to know their ideas had been set in stone. I doubt if they would still be doing things the same way if they were here today.

When I looked at the ministry of Jesus, I saw something completely different. He could have sent a team of angels from heaven, but instead he picked twelve local men. He put them through a training program and then said, "Now go and do it"—and promised that he would be with them. In other words, he gave them the responsibility, power and authority and sent them to do the work.

The Apostle Paul was similar. He went from place to place, but never once did he ask the Jerusalem or Antioch churches to send him missionaries to manage the churches he was planting. The leaders were normally local people—people he raised up, trained and resourced. In most cases, he stayed with them only a few weeks or months.

I came to believe that the quality and success of missionaries should not be determined by how long they stayed on the field, but by how briefly they stayed, and how strategic they were in developing national leaders and sustainable infrastructure. The purpose of those going had to be clarified: were they meant to go and do the work or were they meant to raise local leaders to do the work? Missionaries and outside workers must be like a scaffolding: once the building is done it, must be removed and relocated to the next site. After training the twelve disciples over three-and-one-half years, Jesus moved on and the mission continued with the local indigenous workers he had trained. These thoughts were reinforced by my business experience. Companies like Coca Cola and McDonald's didn't send Americans all over the world to staff their operations. They went into a country with their vision and trained local people. Then they left them to get on with the job. In less than one hundred years, these companies had achieved things the church had not managed in two thousand. If they followed the traditional mission strategy, where do you think they would be today?

The more I mulled over these ideas, the more excited I became. What if we could train and resource North Indian Christians, instead of Westerners or South Indians, to plant and lead churches among their own people? What if we could expand the numbers until we had a veritable army of church planters, all of them with hearts full of passion for God, the lost, the poor and the needy? What if they planted local churches in local ways? What if Western churches and businesses partnered with and supported them? The possibilities were staggering.

I wasn't sure, however, what to do with these ideas. Jenni may have been brought up in a missions environment, but it was all new to me. At twenty-eight, I felt too young and inexperienced—partly the result of an Indian upbringing that told me respect only comes with age and maturity. So I decided to seek advice and opportunities.

Over several weeks in early 1997, I visited seven different mission organizations. I wanted to explore ways I could join and work with them. Amazingly, there was not one positive response.

One group was focused on another country altogether, with no interest in India. That was fair enough. Another was interested in India but already felt they had their hands full with existing projects. A third group said I couldn't be a missionary in India because I was an Indian—apparently to them returning to your own country wasn't mission work. The fourth group said I could join their denomination and do a few years of extra training, then I could apply and they would consider me.

The fifth group seemed more interested at first. I shared some of my thoughts about how missions needed be done. The response turned cold. "We've been in missions over 150 years, and we've heard a lot of this sort of thing," they said. "But it doesn't work that way. Out there on the field, it's different. And it's hard. Your ideas sound marvelous, but in practical terms, you're just dreaming."

Inwardly I fumed. They hadn't even tried to understand my thinking; they'd just written it off. I felt patronized and discouraged.

With the doors to working through an existing organization so unceremoniously closed, I wondered where to turn next. I was reluctant to face the obvious alternative: starting our own organization. Yet I knew now I had to explore the possibility, and for that I needed advice.

I made an appointment to speak with the director of yet another mission society. I explained what I had in mind. Could he advise me—act as a sort of coach? I had dozens of questions: How do you set up a mission organization? What legalities are involved? How do you run it?

He looked at me strangely. "It's very interesting you should ask me that," he said. "But what makes you think I'd want to help you? The pool for mission support is shrinking, and if I teach you what I know, you'll end up competing with us. I'm not prepared to do that."

I left that room with my blood boiling. I wanted to shout: *But we have the truth! The Bible says it's God's desire that none should perish. We need to be telling everybody, but all you can see is potential competition with your mission!* I felt frustrated, upset and very angry.

Then, I turned to some of my family members who had large ministries in South India to see if they would take up the North Indian challenge. In the past, these same people had done everything they could to get me to support them. Now, all they could do was warn me how dangerous North India would be for Christian work and direct me not to pursue the idea any further. That was the last straw!

Over the next week I located a Christian attorney and learned what I needed to do. I called a dozen friends and we met at John and Diane's house. All agreed to become members of an incorporated association. We discussed the association's purpose and objectives.

We also needed a name. I had an idea. I reminded them of the story in Mark 6 about the time Jesus took his exhausted disciples away for a rest, but the crowds followed them. The Bible records that when Jesus saw the people, he was "moved with compassion for them, because they were like sheep without a shepherd." In fact, his compassion was so overwhelming that he put aside his holiday with his disciples and taught the people.

To me this was one of the most beautiful things Jesus ever did. "The people of India are like sheep without a shepherd," I went on, "and Jesus is moved with compassion for them just as he was for people back then. I suggest we call ourselves 'Compassion For India'."

Everyone agreed.

It took a month for the attorney to finalize the paperwork. While we waited, Jenni and I cleaned out our spare bedroom, got a computer, printer, fax, phone and two desks, one for Jenni (who had now resigned her job as well) and one for me.

At the end of May 1997, an official-looking piece of paper arrived declaring that we were "Compassion For India, Inc." We stood in our little makeshift office in Australia and looked at the certificate and then at each other.

Our looks said: *So what happens next?* The months that followed were something like wandering around a teeming Indian bazaar blindfolded. We were navigating through uncharted territory.

We decided to do our best to raise funds to support what others were doing while we figured out what we were going to do. We compiled a mailing list of 250 friends and relatives and wrote to them, telling them what we were doing and describing some of the things happening in India. We started regular prayer meetings at our home on Saturday afternoons to pray about what we wanted to do.

It would have been easy to get discouraged. Only a few friends appreciated what we were trying to start and offered to help. In the beginning, even our own church showed little interest (though it later became a passionate supporter).

Hardest of all was opposition from my own family back in India. Most of them felt it was far too early for me to take this step. They urged me to get more established, become financially secure and raise a family and get them married before thinking about missions. "Wait until you're fifty," they advised.

But I felt I couldn't wait another day. The words of Rakesh were ringing in my ears: "You're three months late." I was already behind schedule.

While we started to support some work in South India, we kept North India in our vision and prayers. But what to do about it was unclear. Slowly an idea crystallized in my mind. What if we took an Australian team to India? For three weeks we could visit projects we were supporting in the south and then briefly travel up to Delhi. When the team returned home, I could stay on for a few weeks to explore the needs and opportunities in North India further.

Around ten of our friends signed on for the adventure. We left just after Christmas 1997. Excitement was high as we landed at Madras airport. For two weeks or so, we visited orphanages and other projects, then boarded the train for the four-day trip to Delhi. This time there was no first-class air-conditioned compartment; we traveled ordinary class, with all its noises and smells and wall-to-wall people. Everyone had to hang on to their luggage and learn to use squat toilets on a fast-moving train!

Our plan for Delhi was ambitious—to hold a three-night event featuring music and drama, preaching and prayer for the sick. We organized a translator, printed some pamphlets and hired a community hall and PA system. The first night attracted about one hundred people. The team sang worship songs, performed skits, did some clowning and puppetry, and gave testimonies. Then I preached. On the second night, the audience was bigger, and on the final evening around 300 squeezed into the hall.

I was pretty pleased, and not only because people at the meetings responded to the gospel. I had arrived in Delhi feeling rather flat. In the south, I had spoken with two Christian groups about linking up with them so we could work through their organizations in the north. I still hoped an established mission would catch the vision of reaching the millions of the "Hindi Belt." But the response had been very cold: "It's too far away; it's too difficult to manage; the culture is different; the language is different; it's all just too hard."

It became clear to me at last that the only option was to start something from scratch in North India as well as Australia. With these meetings, we were making some kind of beginning at last, however small.

But if I was pleased about that, I also felt incredibly daunted. What did I know about putting together an international mission enterprise? In a land where you have to be middle-aged and greying before anyone will

100

> BE CONFIDENT IN YOUR PROVIDER. IF GOD GAVE YOU A VISION, HE WILL BE RESPONSIBLE TO PROVIDE FOR IT. HE WILL NEVER HOLD YOU RESPONSIBLE FOR NOT DOING SOMETHING THAT HE DID NOT MAKE PROVISION FOR.

listen to you, who would pay me any attention? How could I tackle the legal minefield of registering a Christian organization and getting approval to receive international funds from a bureaucracy controlled by militant Hindu groups? The challenge was, frankly, terrifying.

God must have seen that my flagging faith needed more encouragement. He sent it in the form of three very unlikely men.

The first of these approached me after one of the Delhi meetings. He didn't look like a messenger from God. He looked more like a bodybuilder—5'8", broad-chested, 245 pounds.

"So you're Jossy," he said.

I admitted I was.

"And you're from South India."

"That's right."

"But you're also from Australia."

"Yes. I'm an Indian who lives in Australia."

I wondered where he was going with this.

"And are you married to an Australian lady?"

Jenni was part of the group and rather conspicuous since she was seven months pregnant, but he wouldn't have known we were married. "Yes, I am," I replied.

"And have you come here to start a ministry?"

What is this? I thought. Perhaps he's not a bodybuilder, but an intelligence officer sent to check me out and put me on a blacklist!

Feeling somewhat intimidated, I said, "You need to speak to my lawyer."

He smiled and replied, "No need for that." I listened nervously while he asked a few more questions—questions that suggested he knew things I hadn't shared with anybody else. I was even more puzzled because he got more and more emotional as we spoke.

After some moments I broke in. "Wait a minute. How do you know these things? What's going on?"

His eyes filled with tears. "Two years ago, somebody gave me a prophetic word," he explained. "He said, 'You will meet an Indian guy who will come from Australia, he will be married to an Australian lady, and he will be coming to North India to start a ministry. You should do whatever you can to assist him.'"

That got my attention.

It turned out that the man I was talking to, Shibu, was an evangelist from South India who had worked in the north for several years. He had no support, no infrastructure—just his own two feet carrying him house to house, sharing the gospel.

Shibu was adamant that God had spoken to him, and I didn't doubt it. His offer of help was obviously genuine. But I explained that I wasn't ready to start a ministry. I had no idea of when, where or how. Astonished as I was by what he had said, I had nothing concrete to tell him.

"Let's continue to seek the Lord," I said noncommittally.

The more I thought about what Shibu had said, the more significant it seemed. I didn't feel ready to start a ministry in a region where I didn't know anyone or speak the language, yet it was certainly in my heart to do so. And apparently it was in God's heart, too.

What really took me aback was the timing of the prophecy. Shibu had received it two years before—at the time I was in my faith crisis. Even then, I now realized, God knew what would happen in the future and was preparing for it.

This gave my spirit a terrific shot of confidence. My burden for North India seemed to face a hundred hurdles: we didn't know the language or culture, we didn't understand the geography, and we had no contacts or influence. But through Shibu, God said loud and clear: "Don't worry about all that. I am with you. I can organize everything you need."

The second man in God's unlikely trio confirmed this. He too came to the meetings. A fit, clean-shaven man in his forties with grey hair and an easy-going personality, Thomas was a family friend from South India who lived in Delhi. After abandoning his faith as a young man, he had recently gone through a spiritual renewal, thanks to the prayers of his wife.

In our meetings, his heart was stirred. "I want to be involved in something more than just the normal," he told me. "I'm not a preacher or a teacher. But if you need me I'm prepared to commit 100% of my time and skills to whatever you want done. I volunteer."

Indeed, his skills were impressive. He had been employed in the federal police force for twenty-five years, so was both street-smart and familiar with legal matters. He was an experienced accountant. He spoke Hindi, English and Malayalam. And thanks to years of travel as a police inspector, he knew northern India like his own backyard.

Most importantly, he had a great heart to serve.

I didn't know what to make of it all, but one thing stood out to me as I went to see Jenni and the other team members off at Delhi airport. Somehow, working in North India would be achievable. If God could bring along one Shibu and one Thomas, he could bring along hundreds.

I now had six weeks in front of me to explore North India. I wanted to get a picture of it in my mind—its people, its character, its needs.

I also wanted to find out what was already being done to preach the gospel. What strategies were proving effective? Were people responsive? Was there opposition? And I wanted to research the legal requirements for starting an organization in North India.

The only places I'd really seen so far were Delhi and Agra. North India was much bigger than that. I discussed what I could do with Thomas, but I didn't formulate a tight itinerary. He gave me a few addresses and a map showing the major cities I wanted to visit. Beyond that, it would be an unplanned adventure with no mobile phones, GPS or Internet.

This was probably just as well, because the third man God sent my way—the man I would be traveling with—was in some ways the most unconventional and unlikely one of all.

CHAPTER 8 LEADERSHIP LESSONS

+ Keep running! Good and well-meaning people will try to talk you out of your vision or reduce the size. Don't allow them to confuse what God has spoken to you. They have neither seen nor heard what the Lord has told you. Keep running with what you have received.

+ Jump the hurdles. The leadership race is like running hurdles— unless you jump over the obstacles along the way, you won't reach the finishing line.

+ Be confident in your Provider. If God gave you a vision, he will be responsible to provide for it. He will never hold you responsible for not doing something that he did not make provision for.

+ Respond strategically. Allow your strategies to continue to change and evolve. Hold tight to your vision as you pay attention to the current culture, context and times. Results will speak to the effectiveness of your strategies. If you are not getting the right result, don't question the vision, rather change the strategies.

+ Act for such a time as this. Doing new things does not mean people in the past did it the wrong way. They did what was right for their times. Now, it is your turn to do what is right for your times.

CHAPTER 8 REFLECTION QUESTIONS

1 Have people you love and respect tried to talk you out of something you believed to be true? Did you give in?

2 What is your natural reaction when hurdles are placed before you? What can you do to change your approach next time?

3 When was the last time you intentionally measured the effectiveness of your strategies? Have you established specific metrics you can use to measure results in an ongoing way?

9 | JOURNEY THROUGH A LOST WORLD

On a cloudy Adelaide afternoon eight months earlier, I was standing in the expo area of the Australian Christian Churches national conference and feeling rather glum.

All around me were the magnificent exhibits of other Christian organizations, complete with multimedia displays and piles of glossy, full-color materials. I looked at Compassion For India's simple plywood stand, with its Velcro-attached photographs, basic one-color brochure and photocopied newsletters. It seemed very inferior.

I'd come to the conference brimming with enthusiasm to promote the vision of reaching Asia's unreached millions. But very few people had noticed. Enthusiastic singing floated out from the session underway in the meeting hall, but my heart felt as heavy as lead.

Look at our pathetic display, I grumbled silently. *Nobody's interested. How will I ever communicate God's heart for the lost and the plight and needs of a desperate world to the sophisticated, high-tech West?*

I went outside to get some fresh air and space to think.

While I was walking around, I noticed a guy of about twenty years of age pushing a bicycle. He had obviously just arrived. But he didn't look like a regular conference delegate. Around 5'6" and rather slight, he was unshaven and his clothes looked travel-worn.

I went up to him and we got talking.

His name was Stephane, a native of Switzerland. In broken English, he told me he came to Australia to work on a farm in Tasmania. After that, he rode a pushbike around the island (more than a 620 miles) before pedaling all the way from Melbourne to Adelaide (another 500 miles). Since even driving to Adelaide made me exhausted, I must say I was impressed.

Stephane also explained that while camping in the bush in Tasmania, he had an encounter with Jesus. Now he was searching and trying to learn more. Somewhere he heard about the conference and decided to check it out. I invited him to come and see our display.

We finished talking and parted, but next day he turned up again. He didn't know anything about missions and showed little interest. Later he confessed that he didn't like Asia much, but he put one of our homemade business cards in his pocket.

"When you come back through Melbourne, we'd love to see you," I said. "If we can be of any help, just let us know."

The conference ended and I returned home, quickly forgetting about the athletic young man. Then one day, several weeks later, the phone rang and I heard Stephane's thick French accent on the line. He asked if he could come and pitch his tent in our backyard. I offered him a bed, but he said he had four friends with him.

"No problem," I said. "When are you coming?"

"This evening!" he replied.

I later discovered he hadn't wanted anything to do with the Indian mission junkie. But with every backpacker accommodation place in Melbourne full, he had already slept under a bridge for two nights. The late autumn cold finally made him desperate enough to call us.

Stephane and his companions had purchased a decrepit old Volvo with no reverse gear and smoke billowing from the exhaust. A colorful assortment of luggage was piled on the roof. All of them came from Europe—a friendly bunch of low-budget backpackers living on the road. For a week or so, they took over our lounge room.

We had a great time. I still laugh at what the neighbors must have thought! We lived in a quiet suburban court, and the sight of five scruffy guys (one with dreadlocks) pushing their car backwards to turn it around was pretty unusual. We played games and talked till late into the night. As Stephane relaxed, he asked more and more questions about God, the Bible and missions. We tried to explain everything in language he could understand.

Finally the day came for them to leave. I don't know why, but suddenly I found myself wanting to invite him to come with our group to India. It was a strange thing to do, but somehow it seemed appropriate.

Naturally, he was surprised. "Where in India will you be visiting?" he asked. I couldn't tell him exactly. He was noncommittal. Perhaps he would come, perhaps he wouldn't. He would think about it.

He asked how he could find me there if he decided to come after we left. The only contact I had in Delhi was for Thomas, the ex-policeman who had offered to help us get started in North India, so I gave him this address.

Months passed and I didn't hear from Stephane again. As our departure date approached, I managed to contact him in the Northern Territory. The Volvo had carried its freewheeling crew a long way before sand had killed the engine. His plans were as vague as ever.

"Don't worry about me," he said casually. "If I come, I come. Otherwise, I don't!"

Well, that's the end of that, I thought.

Our team trip went ahead, ending with the series of meetings in Delhi I have described. After Thomas offered his help one night, I was eager to talk about possibilities further, so we agreed to get together next day. He came to collect me at our hotel and take me to his home.

Getting to Thomas' was easier said than done, however. The colony where he lived was in one of the largest slums in India—a vast cluttered jungle of over a million people. A few steps into the tangle of streets and I was completely lost.

We walked for some time, twisting and turning, jumping over filthy puddles and dodging cows, pigs, bicycles and people. At one point, we crossed a tip area covered with animal skeletons and vultures. Eventually we moved from a Hindu area to a Muslim one where open-air butcheries lined the street, swarming with flies. Mosques boomed out chants and readings from loudspeakers. The hot, sticky air seemed heavy with spiritual oppression.

Finally, we arrived at Thomas' one-room house. Ushering me indoors, he offered me a seat and made us chai. The long walk in had left me drained, but as we settled down to talk, excitement returned. At last, I'd found someone eager to share my dreams.

After a while, we were interrupted by a knock at the door. Thomas rose to open it. A thin westerner with blonde hair stood outside.

"I am Stephane," he said, "and I am looking for Jossy."

No one will ever convince me that my young Swiss friend's arrival was anything short of a miracle. He was booked to go to Chennai in South India, but the plane was diverted to Delhi and he decided to get off. Then somehow he found his way through the slum—crisscrossing it for hours, asking for directions in halting English. All of that was astonishing enough. But that he should come on the very day I was there surpassed belief.

"Wow, man, where did you come from?" I asked.

"I just come," he said.

"How long are you here for?"

"How long are *you* here for?"

"I don't know exactly. Maybe a couple of months."

"Me too. A couple of months."

To all appearances it looked as though Stephane was just drifting in his usual resourceful way. But by now it was obvious to me that God was deeply at work in his life. His backpacking odyssey had become a spiritual journey, and now God had drawn him to India.

We poured more chai and I explained what I was planning. "I'm just going to travel," I said. "Anywhere and everywhere. I want to see what North India is like—out in the villages and small towns. I want to try to find Christians doing ministry there, if there are any." I glanced at Thomas and back to Stephane. "I'd love to have a companion. Will you come with me?"

Stephane shrugged. "Why not?" he said.

Over the next six weeks Stephane and I traveled through most of the states of India. We'd catch a train, grab a taxi, board a bus—all the time trying to get to places where we could touch the real India. We slept on public transport, at taxi ranks, even by the side of the road—just pulling up our blankets to fend off the mosquitoes.

We had many unforgettable experiences. One night, sleeping in the open, I felt water falling on me. It must be raining, I thought. I opened my eyes and looked up at a dog urinating. Another night we slept in a parking lot among dozens of taxis. I nestled down beside one to get out of the wind, but before I woke next morning, the driver started the engine and gave me a mouthful of diesel fumes.

It was a gypsy-like journey, and no one could have been a better companion than Stephane. I'd never done anything like it in my life, so his experience of traveling rough was invaluable. I already knew he was athletic—he had been a competition mountain biker and snowboarding teacher in Europe—and now I discovered he was practical and gutsy, as well. Nothing fazed him. Without his friendship and company, I honestly believe I wouldn't have lasted a week.

Immersing ourselves in the life of India was like leaping into a gigantic whirlpool. Millions of human beings swirled around us, threatening to swamp us with sensory and spiritual overload. Behind everything was the beat of India's dark spirituality, as incessant as a drum thudding in a Hindu temple.

The variety of experiences was phenomenal. In Varanasi, the holy city of Hinduism, multitudes of pilgrims crowded the banks of the Ganges River and worshipped at innumerable shrines, including one swarming with monkeys. In Deshnoke, they bowed down to thousands of rats in the Karni Mata temple, feeding them and throwing garlands. In the deserts of Rajasthan, people rode on camels and sat around fires smoking hookahs. In Punjab, tall, turbaned Sikhs carried swords and spears and worshipped at the opulent Amritsar temple, plated with 880 pounds (400kg) of gold. In Uttar Pradesh, home to 120 million Muslims, we heard the call to prayer echo through streets where burka-covered women walked. In Orissa, we encountered tribal people living a primitive forest life, spending their days trying to placate the spirits they believed inhabit everything.

Especially confronting was the intense religious devotion evident everywhere. Near-naked Hindu priests fasted until they were skeletal. Men on long pilgrimages prostrated themselves repeatedly along the road. One devotee we came across had sat on a platform in a tree for six years. Another had a long skewer piercing his cheeks and tongue, with idols of Ganesh, the elephant goddess, dangling from each end. I can still picture the wild-eyed man with almost 90 pounds (40kg) of metal tied in his long dreadlocks, struggling to hold his head up as he walked around chanting.

YOU CAN'T OUT-DREAM GOD. IS YOUR VISION GOD-SIZED? WHEN PEOPLE HEAR YOUR VISION, DO THEY KNOW HOW BIG YOUR GOD IS? LEAD IN A WAY THAT INSPIRES THOSE AROUND YOU TO BELIEVE FOR BIGGER AND GREATER THINGS.

Such zeal challenged me deeply. Back in Australia, we Christians thought we were doing brilliantly if we tithed our money or went to church for two hours a week. Here people were literally sacrificing their lives for what they believed.

Wherever we went we asked if there were Christians nearby. We visited churches and met pastors, encountering some extraordinary individuals. We saw the fine work of many Christian organizations—running hospitals and schools, leading community development projects, teaching family planning, digging wells. On the other hand, in many places we found no Christians at all.

One clear evening, we were sitting on the roof of a hotel absolutely exhausted by our continuous travels. We had not enjoyed proper sleep or food in some time and felt very confused. Where do we start? What could we do? Who will help us? The more we talked the more depressed we became. So we decided to pray. While praying, I looked up and the sky was filled with stars. It was then I felt someone whisper in my ear, "That is how many churches Jesus would like to see planted in the dark places of the world."

I turned to Stephane and said, "I know what we are going to do!"

"What?" he asked.

"Stephane, look up," I said. "How many stars do you see?"

"Lots and lots," he replied.

As I stood up, I stated out loud, "We are going to plant that many churches because Jesus said 'I will build my church,' so let's build what Jesus is building."

Stephane stood with me nodding his agreement. We joined hands and we prayed, weeping for the lostness of the people. That night something happened—something hard to explain. Jesus said that if two would agree, it will be done; as Stephane and I agreed, we both felt Jesus say just that, "Done!"

By the end of six weeks, three major changes had taken place. The first was in me: I now had the broad insight into North India I had longed for. The second was in Stephane: his faith had deepened beyond all expectations, and the vision of reaching North India had captured his heart.

"Jossy," he said before we parted, "I think this is the kind of thing I want to do with the rest of my life."

Third, there was clarity about what we were to do, even though the how was still unknown. It was time to head home.

I returned to Australia at the beginning of March 1998, just in time for the birth of our first child, Jemimah. Stephane flew back to Switzerland and immediately enrolled in a Bible college in Denmark. In November that year, when we officially started our work on the ground in North India as Compassion For India, Stephane was there too, along with his pastor. My young companion was taking the first steps that would eventually lead to his organizing short-term Swiss teams to visit India. Ultimately, he would set up our Swiss Empart office and become one of the most passionate communicators of the Empart vision.

I marvel now at how God did things back then. At the very moment I was lamenting our miserable Adelaide conference display, God was opening an enormous door. Never underestimate Him or the people He brings into your life—however unlikely they might seem.

When I returned to Australia, I found that many images from my journey with Stephane had been imprinted deeply in my heart; there were images of Hindus and Muslims, Sikhs and Buddhists, animists and Jains that I still carry with me. These people had very different beliefs, yet to me they had one thing in common: they were all searching.

My head rang with a cacophony of bells and chants and songs and prayer calls telling me that the people of North India were desperate to find their way back to God.

One day later that year, on another trip to India, I was in a city in Uttar Pradesh taking a morning walk with a local brother. We were passing a Hindu temple when the loud ringing of bells and billowing of smoke caught our attention.

Intrigued, we stopped to look.

A bearded man of about forty was standing in front of the statue of an idol. He was stripped to the waist. Beside him stood a boy of about twelve, similarly stripped. The boy was holding a six-month-old baby.

The man was whipping himself with a stiff leather strap, and the boy was whipping himself and the baby. They were chanting as the blows fell.

I stared in astonishment and revulsion. As the baby screamed and blood oozed from their self-inflicted wounds, the man scooped it into a stainless steel bowl. Then he turned and laid the bowl before the idol. The statue was huge, perhaps six-and-one-half feet high with four arms. One hand held a big sword and another held a severed head. Hanging out, its tongue was painted a vivid red.

> BE WILLING. BEFORE GOD WILL GIVE YOU OTHERS TO HELP, HE LIKES TO SEE HOW READY YOU ARE TO GET YOUR HANDS DIRTY, LEARN NEW SKILLS AND YOUR WILLINGNESS TO DO THE LITTLE THINGS.

This represented Kali, the bloodthirsty goddess of death and destruction. Scarcely able to believe what we had witnessed, we waited for the man and his little group to come out of the temple. His name was Rao and the boys were his sons. With my companion interpreting, I asked him what they had been doing. A big smile broke across his face.

"We came to offer our blood to the goddess so that our sins will be forgiven," he explained enthusiastically.

My mind lurched. "Why did you do that?" I said.

"Because our scripture tells us that without blood there is no forgiveness of sins."

His answer broke my heart. Rao was echoing exactly what the Bible says: "Without the shedding of blood there is no forgiveness" (Hebrews 9:22). He had brought the males in his family to offer their blood so that the family's sins would be forgiven and their next reincarnation would be better. They had never heard that Jesus came and shed his blood so that they didn't have to offer theirs any more.

Rao clearly thought he and his sons had done something wonderful. Suddenly, it hit me: he was not a cruel man, but a man acting out of sincere conviction—a man with a desperate hunger for salvation.

In several Indian religions, the word for salvation is *mukti*, "release." I had now seen vast numbers of men and women like Rao earnestly searching for *mukti*. In the West, most people seem uninterested in religion, and Western Christians tend to think the whole world is the same. This is untrue. The fact is that a billion Hindus are actively searching for salvation. So are a billion Muslims. So are untold numbers of Buddhists, Sikhs and many others.

Encountering Rao ignited something in me. It was as if everything I saw in my journey with Stephane laid the fire and now God sent the flame.

A new passion to preach the gospel blazed up in my heart. A world full of people like Rao was desperately hungry for Truth, and now I felt desperate to tell it.

Back home from my journey with Stephane, I had to work out what on earth should happen next.

I shared with our core group of friends everything I'd seen. Their excitement confirmed what I was quickly coming to believe—that we needed to meet the challenge head on.

The prospect both overwhelmed and energized me. The workload would be gigantic. Nonetheless, the kind of two-way relationship I envisioned—with Australian and Asian Christians partnering to reach the unreached—would be revolutionary.

After lots of prayers and discussions, we cranked up the pace and got down to work. Everyone was asking me what to do, how to do it. When I wondered why they were asking me, they reminded me that I was the leader. Even though I didn't have all the answers, I decided that the things that I did not know were not going to hold me back from pursuing my destiny.

Too often, we wait for everything to emerge before we embrace our calling. But we were past that. We just had to jump in. I kept telling my little team: "Don't let the little things you don't know hold you back from the big things you know to be true. According to 2 Peter, God desires that no one should perish. So, you don't have to pray to see if you should rescue perishing people—it is God's will. Just do what you can with what you have and then you will see the God of miracles appear to do his part. While we wait for God to make the first move, he is waiting for us."

Nothing in creation is made for itself, including you and me. Most of nature seems to understand and submit to this, but we seem to rebel—wanting to live for ourselves and do things for ourselves. This is why Jesus invites us to die to self, so that we can live in him. To live a life of significance is to give yourself away—but not just anywhere and everywhere. The Bible makes it clear that you were created by God in a unique way (Psalm 139). He has prepared you for good works (Ephesians 2:10). Our challenge is to discover and align all that we are and all that we have to that which God has already prepared.

There was much to be done. Each day, starting around 7 a.m., we collected the mail, recorded donations, wrote receipts, composed thank you letters, deposited checks and sent money to India. We followed up supporters, coordinated mailings and organized project reports and photographs for sponsors. We visited churches and conferences, preparing all the materials and setting up displays. We started to plan, organize and lead short-term mission teams. At the same time, we had to develop strategies for the growing ministry in the field and work out ways to generate financial and prayer support. We regularly finished work well after midnight. In the process, there was lot of "dying" we had to do: the comfort, security and infrastructure of a big business was gone. I had to get my hands dirty—learning to do jobs that were previously done for me.

After my return trip to India in May 1998, when I met with Thomas and the four other leaders God had placed on my heart, the task of meeting the legal requirements to operate in India joined the list. Our life felt like a cricket match, only we were playing all positions—bowling, batting, fielding, coaching and umpiring—at the same time.

Though I was thankful once again for the work ethic that my grandfather taught me, admittedly, we were sagging under the load. With a new baby now in the picture, I wondered how long we could sustain the pace.

Then, something wonderful happened. God began to bring volunteers with a variety of skills. Jenni and I jumped up and down in the living room each time someone signed up.

To accommodate the ministry's expanding needs, we moved a table into our main bedroom so Jenni could work there. The rest of the house quickly filled with leaflets, correspondence, newsletters, files and photos.

After a few months Ray, a retired builder, looked at us—crammed in like bananas in a box—and made a suggestion: "Why don't you build an office behind your house?" His initial plan for a 19' x 16' room quickly grew to twice that size and incorporated a bathroom and small kitchen. The decision to proceed with something so big was not easy. Were we being overly-ambitious? Was it responsible stewardship of God's resources? We finally went ahead in the belief there was a good chance we would need the extra space in five years' time.

The room was built entirely by volunteers. When we moved in, our four desks looked lost in the huge space. But it was a relief to be out of the cramped conditions in the house.

Shortly after that, someone volunteered to put in a second-hand phone system. We had been using our home phone up to this point. He installed it one day while Jenni and I were out. When we came home, we no sooner walked in the front door than there was a crash above our heads and our friend came down through the ceiling in a rain of plaster—still holding the phone cord. All I could do was laugh. Jenni was not amused.

Our prediction of five years turned out to be wildly inaccurate. In less than twelve months the new room was completely packed out and we had overflowed back into the house. Those were wonderful days. We were like a little community, a family. Everyone chipped in to help everyone else. Each day Jenni would prepare lunch for the team while young Jemimah crawled around people's feet. When the numbers grew too big for everyone to sit together for the meal, we extended our dining and living room.

For us, the significance of all these people wasn't just that they shared the workload. They had caught the vision. The fact that people believed in us enough to sacrifice their time, even their jobs, was precious. The confidence this gave us was an incredible blessing.

We sent all the money we received to support national workers. In the early days, operating costs were largely covered from our personal savings, but that approach wasn't sustainable long-term. Financial limitations made it difficult to employ skilled people when we needed them.

Hard as it was, however, this forced us to depend more on God. From the start of the ministry, Jenni and I felt that we should not take any money from the ministry. Rather, we believed that we should serve freely, trusting God for our needs. As the leader of Empart, I felt if I couldn't trust God to provide for our family, how could I trust God to provide for planting 100,000 churches?

It was a vital lesson, helping me to understand the way of life that would eventually become daily reality for the thousands of evangelists, church planters, pastors and believers that would emerge in Asia.

By this stage, midway through 1999, I was juggling my time between India and Australia. In Delhi and Chandigarh, I worked on building our five-man team, meeting with them in their homes and wrestling with the dream of planting 100,000 churches. In Australia, I traveled wherever I could, casting the vision and enlisting support. I was happy to sit with anyone who would listen—even one person—and share my heart.

On one such trip, Jenni and I visited Launceston (Australia) to speak at New Life Church. At the end of the worship time, the pastor, Don, said, "Before Jossy comes to speak, is today anybody's birthday? I'd like to pray for them."

To my surprise Jenni's hand shot into the air. "Yes, today is Jossy's birthday!" she called out. We'd both forgotten.

Another person had a birthday too, so Don brought us both to the front. As he was praying for me, he suddenly started to describe a picture in his mind.

"I see you in India," he said. "I see huge concrete pillars and concrete roofs. I see concrete floors everywhere. I see lots of rice fields all around. And I see thousands of people coming into this place. I see you standing there and preaching the gospel. I see people worshipping there. I see God doing amazing things."

Driving away from the church after the service, Jenni and I discussed Don's unusual picture. Neither of us could make much of it. With a mental shrug, I filed it away in the back of my brain.

Quite frankly, it just seemed a bit strange to me. Then again, I suppose my own vision of planting 100,000 churches seemed outrageous to some people, especially when we only had five people working to make that happen.

CHAPTER 9 LEADERSHIP LESSONS

+ Keep the big picture. Don't let the little things you don't know hold you back from the big things you know to be true.

+ You can't out-dream God. Is your vision God-sized? When people hear your vision do they know how big your God is? Lead in a way that inspires those around you to believe for bigger and greater things.

+ Start with what you have. Do what you can with what you have and then you will see the God of miracles appear and do his part. Don't be afraid to make the first move; God always rewards actions of faith.

+ Be willing. Before God will give you others to help, he likes to see how ready you are to get your hands dirty, learn new skills and your willingness to do the little things.

CHAPTER 9 REFLECTION QUESTIONS

1 Think of something that you want to do but have not started yet? Why? What should be your next action steps? Write them down.

2 Have earthly practicalities caused you to forget the heavenly possibilities? Journal around this thought.

3 Are you investing and giving of yourself in the right place? For the right cause? In light of eternity, are you doing what you are called to do?

10 TURNING VISION INTO ACTION

It's one thing to dream of transforming 100,000 communities by planting churches. But how do you actually do it?

I had seen how it's done in the West. An established church in one part of a city would identify a new location, find a qualified leader, raise funds, build a team and create a marketing plan. Then, the fledgling crew would be sent off to another part of the city where they would rent a building on Sundays and staff up with youth, children's and worship pastors to serve the people. Within a year or two the newly planted church would have their own campus, building, ministry departments and a thriving congregation.

While that is good and may work in a Christian cultural context, I knew this was not going to work in North India. Even if it did, how many churches could we plant based on that model? More importantly, is this what Jesus wanted to do in Asia? When Jesus said, "I will build my church," what did he mean for us in Asia? How is he going to build his church? Now new questions began to fill my mind—not about the what, but about the how. We knew we couldn't copy Western methods. Since the traditional means of church planting in North India had not been very effective, we would have to create a new model. To do so, we decided to go to the original: the gospels and the early church. As we studied the Bible we realized that it was not a new model that we needed after all, rather we needed to go back to the old model: yes, a two thousand-year-old model—Jesus' model.

SUCCEED WITH CHARACTER. LEADERS DON'T FAIL BECAUSE OF LACK OF INFORMATION BUT BECAUSE OF LACK OF CHARACTER. SO TAKE TIME TO DEVELOP CHARACTER IN YOUR PEOPLE. THIS MAY NOT BE POSSIBLE WITHOUT SHARING YOUR LIVES TOGETHER SO BE WILLING TO BE TRANSPARENT AND VULNERABLE.

Here's why: over time, different cultures and civilizations created their interpretations of Jesus' church model. Because of this, the church we have today is like a photocopy of a photocopy—the more copies we make, the less they reflect the primary image. As the original text fades away, these copies (churches) become more and more vague, making it hard to understand what they are saying. Returning to the gospels and the book of Acts provides a clear image of the original design for planting churches. So the Indian leadership and I agreed to read, study and meditate the way of Jesus and the early church. In fact, ever since that early agreement, all our key leaders read and listen to the book of Acts together nearly every month. Doing this helps us stay close to the original model.

Whenever I returned to North India, I would meet with my team of five, spending several days together in one of their tiny one-bedroom homes. Typically, there was no running water and only three or four hours of electricity each day. For days at a time, we would study the way of Jesus and the early church, pray and strategize together. We ate on plates held in our laps and slept on the floor at night.

This time, we were back in Thomas' small house in Delhi. The North Indian summer was stifling, but the faces of the five brothers squeezed into the room with me were eager.

The challenges we were now grappling with was to balance our compassionate desire to bring social transformation with Jesus' command to preach the gospel and make disciples. We needed *specific* answers for our context—where poverty and human misery is pushed into your face. At least on the surface, poverty and related causes seemed to be the most urgent need. In the West, where the media is often filled with news of earthquakes and famines, "compassion" seems to translate into giving money to help people in trouble. We thought it would be a lot easier to raise money from the West for these causes than for preaching the gospel. But, if we gave into that mindset, we knew we could never explain to Jesus why we ignored his command to preach the gospel.

As we started to dig deep into the scriptures, we began to see a different perspective.

Studying Mark 6, we found it. Here, Jesus was moved with compassion for the crowds "because they were like sheep without a shepherd." His immediate response, the Bible says, was to teach them. He didn't first heal them because they were sick or feed them because they were hungry. He taught them because they were lost. That was his number one priority.

"We shouldn't be moved primarily by poverty and hunger, dreadful as it is," I explained. "We should be moved by the things that moved Jesus. As he looked at the crowd, compassion flooded his heart; these people were like sheep without a shepherd and needed to know him."

But that wasn't all that Jesus did. After he had finished teaching, his disciples drew his attention to the people's need for food. Jesus' response was unexpected: "You give them something to eat." When they complained that they couldn't, Jesus provided the miraculous resources to them through the loaves and fishes.

"I believe the principle here is that the church needs to look after the people who are in its hands," I said. "First, Jesus preached the gospel. Then he organized and resourced his disciples to distribute God's provision to the community. That's what we need to do. We need to preach the gospel as our top priority, but we also need to structure social programs through the local churches and disciples."

It is not either just about preaching nor is it just about meeting a need; we need to do both social and spiritual transformation. Jesus never separated the Good Commandment and the Great Commission; to him these were the two sides of the same coin.

As I saw it, these two approaches went hand in hand. Neither Jesus nor the early church separated them, preaching and compassionate care always worked together. But in the West we have rationalized separating the two. And, by doing so, we have removed the goodness out of greatness. We should never allow the last words of Jesus to be compromised. No one should expect to benefit from Christian love and compassion without being presented the truth about the One who compels us with that love and compassion. If you are giving me something I should know your motivation; if your motivation is Jesus, then I need to know it is Jesus who motivates you. The message has to be clearly understood. Otherwise, we miss the point.

"Does that mean we should only help people who become Christians?" many have asked.

My response: "No. Whether people receive the message or not is their choice. We don't say, 'You have to become a Christian to benefit from these programs.' But we do say, 'You need to understand why we do this. It's up to you whether you embrace the message or just take the benefit.'"

Christ-like compassion compels us to care for the lost and the needy, giving people the answer to both problems.

In November 1998, the official launch of the ministry had catapulted us into a period of intense prayer, reflection and strategizing. Throughout 1999 the five Indian leaders and I slowly laid the foundations of the ministry. Working hard, we clarified the principles and values that would undergird the movement we hoped to build.

The key to our first principle lay in Jesus' Great Commission: "All authority in heaven and on earth has been given to me. Therefore go and make disciples of all nations, baptizing them in the name of the Father and of the Son and of the Holy Spirit, and teaching them to obey everything I have commanded you" (Matthew 28:18–20).

The heart of the Great Commission lies in the words "make disciples." Until recently, most strategies to accomplish it have been developed by people from the West. As a natural consequence, the methods used were largely based on an understanding and perspective of Western culture. However, Asia operates according to a very different cultural and religious framework. Just as we needed to define a contextual model of church here, we also had to discover what the implementation of the Great Commission would look like in our specific context.

Thanks again to my exposure in business, I was quick to recognize that many multinational corporations have done a far better job at this than the church. Take the McDonald's example: before you walk into a McDonald's restaurant in India, right outside the door you will see a sign that reads, "We don't use beef or pork in our restaurants." Once inside, you will notice the menu is quite different. You'll find Veg McMuffin, Veg Supreme McMuffin,

McAloo Tikki, Masala Grill Veg, Veg Maharaja Mac and a host of other products tailor-made for the culture and context of their customers.

If we are to see the mission of Jesus fulfilled, we can't have "my way or the highway" or "take it or leave it" attitudes. Back to the example of McDonald's: their strategic adaptations to the Indian market do not compromise their vision and mission. They are agile and flexible, acculturating in ways that welcome and value their customers. They give people what they are hungry for. Not surprisingly, there are often long lines at some of their restaurants, even running out into the streets.

Sadly, many Christian churches in the West sit empty today. In comparison, everywhere Jesus or Paul went, they drew McDonald's-like crowds. They met people right where they found them. It seems that multinationals have learned to adapt more quickly and more effectively than the church.

If we were to make disciples, we had to consider the current setting we were entering, especially its religious aspects.

In India we knew it was easy to motivate people to put up their hand to follow Christ. They already believed in 300 million gods, so one more was neither here nor there. But such a "decision" did not make a disciple, as became obvious if you challenged them to renounce all other gods and accept Jesus as the only Lord and Savior.

For an Indian, true discipleship required a massive cultural and mental shift that simply couldn't be accomplished overnight.

Hinduism is the majority religion of India and it shapes every aspect of people's lives. If I am a Hindu, the caste system tells me my place in the social order, from those at the top (Brahmins) to those at the bottom (Dalits). In addition, my belief in karma gives me the key to my personal destiny. Karma says that whatever my circumstances, I am either enjoying the benefits of my good works in my last life or suffering the consequences of my bad works.

This leads to a pervasive fatalism. I will have little motivation to improve my fortunes; indeed, to do so may earn me more bad karma for trying to circumvent my just punishment. Similarly, helping someone else may interfere with his or her punishment, again bringing me bad karma. All I can do is to accept my lot and work for a better reincarnation next time.

I do this by attending to my religious obligations. Making offerings at the temple, praying to the gods, participating in the rituals, festivals and sacrifices, this is what will bring me good karma and secure a better rebirth. In Hinduism, a good man is not someone who helps others, but someone who fulfills his religious obligations.

Thus even the poorest, most uneducated Hindu is caught in a web of mind-numbing complexity. His conclusion: "I have no future. I deserve what I have. This misery is my lot in life, so I will simply beg until I die." He suffers and his children suffer, generation after generation.

This conclusion is reinforced by the general attitude to those at the bottom. In Hinduism, Dalits have less dignity and worth than cows, elephants, snakes or even rats.

Without a doubt, the gospel is the most powerful tool to transform lives and societies. But unless we address the root issues, packaging and presenting the gospel in a culturally relevant and appropriate way, we will never cure the disease. How long does it take to renew a mind steeped in such a worldview? A two-or-three night evangelistic campaign won't do it. Beliefs are much more powerful than we like to admit. Fulfilling the Great Commission requires much more than using the techniques that work in a Western nation and copying them around the world.

To make disciples in India involves changing the thinking of thousands of years; it necessitates valuing people just as they are. What is true for Hindus, we realized, is equally true for Sikhs, Muslims and others. So we determined that our first principle would center on making disciples; that is, we would commit to the difficult, long-term process of transforming the way people think and, therefore, behave.

Once this first principle of making disciples was established, it led naturally to the next: the priority of church planting.

We knew we couldn't effectively make disciples without the existence of local churches to sustain them. We needed a means that would also ensure those churches remained healthy. Unquestionably, disciples are made by the supernatural intervention of the Holy Spirit, but Jesus gave each of his followers a part, too. Discipleship requires teaching, training, relationship and fellowship. It is a life-long process among a community of believers, the local church.

Clearly, we saw that new Christians needed to be plugged into fellowships led by those who could bring them to maturity of faith. Our goal would be to plant churches through local people, for local people, using local languages and worshiping God in local ways.

Another consideration was just as vital: those who come to Christ in India are often alienated from their community. In a village culture, that is disastrous. The sense of belonging is a critical human need. Church planting, then, is not just a nice religious idea; it is a necessity. We needed to create communities where brothers and sisters belong, where they are cared for and where they have a future.

We decided that everything we did would emanate from a local church. Whether evangelizing or training church planters, discipling new believers or caring for orphans, the underlying structure was to be the local church.

In the words of Bill Hybels, founder of Willow Creek Community Church, "The local church is the hope of the world." I too believe the church offers the greatest hope to the world. Governments alone can't solve the world's biggest problems like poverty, disease, racial and ethnic conflict, and illiteracy. In these and other areas, Christian leaders and local churches can, and should, help in strategic and significant ways.

Moreover, these churches would be churches for the entire community; caste or social group could not segregate them. The only thing necessary for a person to become a member would be that he or she renounce all other gods and declare the lordship of Christ.

In the past, as foreign missionaries were refused entry to India, missionaries from South India had often stepped into the vacated space and enforced their cultural standards on North Indian converts. This created enormous barriers. For example, when South Indians insist that a Christian man could not have long hair, they have made it almost impossible for a Sikh, whose culture says he must never cut his hair, to come to Christ. Likewise, when they insist women should not wear jewelry, they unwittingly make it difficult for a married woman to choose to follow Christ. In North Indian culture, a married woman only removes her jewelry if she is divorcing her husband!

The pattern that Jesus set was entirely different. He called the fishermen and they immediately followed him. He didn't tell them to get a haircut first. He said to Zacchaeus, "I must stay at your house today." He didn't say tomorrow after you've repented and cleared out all the junk. Radical transformations should take place, but that should be the result of the outworking of Christ living in people, not as a condition for following God.

The same applies to worship styles and other facets of church life. Cultures within North India vary substantially, so we decided we would not expect all churches to follow one set of practices. The outworking of biblical principles in each place had to be discovered by the local people within their own cultural framework.

Our goal was to empower, not impose. "Empowering" involves providing mentoring, training and spiritual covering through relationship. We would also provide legal covering for the local churches and moral accountability for the church planters.

We went further: we decided that we wouldn't try to control pastors or transfer them from church to church. If a man pioneered a work, it was his work. God had appointed him to that place, and only God had the authority to take him out of it. (The only exception would be gross negligence of biblical principles, in which case we would assist the local church in resolving the problem.)

But we didn't just want to plant individual churches; we knew if we did that the unreached millions would never be reached. We wanted to ignite a church planting movement like the one described in the book of Acts. This led us to some further key principles.

The first principle to ignite this movement was that all our strategies had to be easily multipliable. Taj Mahals can be admired but not multiplied; we didn't want the admiration, we wanted multiplication. Any church should be able to say, "we could do that" and adapt our model to their needs. This was particularly true of social programs. The social programs should be administered through the local church and be of benefit to both the Kingdom of God and the community, as well as be readily multipliable.

The centers to train pioneer church planters that we envisioned also needed to be multipliable. We'd never train thousands of church planters by building one big institution like a seminary. We needed a model of training that could instruct local people in their own language without removing them from their cultural context. This would also help to preserve cultural relevance: people could be trained on location rather than taken out of their context and introduced to foreign cultures and lifestyles.

But how exactly would we train church planters? Here we came to the nub of things.

As before, we looked to Jesus' example. How did he train his team? First, he selected them and then he lived with them. They traveled together, fished together, cooked together, prayed together. In the middle of all this, he taught them and ministered with them. Most of the time he concentrated on a small group so he could relate to them one-on-one and work on their character.

Paul did something similar. This great scholar, who knew the Jewish educational system inside out, never set up a seminary. Wherever he planted churches, he appointed elders and deacons who were local people who spoke the local language, understood the local customs and had local networks. Then he trained them on the job. Some, like Timothy, he took with him so he could mentor them, just as Jesus did.

This became the biblical training model: training in the context of real life, focusing on biblical principles and practical Kingdom work, which equates to character development. I was convinced this model had been largely lost in the West, where the church had embraced a secular educational approach. I had seen scores of people earn theology degrees, but I knew that fewer than 10% of Bible college graduates in Australia end up in any form of ministry. An intellectual knowledge of theology would not be enough. Leaders don't fail because of lack of information, they fail because they lack character.

How might such training work? We sketched out possibilities.

Suppose a group of students, twenty or so, lived for a year with an experienced leader and his family. They would be together twenty-four hours a day, seven days a week. The students would learn by observing the pastor. How does he live? How does he relate to his family? What is his daily and weekly routine?

The pastor's own church would be in the same place, probably using the same building. So the students would be involved in the church program. They would wrestle with questions like: How does a church function? How

EMPOWER, DON'T IMPOSE. A LEADER MUST INSTILL THE "WHY" AND "WHAT" IN EVERYONE'S HEART AND MIND, AND THEN LEAVE ROOM FOR THEM TO GRAPPLE WITH THE "HOW" IN THEIR CONTEXT. THIS CREATES A CULTURE OF EMPOWERED PEOPLE. AND IN THE END, MEASURE THE SUCCESS OF THE "WHAT" NOT THE "HOW".

> CATALYZE GROWTH. A REPLICABLE MODEL CATALYZES GROWTH EXPONENTIALLY. THIS IS ONE OF THE GREATEST SECRETS BEHIND THE MODEL OF JESUS. WHAT HE DID, EACH OF HIS DISCIPLES ALSO COULD DO.

does the pastor pray for people and counsel them? How does he handle church issues?

This relational mentoring could be supplemented by more formal learning. Other pastors could come and teach, covering both biblical and practical subjects. These pastors would not be professional teachers but practitioners, passing on what actually worked for them.

As well as classroom learning, the students would learn skills such as how to cut hair, make candles and soap, start schools, and offer first aid. That way, when they go into villages they would be able to give holistic leadership for both the spiritual and social needs of that community.

In the evenings and on weekends, trainees could go with one of the pastors or by themselves to do practical evangelism and or social services in the community. As a team, their goal would be to plant two or three new churches by the time their training finished. Doing this would give them the opportunity to apply what they were learning right away rather than waiting until after graduation.

According to this method, by the end of the year they would have observed, studied, learned and implemented. They would have seen the book of Acts lived out before their eyes. Close living with others would have rubbed the roughest edges off each one's character. All of this was designed to give them great confidence as they launched into whatever work God gave them to do.

Of course, to accomplish all this we would need to rent or build a suitable building. It would need to be multipurpose housing for both the pastor's family and the students, including a large room or hall to use for classes and church gatherings. Any social program run by the church would also be based from that building.

And so our ideas and strategies gradually took shape. At the same time, the six of us did ministry of various kinds in villages and worked hard to network with existing church planters. I visited to encourage, pray with, and teach them. My deepest desire was to serve the servants, to help them become more fruitful.

By the end of 1999, we were ready to begin in earnest. The next twelve months would be a year of experimentation.

First we set up our initial church planter-training center in Chandigarh, 150 miles north of Delhi. Here we put our ideas into action on a small scale, seeing if they were feasible.

Then we wanted to do something about homeless and needy children, including orphans (of which India had over 12 million). Being unhappy with the traditional institutional model, we decided to try something new: we would have a pastor take a group of children into his home to live with his family.

Other possibilities we explored included tailoring training, health care through temporary medical camps, literacy programs and a traveling film ministry.

And that wasn't all. We were also starting to play with an exciting new idea: staging a large Christian convention in Punjab at the end of 2000. We wanted to bring hundreds, possibly thousands, of people together to celebrate their faith in Christ.

There were two motivations for this. The first was the inferiority complex I'd observed among believers in North India. The North Indian Christian community was only 0.14% of the total population, with most churches being just twenty or thirty believers meeting in houses. The general population saw it as weak and insignificant, and believers themselves perceived the Christian community to be small and powerless. If 2,000 people came together and worshiped Jesus, we believed it would give them a tremendous morale boost.

The political power brokers would also have to take notice. This was our second motivation. As long as Indian politicians saw Christians as a tiny minority, they would ignore them. But a significant gathering of believers might change that perception and give the Christian community some important political leverage.

As it turned out, the idea to build more connection with politicians received a huge boost in a second event planned for 2000. God initiated it, putting me in the right place at the right time and then doing something totally unexpected.

I've never set out to hob-nob with dignitaries, but one day early in 1999 someone offered to arrange a meeting for me with the Chief Minister of the Punjab, Shri Prakash Singh Badal. I enthusiastically agreed.

The meeting was scheduled at Shri Badal's office in Punjab's capital, Chandigarh. Politics in India can be a violent business so security was tight. After stepping through a metal detector and having our bags x-rayed, we were patted down by guards and sniffed by dogs. Then we were shown into his office.

The Chief Minister greeted us with a warm smile. He was very tall but not intimidating. His manner was easy-going, even gentle. His personal assistant was also in the room.

We chatted for a while, simply enjoying the conversation. I had no particular agenda other than to see what God might do with this unexpected opportunity. Eventually Shri Badal looked up, signaling a change in direction.

"So, Chacko, what can I do for you?"

I had no reply ready but an idea popped into my mind. "Well, next year is the 2,000th birthday of Jesus Christ, who is my Lord and Savior. I'd love to do something to celebrate his birthday."

Shri Badal looked intrigued. "That's very interesting. What would you like to do?"

"Oh," I said, thinking fast, "it would be great to have a big meeting with lots of people, and have a big cake and a big time of celebration."

"So what would you need for that?' He nodded to his PA to take notes.

"We'd need a venue."

"How big a ground?"

"Big enough for maybe 30,000-40,000 people."

"Okay. What else?"

"We'd need security, and all the permissions and clearances necessary to put on an event like that."

"Of course."

"And," I said, taking a deep breath, "it would be great to have all your cabinet ministers come along to celebrate the occasion."

The Chief Minister's response was enthusiastic. To my amazement, he quickly decided the celebration would not only occur but also would also

> BE AGILE. WHILE THE VISION AND MISSION SHOULD NEVER CHANGE, YOUR STRATEGIES NEED TO BE AGILE, CONTINUALLY ADAPTING TO MEET THE CULTURE, CONTEXT AND TIMES. A LEADER WHO IS BOUND TO SPECIFIC STRATEGIES WILL DIE WITH HIS OR HER VISION, WHILE AGILE LEADERS WILL ENJOY WATCHING THEIR VISION THRIVE BEYOND THEIR LIFETIME.

be organized and funded by the government. He would make sure that it be promoted widely in the media and have his personal backing.

"And Chacko," he asked, "would you come and speak at this meeting? Would you come and tell everybody about the birth of Jesus, why he came and what happened when he did?"

"I'd love to," I replied.

I left the meeting with my head whirling. Why would Shri Badal, a devout Sikh, want his government to be associated with a celebration of the birth of Jesus Christ? And why would he ask me, a South Indian Australian he'd only just met, to participate? It was totally beyond my understanding.

It had to be God. And I already sensed that what had happened in that office would have more implications than I could see.

CHAPTER 10 LEADERSHIP LESSONS

+ Succeed with character. Leaders don't fail because of lack of information but because of lack of character. So take time to develop character in your people. This may not be possible without sharing your lives together so be willing to be transparent and vulnerable.

+ Be clear. Know and articulate your values and principles clearly, not just the vision and mission.

+ Empower, don't impose. A leader must instill the "Why" and "What" in everyone's heart and mind, and then leave room for them to grapple with the "How" in their context. This creates a culture of empowered people. And in the end, measure the success of the "What" not the "How."

+ Catalyze growth. A replicable model catalyzes growth exponentially. This is one of the greatest secrets behind the model of Jesus. What he did, each of his disciples also could do.

+ Be agile. While the vision and mission should never change, your strategies need to be agile, continually adapting to meet the culture, context and times. A leader who is bound to specific strategies will die with his or her vision, while agile leaders will enjoy watching their vision thrive beyond their lifetime.

CHAPTER 10 REFLECTION QUESTIONS

1 What areas of your character could cause you to fail? Who is going to help you avoid that failure?

2 How does your model of leadership, training and making disciples compare to that of Jesus?

3 Take time to review your strategies within your culture, context and time. Are they culturally relevant and agile? What changes are required to get the results you desire?

4 What are the things holding you back from seeing exponential growth? How replicable is your model?

11 MIRACLES AND MISERY

The Punjab Christian Festival and the Jesus birthday celebration were still a year away, and right now there were more pressing concerns. Between training the team in India and overseeing the ministry base back in Australia, I was fully stretched. And as often happens when the Kingdom of God starts to advance, obstacles mysteriously appeared in our path.

Problems sprang up on several fronts. One was the deep spiritual oppressiveness that hangs over parts of India.

Every time I made the journey into the sprawling slum where Thomas lived, heaviness descended on me like a fog. No taxi could make it through the potholed streets, so I usually hired someone to carry my luggage and walked in. Even on bright summer days the sense of darkness pressed down more and more with every step. Inevitably, I would arrive at Thomas' door deflated. Our work there was always conducted within sound of the Islamic calls to prayer that echoed through the neighborhood five times a day.

Then there was my health. Whenever I went to India, I came down sick. On every single trip I struggled with the infamous "Delhi belly," often accompanied by a high fever. Once I even caught hepatitis. Many times I contracted mystery illnesses that the doctors could not diagnose.

Even more seriously, we faced mounting opposition—both from the opponents of Christianity and from its friends.

The actions of those who hated "Western religion" were to be expected. At the time, fundamentalist fervor was growing in many religious communities. An anti-Christian spirit was flowering into acts of outright belligerence.

I had several experiences of this myself. One time, we were attacked while driving our new van outside Chandigarh. Another confrontation occurred in a village in the state of Haryana during a trip with an Australian team.

We were on a kind of gospel tour, traveling by taxi from village to village. With the help of Hindi translators, we put on a lively open-air program with music and puppets. Usually we distributed tracts and I shared a gospel message.

This specific afternoon we set up in the middle of a village. A crowd of about twenty adults and thirty children stood around listening. We presented our program and I began to preach.

As I went on, however, four or five young men started to yell abuse.

I stopped speaking and went with my translator to talk to them. Their accusations grew wilder and wilder as their anger flared.

"You have no right to go around India preaching this white man's religion!"

"We're Indians! We're Hindus!"

"You've betrayed India!"

"You're worse than a dog!"

"You shouldn't be living!"

As they shouted, the team was bundled into a taxi and driven to safety.

I tried to talk to the men as calmly as possible, but the situation quickly got out of hand. The one who appeared to be the ringleader pushed me in the chest, then swung his fist and hit me in the stomach. My translator was pushed and struck. Things would have become even nastier if some older villagers hadn't leapt in and calmed the young men down.

This episode rattled me badly. As with the attack on the van, it made me wonder whether we could go on. But we did, and six months later I heard the most extraordinary news. The leader of the protestors, the very man who had screamed in my face and punched me, had walked into a traditional Church of North India church one day and given his life to Christ.

Experiences like this made me feel that every trip to India could be my last. Jenni and I had to come to terms with this. I didn't have the white skin that made people think twice before attacking Westerners to avoid international wrath. I didn't go looking for trouble, but if it found me… well…my life was in God's hands. I live my life with the conviction that God has numbered my days, and without His knowledge not even a hair of my head falls out.

Alarming as this kind of opposition was, in some ways another kind of hostility was harder still—that from other Christians.

Our determination not to impose cultural restrictions on new believers was one flash point. Once we started baptizing women with jewelry and men with long hair, some other Christians labeled us a cult. Pastors were ordered by their church leadership not to have fellowship with our church planters. Because of my youth and inexperience, many Christian leaders felt that I wasn't qualified for leadership.

Hardest of all for me was increased antagonism within my own family. They felt strongly that our move into North India was wrong. They could not understand why I was investing so much time and money and risking my life for a people and culture that was not ours. They pleaded with me to do it in the South where at least it will enhance our family name and social standing. When our ministry ignored their pleas, letters were sent to all the people they knew, warning them against supporting me. Among other allegations, they said I had rebelled against family authority, which in India is a serious offence.

At the time I consulted three senior pastors in Melbourne about what to do. All advised me the same way: "Don't try to defend yourself. 'Vengeance is mine, says the Lord.' Leave it with God. Just keep doing what you believe God has called you to do. And keep blessing them."

In the years since that letter, we made no progress in reconciling, despite numerous attempts. This gave great pain to Jenni and me. But the lesson we learned was a powerful one: don't take revenge—simply keep praying God's blessings on everyone. This enabled us to face not only family opposition, but also the other animosity and rumor mongering that, sadly, seems to be part of ministry life.

By God's grace, as others saw the fruit of our ministry, they also began to see our heart. Slowly people realized they could rejoice in how God was blessing us without compromising their own work. The time eventually came when many recognized the new thing God was doing and even modified their own practices in the light of it.

It is a great relief when Christians realize their battle is against the powers of darkness, not against each other.

Meanwhile, back in North India, our five leaders got the ball rolling on preparations for the Punjab Christian Festival. First, they went to South India for some training from leaders who had experience organizing annual church conferences of 25,000 people. Second, I asked them to shortlist possible venues around Punjab capable of hosting a few thousand people for four days.

Early in 2000, I returned to India. The guys had done their job well and had three possible sites to show me. The first one was in a district called Gurdaspur on the border with Pakistan, a six hour drive northwest of Chandigarh.

When we arrived, we turned off the main highway and drove towards a massive open-sided concrete facility. As I looked at it, something incredible happened. The picture that Pastor Don in Launceston saw when he prayed for me nine months before came back to me: "I see huge concrete pillars and concrete roofs. I see concrete floors everywhere. I see lots of rice fields all around." I looked around at the rice fields nearby, then at the acres of open concrete apron stretching in all directions. It was exactly what he'd described.

"Who owns this place?" I asked.

Thomas explained it was a government grain distribution depot that served farmers across Punjab. The farmers sold their rice and wheat to various co-ops and societies, which in turn sold the grain to the government. Grain was shipped here to be sorted, packaged and stored, before it was distributed all over India and the world.

Thousands of bags of grain stood in towering stacks all around us. Trucks rumbled in and out. The area swarmed with workers. I took it all in and I knew—this was our venue.

POWER OF UNITY. IF THE DORMANT ENERGY OF CHRISTIANITY CAN BE RELEASED INTO ACTIVE ENERGY THROUGH UNITY, THE CHURCH CAN AND WILL CHANGE THE WORLD.

"I don't think we need to look at the other two places," I said. "This is it."
The others were skeptical. "I doubt whether we could get it," one of
them said.

"It would be far too difficult," another agreed. "We'd have to get so
many permissions and approvals it would take forever."

"And they wouldn't give it for a religious function anyway. If they gave it
to one group, they'd have to give it to everyone."

I surveyed the scene again. In my mind's eye, I saw a big stage in the
undercover area, with scores of tents and thousands of people milling
around. "Let's pray," I said. "Let's talk to anyone and everyone we know in
any position of influence. Let's believe God is going to give this to us."

It wasn't easy, but the men set to work. Several weeks later, when I was
back in Australia, I got a phone call from Thomas. The news was good, he
said. With the help of a government minister we knew well, approval had
been granted for us to use the facility during the first week in September.

I was over the moon. Our prayers had been answered.

"And how much will it cost?" I asked.

I could almost hear his big grin coming through the phone. "Nothing."

"What? What do you mean?"

The government had offered to give us the site for a whole week at no cost.

Arranging the festival venue a great start, but it would still require
a massive amount of work to make it happen. We were eager for the
entire Body of Christ in Punjab to do it together. I traveled from Australia
four times to meet with leaders from seventeen denominations. They
unanimously endorsed the vision.

The logistics were mind-boggling. We had no idea how many people
would come, but we had to plan for several thousand. We arranged tents
and booked as much accommodation around the area as we could. We
organized transport to bring people from the railway and bus station five
miles away. We sourced food supplies and cooking equipment, carpets and
lights, sound systems and an army of young, eager volunteers.

By the first day of the festival, September 5, 2000, the grain depot had
been transformed. At the center of the site stood a meeting tent capable of
holding 5,000 people. A six and one-half foot high stage took up one end
and carpet (donated by the local mayor) covered the concrete floor. Outside
the tent was room for another 5,000. Five hundred fluorescent tubes fixed
to bamboo poles crisscrossed the area, and nearby a miniature city of

kitchens, food-serving areas and accommodation tents had sprung up.

The first meeting was scheduled for 6:30 p.m. that evening and people would be arriving all day. How many would come?

I was so anxious and excited I didn't know what to do. All morning I walked up and down in my hotel room, waiting for the dream to become reality.

One concern in particular weighed heavily on me. From the moment I first saw sheets of lightning brighten the sky at 5 a.m., I had been praying fervently that the festival would be spared. Through the day the wind started to gust and torrential rain bucketed down. I watched out of my hotel window in dismay.

Around 4:30 p.m. the phone rang. The agitated voice of one of our leaders told me the worst. The storm's onslaught had abated, but it had wreaked havoc. The whole tent and stage had collapsed.

I jumped into a taxi with Thomas and raced to the site. It was like a scene from a disaster movie. The fallen tent covered a tangled mass of soaked carpet, shattered fluorescent tubes, smashed sound and lighting equipment and live electric wires. I was told one of our volunteers had been thrown through the air after touching a cable. Others had received shocks. Someone had tripped over and suffered what looked like a broken arm.

And the first meeting of the festival was only one and one-half hours away.

I winced as an appalling irony struck me: the passage of Scripture I had planned to speak on was the story of Jesus calming the storm. I had been all fired up to preach about his awesome power, a power so great that even the winds and waves obeyed him. I stood amongst the wreckage of the festival, tears welling in my eyes, and thought: this is the devil's biggest attack.

For me it was too much. All those months of work had been reduced to sodden rubble. I grabbed one of the leaders and said, "It's over. I can't do it. Forget about everything. Let's just pack up and go."

I turned to get into the taxi, but another of our leaders stopped me. His faced was determined. "Give us two hours and we'll get everything happening again," he said.

"You must be joking," I protested.

"No. We can't let the devil win on this."

Immediately I heard his words, something clicked in my spirit. All of a sudden enthusiasm and vision came surging back. I gathered the team together, about 300 people, and told them to ring or visit every church nearby and get as many helpers as they could. We all got together and prayed.

For the next hour or so we worked frantically, clearing away debris and setting up an impromptu stage under a section of the permanent concrete roofing. The rented PA and lighting systems were useless, but the guy who owned them, a Sikh, offered to get replacements from another town. After a herculean effort, by eight o'clock we were ready to start the festival.

Three thousand people were there that night. I still preached my message about Jesus calming the storm, and as far as I was concerned, he had done it again. He had turned catastrophe into triumph.

I've thought a lot about that day since then. I believe it was a test of faith—a test of our commitment, our desire, our stickability. Any vision that is not tested will remain a hollow dream. Most people give up when tests come, and if it hadn't been for my brother speaking when he did, I would have given up too. Through this I learned the importance of having the right people around a leader who can speak into his life.

The first Punjab Christian Festival led to a second one twelve months later, and then a third. Each year since then it has grown in size and influence.

The festival is primarily for Christians, bringing them together from all walks of life to celebrate Jesus and challenge them about the Great Commission. Yet a surprising number of Sikhs and Hindus also attend. Many come to faith in Christ. One man I met became a Christian one year, committed his life to serve the Lord the following year and the third year joined our training center to become a church planter. Another man who became a Christian at the festival gave me the joy of performing his marriage—to a girl who had also been saved at the festival!

The storm in 2001 was only the first of many challenges. Several times since then the festival has been threatened by bad weather. But people literally stood and prayed, then watched as the rain fell all around the ground, but not on the meeting. The fourth time this happened the local newspaper put it on the front page, declaring, "Their God must be real!"

We've also faced enormous logistical challenges. Feeding all those people requires thousands of kilograms of rice, dahl (lentil curry) and rhoti (Indian bread). Providing accommodation requires us to hire out every auditorium, school and marriage palace in the district.

But where the needs are many, so are God's miracles of provision. One year, for example, a Hindu gave over 11,000 pounds of rice as a contribution. The Sikh man we hired to manage the lighting and PA equipment charged us only 30% of the normal cost. Now this kind of thing is common, and it illustrates how God will use anybody, not just Christians. When God says he will provide, he does not mean only through offering bags or Christians.

The ongoing availability of the venue itself is a miracle. Counting set-up and dismantling time, the festival disrupts the depot's schedule for up to four weeks. During the main week of the festival, all work grinds to a halt. Yet they happily let us return year after year.

Not everyone appreciates such a strong show of Christian faith, of course. We have both our own security volunteers and police security—and we need them. One year an angry militant tried to drive a four-wheel drive straight into a meeting. Our security team blocked him with other vehicles until the police arrived, but he drove the car into the rice paddies and escaped on foot.

On another occasion, I was preaching in a meeting when some of our security personnel marched into the crowd just ten feet in front of me. They plucked an agitated young man from his seat and dragged him out. Something about his behavior had aroused their suspicions. They found a large knife taped under his jacket. He said he had been paid by militants to stab me.

Such threats of violence are not uncommon. We have quite a collection of weapons confiscated from would-be troublemakers. Another year, two truckloads of young men armed with sticks and swords tried to disrupt the meetings, screaming abuse and threats. Fortunately the government minister responsible for minority communities was in the audience, and a mobile phone call from him brought a contingent of India's elite counter-terrorism commandos, the Black Cats, to the scene. They bundled the troublemakers into trucks and took them away.

One of the worst incidents occurred in 2001 when our staff and volunteers were packing up after the festival. That evening a violent anti-Christian mob attacked the rented house where the main team was staying. A number of our leaders were beaten with sticks. Somehow the gang climbed onto the roof, and as our people were chased out of the house, the attackers dropped rocks on them. A 33 pound (15kg) rock struck the shoulder of Pastor Abraham, one of our key leaders, missing his head by inches. Several of our guys had to be hospitalized.

IMPORTANCE OF YOUR VISION BEING TESTED. ANY VISION
THAT IS NOT TESTED WILL REMAIN A HOLLOW DREAM.

But the militants didn't reckon on the reaction of the local townspeople. When word got out that the Punjab Christian Festival leaders had been targeted, hundreds of residents filled the streets and brought the town to a standstill. The local police inspector came, but the protestors declared they wouldn't move until the attackers had been brought before the crowd to apologize. After a brief and intense manhunt, two or three men were arrested. Within a couple of hours, the people had the public apology they wanted.

This experience showed us the level of unity and support we had in the community, which had experienced God's blessing through the festival. If the dormant energy of Christianity can be released into active energy, through unity the church can and will change the world.

It also reminded us that God's promise never to leave us or forsake us had to be a reality we lived by, not just a pious platitude.

Such festivals are now an established fixture on the Christian calendar in many places, with tens of thousands in attendance. In keeping with Empart's policy of encouraging indigenous leadership and self-sufficiency, these festivals are now organized and funded entirely by local people, who celebrate their faith and local culture.

The festival has done a number of important things for believers. First, as we hoped it would, it has shown them that the church of Christ is vibrant and alive—that their little house churches of twenty to thirty people are part of something much, much bigger. Second, it has provided an opportunity for Christians from different backgrounds to come together and express their unity in Christ. Third, it has raised the profile of Christians, especially with political leaders. The numbers represented by the festival have made many leaders very happy to talk to us.

The most significant effect, however, is something far deeper. One night an elderly man pulled me aside. I knew him as Pastor Samuel, a pioneer church planter who had been laboring in Punjab for over fifty years.

"Pastor Jossy, I want to tell you something," he began, his voice husky with age and countless sermons. "Since the start of this festival I've been coming every year, and I've seen a significant change in the spiritual climate of this region. More people are being saved. We're experiencing more healings and miracles. Most of the churches are growing. In all my years of ministry I've never seen anything like it."

He reached up to wipe tears from his eyes. "Thank you for giving us your leadership and support. In heaven you will know what you have done."

That's what it's all about. When Christians come together in unity, blessing is not left to chance, but God makes sure it happens (Psalm 133).

The Punjab Christian Festival and other festivals have given wonderful opportunities for our leaders to utilize their gifts. Many church planters from across Asia have attended and learned important skills in areas such as leadership, management and administration. But above all, the festivals have given us enormous confidence in God's ability to open doors. If we have his favor, nothing is impossible.

CHAPTER 11 LEADERSHIP LESSONS

+ Importance of your vision being tested. Any vision that is not tested will remain a hollow dream.

+ Power of unity. If the dormant energy of Christianity can be released into active energy through unity, the church can and will change the world.

+ Blessing in unity. When Christians come together in unity, blessing is not left to chance, but God makes sure it happens.

+ Provision. When God says he will provide, he does not mean only through offering bags or Christians.

CHAPTER 11 REFLECTION QUESTIONS

1 What would the expression of Christ-like unity look like in your city or town? What are the things holding you back from connecting with others in meaningful ways?

2 How do you view tests, trials and difficulties? Have any of them caused you to abandon your dreams? What can you do to resurrect those dreams?

3 Does the lack of provision stop or hinder you from taking steps of faith towards your goals? Where do you look for your provisions?

12 ENCOURAGE THE CLEANERS

No sooner had we finished cleaning up after the first Punjab Christian Festival, than it was time to get ready for Jesus Christ Javanti 2000 (Javanti means "birthday"). Chief Minister Shri Badal had been as good as his word. Everything was arranged. As my colleagues and I drove north on our way through Punjab, we marveled again at the door God had opened and the unexpected person he had used to open it.

The celebration was held in a big open field. The event was massive. Nearly forty thousand people came from all over the state, and not just Christians. Sikhs and Hindus flocked in as well. Indians love big festivals.

Security was tight and no wonder. The whole cabinet and many other politicians were coming. Apart from the dangers of cross-border terrorism from nearby Pakistan, there is a history of sometimes violent political struggle in Punjab itself, where many people want independence from India, making politics a hazardous occupation.

Five thousand police patrolled the enormous outdoor venue. When the chief minister arrived by helicopter, he and other dignitaries were ushered up onto the main stage. Journalists and television cameras stared up from the audience, ready to broadcast the event across Punjab.

And there, in the middle of all these VIPs, I took my seat. I felt very small and out of place.

The program of music and drama was lively, full of the kind of color and vitality that Indians adore. Then the time came for me to speak. I walked to the podium. Because the Chief Minister was a very tall man, the bulletproof glass around it had been built higher than my head. I gazed out at the vast crowd and breathed a silent prayer. I knew I was a non-entity to them, but I desperately wanted to touch their hearts.

My task was to explain why we were celebrating Jesus' birthday. Using John 3:16, I told them as clearly as I knew how about the love of God, a love so compelling that he sent his only Son into the world. My words boomed out through the gigantic sound system, echoed by my Punjabi translator. *What are all those thousands of people thinking?* I wondered.

Eventually, I finished and sat down. Shri Bagal rose to his feet.

"What this young man has just told you is a very powerful message, and all of you need to seriously consider its implications," he said. "If we lived by the teachings of Christ, we would have a much better society." He explained some of the benefits he saw, including no crime. "Every one of us should study and understand Jesus Christ more," he concluded.

This ringing endorsement of Jesus by the most powerful Sikh politician in Punjab was the most incredible part of an incredible day.

After that, I received a very warm reception. Everyone wanted to know who this preacher was who had shared the stage with the Chief Minister. This opened many new opportunities. From being nobodies on the Indian scene, we were suddenly the people in demand.

I returned to Australia to face a different kind of challenge. We now had up to thirty people involved in the team at various levels, with eight to ten people working regularly in our office at home, and all of them drove cars to work. Our small cul-de-sac simply couldn't provide enough parking spaces.

The neighbors were very nice about it. They didn't complain to the council. But after several spoke to us, we knew the situation couldn't continue.

Jenni had been thinking about this when she noticed an advertisement in the local newspaper. A factory-office complex in nearby Croydon was up for sale. She urged me to look at it. We had no money to buy a single brick because we were sending all the money to support the work in India, but I took down the phone number and called the real estate agent anyway.

FOSTER OWNERSHIP. WHEN YOU ALLOW OTHERS TO
HAVE OWNERSHIP OF YOUR VISION, IT INCREASES THEIR
ENGAGEMENT AND SATISFACTION. THIS ENSURES LONG
TERM SUCCESS OF THE VISION.

I met him at 14 Railway Crescent. He showed me around the property, which actually consisted of two factories about 2,700 square-feet each. They were thirty-five years old and had once been the national offices of Panasonic and, later, Penguin Books. The buildings would require a lot of renovation, but I could immediately see the potential.

Inside, a man and a woman were busy cleaning one of the factories. "We're cleaning it up because someone else is interested," said the agent, trying to pressure me. "In fact, we've already had an offer."

"How much are you asking?" I said.

"For a quick sale, it has been reduced to $280,000(AUD)."

Out in the parking lot I explained our circumstances. "Look, it is a very good price, but we run a non-profit charitable organization out of my home. We desperately need an office but we haven't got any money. So if somebody else is interested in buying, you'd better sell it to them."

He looked at me coldly. "Thanks for wasting my time," he said as he got into his car and left.

I climbed into my own car and drove away, praying hard.

A mile or so down the road an odd thought struck me: Go back and encourage the cleaners. It was just a whisper at the back of my brain. I ignored it. But the further I drove, the more persistent it became. "Okay," I said finally, feeling very foolish. I did a U-turn and drove back, trying to role-play in my mind what on earth I would say.

I knocked on the factory door and called out. The male cleaner answered the door. Rather embarrassed, I said I just wanted to tell him what a great job he was doing cleaning the place, adding that I'd like to pray that God would bless his cleaning business.

He smiled broadly. "Sorry, but we don't have a cleaning business. We're actually the owners. And you must be a Christian," he added, his smile getting even broader. "So are we!"

He introduced himself as George and took me to meet the other cleaner, his wife Bev. They explained why they were selling the two units: to help missionary friends in Vanuatu build a boat to take the gospel from island to island. They were interested in what I told them about our ministry and offered to pray for us. I left my name and number with them.

A few days later, I departed for a meeting in Singapore, forgetting all about Railway Crescent. But George and Bev didn't forget about us. While I was away, they called Jenni. They had received a number of offers for the property but felt unsettled about selling. They wanted to talk to us and were prepared to put the sale on hold until I got back.

Arriving home to this news, I jumped straight on the phone. George and Bev came to lunch and met our staff and volunteers. Over coffee after the meal, we discussed Railway Crescent. They felt strongly we should consider buying it. I admitted we would dearly love to, but we had no way of financing it. Finally, we agreed to set aside a Saturday when we would all pray and ask God what to do.

That day, our team headed for a retreat center in the mountains to fast and pray. At the end of the time, we were admittedly disappointed that nothing spectacular happened, no phone calls saying, "Here is the money." But I did share one persistent impression.

"All day this figure has been floating around in my head: 160,000," I said. "I don't know what it means. But if it's meant to be an offer, it's nowhere near what the place is worth or what it's on the market for."

Back home that evening, the thought grew stronger.

"I think we should make an offer of $160,000(AUD)," I told Jenni.

She said, "Just be sure it's from God, otherwise George and Bev will take it as an insult and we'll look ridiculous."

EXPECT MIRACLES. GOD DOESN'T SHARE THE PHYSICAL AND CIRCUMSTANTIAL LIMITATIONS WE DO. THOUGH IT'S HARD TO DO IN A MOMENT OF NEED, A LEADER SHOULD BE THE FIRST TO EXPECT THE MIRACLE.

We had arranged to meet them for lunch again the next day. For their part, they had each spent Saturday alone, asking God what they should do.

"So what happened?" I began.

George leapt straight in, "I'll start. Yesterday I spent all day seeking the Lord, and there are three things I want to say. Number one: God's hand is on your ministry. Number two: Railway Crescent belongs to you. Number three: we should sell it to you for $160,000."

Jenni was in tears as I told them that this was exactly the figure I had decided to offer them. A sense of awe came over us. We immediately stopped to thank God and praise him. Then, conscious that we had no money, I made one further suggestion: "If this is from God, then I think we should ask him to give us at least 10% of the $160,000, within the next ten days. It will have to be non-designated money, not money given for India. We won't ask anyone, we won't write to anyone, we won't tell anyone, we will just ask God."

Amazingly, over the next ten days we were given $20,000 in non-designated gifts. With God as our financier, we signed the contract to buy the property.

We moved the office to Railway Crescent in early December 2000, just a few weeks before the birth of our second child, Jacob. We couldn't afford renovations, so we simply shifted everything into one of the factories and set up on the bright red carpet tiles. They made an interesting contrast with the mission brown walls.

A week after the move, a middle-aged man named Adrian came to the door. He asked if we were Christians and whether we had bought the place. When I answered yes, he lifted his hands in the air and started praising God. He lived nearby, and explained how, as he had driven past the building with its "For Sale" sign, he had prayed that Christians would buy it for Kingdom purposes.

Then he asked if we had anyone to help us with our computer needs. I answered no. He said his sixteen-year-old son Bobby was a computer whiz, and the next day he brought him to meet us. Soon Bobby was volunteering after school and on weekends. Using old computers and parts he picked up here and there, he gradually built us a fully networked system. He eventually went on to become our full-time IT manager, still serving with Empart.

All along the way, God has faithfully provided what we needed. We borrowed the balance of the purchase price from the bank, but thanks to the help of many people the loan was paid off within eighteen months and we were debt-free.

Throughout 2001, as interest in the ministry took root in more and more churches, we worked hard to keep pace with the growth. The sacrifice of our volunteers was inspirational. Despite the fact that we had limited heating, it wasn't unusual to go by the office at night or on weekends and find someone working away in a cold, dull corner. People's level of ownership was extraordinary!

Towards the end of 2001, we ran out of room again. We calculated that by ripping out the existing partitions and creating an open office we would double our work area. So we talked to Mobile Mission Maintenance (MMM), an organization that coordinates volunteer tradespeople to assist churches and missions with building projects. They agreed to help for a couple of weeks. While we were at it, we wanted to replace the red carpet and give the walls a fresh coat of paint.

Moving all the furniture out, we began to tear down the partitions and ripped up the carpet. Then, just as we were about to start painting the walls, the floor literally collapsed beneath us. Floorboards, joists and beams were all completely rotten. It took the MMM workers about ten seconds to realize we could do nothing more without replacing the entire structure.

I was devastated. Unable even to stay in the building, I went and sat in my car, holding my head in my hands. *Oh God, what are we going to do?*

For perhaps fifteen minutes I sat there, praying desperately. I had never felt so hopeless. Then my concentration was distracted. A car was turning into the parking lot.

It pulled up and a man climbed out. I knew him as one of our supporters, but he had never visited us before. I went to meet him.

"So what are you guys doing?" he asked, intrigued by the obvious signs of building activity.

"Come in and see."

As he surveyed the wreckage of the floor, he asked what we were going to do. I admitted I had no idea. I explained what we had planned to do and what we would now have to do. He nodded sympathetically.

"Well," he said after I finished, "the floor's on me. I'll pay for whatever needs to be done."

Thankfully the MMM team, due to leave us after two weeks, was able to stay another month because their next job was canceled. We gutted the whole building and rebuilt it. God miraculously provided workers. The only people we had to pay were the carpet layers and the men who

BUILD ALTARS IN THE DESERT. TAKE TIME TO REMEMBER AND
CELEBRATE GOD'S PROTECTION AND PROVISION IN THE PAST.

installed the air conditioning. Even the people we bought the carpet
from (not Christians) took 50% off the price when they heard what we
were doing. Since then, we have purchased two other adjacent properties
and extended to accommodate the ongoing growth of the ministry; in
each case, God's unseen hand was at work.

To us it seemed that God really was guiding our steps as he had
promised. He even had the disasters covered. The miracles weren't confined
to India.

The first Punjab Christian Festival and our move into Railway Crescent
happened when our experiment in training church planters in Chandigarh
was just a few months old. Our initial intake consisted of eleven
extraordinary young men who were prepared to risk literally everything
to take the gospel where it had never been heard. Their training was a
team effort as we tried various approaches to see what worked best. The
center itself had to move three times in two years when our non-Christian
landlords discovered we were training Christian workers and kicked us out.

That first group was followed by others just like them, and then more
and more, until at the time of writing this edition, we have almost 1,225
trainees in 49 training centers—a total of 5,746 since our inception.

Understanding the limitations of our one-year training, we have also
developed leadership management training centers to instruct overseers
and senior leaders for the ministry.

Women trainees have now been added to the mix, also. In most villages,
the men are absent from home during the day, working in the field while the
women work at home. It is culturally inappropriate for male church planters
to visit women alone. In response, we began to set up special training
centers to train women too. The model is the same as for our men: twenty
to twenty-five ladies live with a leader and his family for one year; their
training focuses on character formation, as well as biblical and practical

skills. We call these leaders "key women" because they are uniquely positioned to unlock doors of opportunity for the gospel. We find that, generally, they are faster relationally and are more effective at nurturing the social and practical needs of the community.

These indigenous workers are some of the most remarkable men and women I have ever met. They are true trailblazers for the gospel. It's time to meet some of them.

CHAPTER 12 LEADERSHIP LESSONS

+ Foster ownership. When you allow others to have ownership of your vision, it increases their engagement and satisfaction. This ensures long term success of the vision.

+ Expect miracles. God doesn't share the physical and circumstantial limitations we do. Though it's hard to do in a moment of need, a leader should be the first to expect the miracle.

+ Be an obedient leader. Obedient to God, that is, even if it doesn't make sense to you, because God has a perspective that you never will.

+ Build altars in the desert. Take time to remember and celebrate God's protection and provision in the past.

CHAPTER 12 REFLECTION QUESTIONS

1 How can you enable others to take more ownership in the vision? Do you need to let go, or do they need to step up, or both?

2 When you experience trials, do you abandon hope or expect miracles? Right now, where do you as the leader need to look for a miracle?

3 How do you rate your obedience to the Lord? Talk to him about your answer.

4 During their years in the wilderness, the Israelites got in the habit of building altars to remind them of the great things God had done. Look back over the last year and make a list of your miracles both big and small. Then, add to this record and give thanks as you go forward.

13 KINGDOM HEROES

The cackle of hens and the bark of a dog floated in through the window as Pastor Paul took the glass of chai from his wife, Padmini. He had been up since dawn, first to pray and then to study his Bible. After that he had gone out into the dusty streets, mixing with his neighbors as they went about their daily lives. Today, a Hindu family had called him in to pray for their child who had a fever, probably malaria.

Now he was back home stretching out his legs. Padmini brought him a simple lunch of rice and dahl. A full afternoon still lay ahead of him as pastor of the small house church he was planting in his village in Rajasthan.

Lying due south of Punjab, Rajasthan is the largest state in India and a stronghold of anti-Christian militants; most of them are passionately dedicated to eradicating small minorities like Christians. Here, Christians make up a mere 0.05% of the population and often live in fear.

As Pastor Paul prepared to leave to visit a family of believers, a banging on the door interrupted him.

He opened it and took a quick, involuntary step backwards. Standing on his doorstep was Rahul, the son of a priest and a prominent militant leader well known for persecuting Christians. The tall, solid man in his late twenties glared at Paul with undisguised hatred.

"You! Christian!" he spat. "You say your god heals people's sicknesses. My wife is dying. We've been to doctors and all the temples. Nothing has helped. I'll give you seven days to pray for her and cure her. If you don't, I'll come back and hurt you."

He turned and stomped away.

Paul had no doubt how serious the threat was. For Rahul's wife to be healed, Paul called on his small congregation to fast and pray with him for seven days. On the seventh day he waited anxiously for the visit he knew would come.

Again there was a knock on the door. Rahul had come as expected, but this time he was not alone. His wife stood beside him, and all the hostility seemed to have gone from his face.

Paul invited them inside, but almost before he had shut the door the pair had fallen to their knees at his feet.

"My wife is completely healed," Rahul said, choking back emotion. "Your god is the true God. From now on, I want to serve your God."

Knowing the dangers posed by the conversion of such a prominent anti-Christian activist, Paul referred Rahul and his wife to a pastor in another area. The depth of the change in Rahul, along with his fierce determination to serve Jesus with the same zeal as he had served his gods soon became evident. The pastor recommended that he attend our church planter training center in Chandigarh.

At this stage, the center was still in an experimental phase which lasted until we began multiplying centers in 2003. Rahul moved in with other trainees, leaving his wife and children at home in the village in Rajasthan.

Rahul threw himself into the training with all the passion of his forceful personality. Eventually the news of his conversion reached the ears of his former associates. Enraged by his betrayal, they attacked his home in the village and burnt it to the ground. His wife and children fled and everything was lost.

Empart leaders urged Rahul to leave training and take care of the situation. He refused. "If I leave my training and go back, then they have won," he said. "I don't want that. I will continue my studies. Jesus will take care of my family."

Rahul completed his training, and I was privileged to be there when he graduated. I asked him where he felt the Lord was sending him. "Back to my own village," he said. Knowing the story, I was concerned for his

> VISION AND RISK GO TOGETHER. IN MOST CASES, IF YOUR
> VISION IS BIG, YOUR RISK WILL BE TOO; IF YOUR VISION IS
> SMALL, THE RISK WILL BE AS WELL. YOUR REWARD WILL MATCH.
> IF YOU ARE NOT WILLING TO DIE FOR YOUR VISION, IT IS NOT
> WORTH LIVING FOR. IF YOU ARE NOT WILLING TO LIVE FOR
> YOUR VISION, IT IS NOT WORTH DYING FOR.

safety. I encouraged him to consider going somewhere else. He stopped me with a question.

"Pastor Jossy, did Jesus know he was going to die on the cross before he came to earth?"

"Yes," I said, "I believe he knew that this was the reason his Father was sending him."

"And did that stop Jesus coming?"

"No, he still came."

"Then if the cross didn't stop Jesus, why should the threat to my life stop me from going back to my village?"

Immediately, I felt humbled by a more profound insight into the meaning of the cross than anything I had read in a theological book.

After we commissioned him, Rahul reunited with his wife and children where they were living with another pastor. Then he and his family returned to their village. They built a small house and started to evangelize. There was no gospel witness in the whole region, but people were attracted by their unusual testimony. Before long, they were running a prayer meeting of thirty or so believers.

Then tragedy struck. Rahul's wife died. The cause was never determined, but the rumor was that she was poisoned.

I was deeply saddened by this, but the next time I met Rahul he put his big arm around my shoulder. "Pastor Jossy, I don't know why you're so concerned," he comforted me. "The Apostle Paul said, 'What will separate me from the love of God?' Nothing is going to stop me from preaching the gospel."

The following year, I met him again. By then he had planted five more churches, baptized 370 people and raised up four other church planters. His next goal was to plant ten new churches, and he had already begun coordinating other church planters in his region. His dream was to see a church in every village in his part of Rajasthan.

Rahul continues his work today, a man transformed from a violent church destroyer to a church planter of apostolic vision. His imposing physical stature and fiery boldness are balanced by a wonderful softness of heart. Seeing the tears stream down his scarred face as he prayed for the people of Rajasthan, I understood how deep his longing was to see them freed from the bondage of idol worship.

It's a longing he has given up everything to see fulfilled.

From the very first, planting churches has been integral to our vision. Jesus said, "I will build my church" (Matthew 16:18), but he wasn't talking about erecting buildings with crosses on top. He was talking about building living communities of believers, linked together by faith in him and pressing on together to meet each other's and the community's spiritual and physical needs.

What is church planting? Strictly speaking, if Jesus is the one who builds the church, then church planting is his job, not ours. So what are we responsible to do? We are commanded to make disciples (Mathew 28:19). I believe that church planting is a result of effective discipleship. That is why when I talk about church planters, I am really talking about effective disciple-makers; these men and women give their lives to make and grow disciples.

Personally, this is what I live for! In the exploding numbers of young church planters in North India and elsewhere in Asia, I have found thousands of men and women like Rahul who not only share my passion, but surpass it. They continually challenge my faith to reach for greater things.

Most church planting takes place at the village level, where 70% of Indians still live. Picture a typical village: a cluster of small mud dwellings

RISK WITH PASSIONATE WISDOM. RISK DWELLS WITH PASSION ON A PRECIPICE CALLED WISDOM. WITHOUT RISK, YOUR VISION CAN'T BE FULFILLED. PASSION CAN FUEL THE GROWTH OF YOUR RISK-TAKING CAPACITY, BUT TEMPER YOUR RISKS WITH WISDOM.

plastered with cow dung sitting in the middle of nowhere, surrounded by rice paddies or other farmland. Dirt roads lead in and out. Dogs and pigs run everywhere, getting under the feet of cows and water buffaloes. The air is filled with the ringing of bells from the Hindu temples, or loud speakers booming out chants and prayers from the mosques.

Several thousand people live there. Most homes are very basic. In poorer areas, these homes are no more than one-room huts made of grass, sticks and trees. In more prosperous areas, people may have mud brick walls or a tiled roof. Usually there is no running water, no electricity and no sewer. During the summer people sleep outside, and in winter they sleep together inside on the floor. Everything is shared and nothing can be claimed as "mine."

Life is noisy, chaotic and busy. Each family has a small plot of land where they work every day. Frequently, this land is owned by big landlords with ties to the feudal kingdoms that dominated India before the British rule. They seldom have the benefit of machinery; these farmers plough the fields using water buffaloes, and they reap and thresh by hand.

The whole of village life is very communal. Everyone gets their water from the village well. All the children live like one big family. People don't expect privacy as they do in the West, instead everyone knows everyone else and is interested in their business.

Many villages are virtually closed communities, which makes breaking into them with the gospel extremely difficult. That being the case, the ideal church planter is someone who is originally from that village. They already speak the language, understand the culture, own a house and most importantly, have relational access to the community. Where church planters come from already established churches, we encourage them to go to people groups that are as close as possible to their own.

Of course this depends on the leading of the Holy Spirit, as does the entire training process. From the moment a leader begins their Empart training, we challenge them to seek the Lord about where to go afterwards. We don't tell them, "Go and start a church in such and such a place." The key to their success is going where God sends them; there He offers provision and favor.

Most of our church planters are young men and women in their early twenties. They have already done an apprenticeship of six months or more with their own pastor who has recommended them for further training.

Frequently they have suffered for their decision to follow Christ. As they head out after training, they go under the oversight of one of our senior leaders who continues to mentor and help them.

We prefer young, first generation Christians for three reasons. First, their initial love for Jesus is still hot. Sadly, it seems that the longer we are Christians, the less we are in love with Jesus. Second, they can relate to the non-Christian community easily and quickly because they have come out of it themselves. Third, they have an adventurous spirit. When we are young, it seems our risk-tolerance is much greater.

We also favor church planters who are unmarried when they first go out. It is easier to slip into a community when you are young and single. The practical and relational cost of moving a family is much higher and their basic needs are much greater than that of a single person. Along with pioneering and growing Kingdom work, a single church planter can marry and raise their family more easily in that context than one who has to be transplanted. It is practical, economical and effective. Despite this, Empart does sometimes enlist married couples; we have many dedicated and successful families in the field.

As a church planter, the first job is to find somewhere to live.

This is not always straight-forward. In a village without a single Christian, people of other religions own all the houses. Often they are suspicious. Even if a landlord does rent out his property, he can come under tremendous pressure from fellow villagers once the church planter's agenda becomes clear. This can lead to the church planter's eviction.

Sometimes, a church planter finds a house but comes up against other serious barriers. One of the hardest is being banned from using the village well. Villagers may see Christians as outcastes who will pollute the whole water system if they touch it, making it impossible for the community to use it. They can then demand large payments to conduct cleansing rituals.

Let us say, though, that a church planter successfully overcomes these hurdles. What do they do next?

Once they have moved in, they visit every house in the village and in nearby villages. They introduce themselves as a priest of the living God, the God who answers prayer. "If you have any needs or want any spiritual advice, here is where to find me," the church planter tells people. Some simple gospel literature is given out, with the church planter's address on the back.

If anyone is receptive on first meeting, the church planter makes a note to pray for him or her and visit again at a later date.

They will also start to help meet the practical needs in the community by teaching literacy, health, hygiene, sewing and other practical skills to the unemployed, caring for orphans and widows, digging water wells, building toilets and helping in any other way to meet the needs of their community.

Prayer meetings and then a spiritual study program will be started in their home. Asian people are very open to spiritual things, so our church planters always offer to pray for and teach spiritual truth and principles to anyone who is interested. When people come, they share with them from the Bible, mostly the gospel stories about Jesus.

Meanwhile, the young church planter prays and fasts for miracles. During training, they have seen God answer earnest prayer for the lost with supernatural acts of love and blessing. If someone is healed or a barren woman has a baby, the whole village quickly hears about it. And when God acts, people want to know more.

Some kind of supernatural breakthrough is the key to pioneering a church among the unreached peoples. In early 2004, we surveyed new Christians in our churches and found that 80% came to faith because they had seen a miraculous act of God or experienced an answer to prayer. Few Indians are interested in debating whether God is the Creator or can incarnate in human form. They simply take such things for granted. Their primary interest is, "Does it work?"

Usually starting with those who receive the miracle, people begin to believe and are baptized, and a new church is born.

We have literally thousands of stories of God's supernatural intervention today. Church planters continually report healings, miracles of provision, and deliverance from demonic spirits. The milky white eyes of a blind man become clear and he sees again. A child comes out of a coma with a loud cry, reaching for her mother.

How do you plant a church in a region where there is not a single Christian and people are hostile to the gospel? The only way is for God to do something that we call "miracles." Miracles are required when we are helpless.

Take, for example, the case of Jyothi. The aunt of one of our church planters, Pastor Manil, Jyothi died unexpectedly. Although she had been lifeless in her bed for two hours, he prayed, "Jesus, if this is your will, restore life to Auntie Jyothi so that your name will be glorified in this village."

As he finished praying, her body moved and her eyes opened. Manil and the rest of the family started bellowing, "Hallelujah! Hallelujah!" The villagers who had gathered outside the house to mourn were startled. All of a sudden Auntie Jyothi interrupted their praises and leapt up screaming. She ran from the house with the family and villagers in hot pursuit. She led them into a nearby forest where she collapsed beside a tree. The villagers knew that tree and they believed it harbored evil spirits. People pressed in as Pastor Manil knelt and took authority over the spirits in Jesus' name. Jyothi rolled around and convulsed violently, and then sat up and smiled. The spirits were gone.

After two such extraordinary examples of Jesus' power, seven non-Christian families immediately told Pastor Manil they wanted to become Christians.

A different story graphically illustrates not only God's intervention but also his protection. It took place in a tribal village in Orissa, India's poorest state, where there are more Hindu temples than anywhere else in the world.

Prakash, the church planter in this village, was a new believer himself. He was only twenty and looked even younger. From the moment he and his wife Madhuri arrived, the village people reacted angrily, harassing and threatening them. He received warning after warning to get out or else.

Prakash, however, believed God had sent him. For nearly twelve months he persevered. Eventually, ten people were meeting regularly with them for worship in an open field. But with this modest growth, the persecution intensified.

One day a group of villagers came to him and announced they were giving him a week to leave the village or face the consequences. He prayed and felt he should stay. When the week was up, they returned.

"Since you refuse to leave," they said, "we will call the witch doctor. He will put a deep curse on you. Then you will die."

Now in tribal societies, witch doctors wield enormous power. They dispense traditional medicines but along with it wreak the evil devastation of the occult in people's lives. Everyone fears them because they know their demonic power is real.

The next day the witch doctor and those who had hired him gathered outside Prakash and Madhuri's house. A bizarre ritual began. Songs and chants and banging gongs echoed through the village. Then a chicken was

> BALANCE YOUR STRUCTURE. WITHOUT STRUCTURE AND
> ACCOUNTABILITY, A MOVEMENT WILL FAIL; IRONICALLY,
> TOO MUCH STRUCTURE AND CONTROL WILL ALSO KILL A
> MOVEMENT.

sacrificed. The witch doctor, in a frenzy of possession, danced around with his long knife, splashing blood on the ground and wiping it on Prakash's house. The young church planter stood at his window, watching.

Finally the witch doctor shouted, "If you don't leave this house by December 1st, the next day you will be dead!"

Prakash was gripped with dismay. He visited his supervisor. The pressure was unbearable, he explained, and he couldn't see how he could stay.

The supervisor understood, but he asked, "Did God clearly lead you to this village?"

"Yes," Prakash replied. "God's call was clear."

"Has He asked you to leave?"

"Well, no…"

Wrestling with his fear, Prakash prayed and his conviction strengthened. *Well, I'm going to die one day anyway, so I might as well die for Jesus.* He decided to stay.

That very day something strange began to happen. The village had been celebrating the Hindu festival of Deepavali, with animal sacrifices and revelry, but during the night a healthy twenty-two year old man unexpectedly died. The small village was shaken, but more was to come. The next day another young man died, followed by a woman. Both had no previous sicknesses. Then a father was found dead in his bed. A thirty year old man ate dinner with his wife and went to sleep but did not wake up the next morning. And young Dhananjay died in his sleep the same night.

A wave of fear swept the village. Had their sacrifices failed to appease the local deity? Had someone cursed them?

At a village council meeting, someone wondered aloud, "Perhaps this is happening because of the way we've treated that young pastor." The council delegated an elder to go to Prakash and ask his forgiveness on behalf of the village. Prakash knew immediately this was the miracle he had been praying for. He embraced the elder and accepted the apology. Then he went through the village, praying from house to house for God's protection from the spirit of death.

The deadline of the witch doctor's curse came and went without effect. For two months, Prakash freely preached in the village. Then, within a single week, more than sixty villagers repented and believed in Jesus. A day of baptism was arranged in the local river. The people brought their idols, charms and religious cloths and burnt them on the riverbank.

Forty-seven elders and their families were baptized that day. Within six months the entire village had chosen to follow Jesus—around 500 people.

A combination of faith, perseverance, willingness to pay the ultimate price, and the supernatural power of God had defeated the powers of darkness. Today Prakash is pastoring two thriving churches and planting a third. He also runs one of our children's homes, caring for fifteen boys from that area.

I don't know what happened to the witch doctor!

Prakesh knew the risk, yet his calling to this particular village was clear. He had a God-sized vision for that tribe, and in order to reach those heights, he had to match the vision with equal risk. Vision and risk go together: the outworking of your vision will be limited to your capacity to embrace risk. In other words, on a scale of 0-100, if your vision is 100 but your risk level is only 60, the reality of your vision will be limited to 60.

The dedication of men like Rahul and Prakash is typical of Empart church planters. They are heroes of the faith, men and women prepared to go to extraordinary lengths to rescue the lost and help the poor and needy.

The advantages of training national Christians are enormous. For the cost of sending one Western missionary, Empart can send from seventy-five to eighty-five national church planters. Each of them can start ministry from the first day. They don't have to overcome culture shock or language barriers. (In contrast, it takes six or seven years for a Western missionary to fully adapt to a new culture.) Further, national church planters don't need visas, insurance, four-wheel drives, mobile phones, laptops or Internet access. They're prepared to go where there are no hospitals, English-speaking schools or roads. One reason the unreached remain unreached is because they often live in remote, difficult regions where few will venture. Our church planters are willing to go wherever God sends them.

We initially estimated we would need about 55,000 workers to fulfill our vision of planting 100,000 churches. But after ten years of working this strategy, we reviewed the output of our church planters. Upon doing so, we discovered that we had underestimated them and revised the estimate of workers needed down to 35,000. To meet this goal, we are now multiplying our training centers. Our vision is for 100 training centers by 2030, each one training 25 young people at a time, creating a total of 2,500 new church planters every year.

Not every church is planted in a village. We have growing churches now in many towns and cities as well. Historically, most mission efforts have been targeted towards the poor, but Jesus had the same compassion on Zacchaeus as on Lazarus. He was able to reach both rich and poor with the same message. In comparison, we often focus our Christian compassion on poverty rather than spiritual lostness. This makes it hard for us to have compassion for the rich even though they might be just as lost as their poverty-stricken neighbor.

A staggering 97% of those who graduate from Empart training go on to plant churches. In fact, on average, each of our graduates plants three churches in their first five years! At the time of writing, we are averaging almost eleven new churches every day, and I look forward to the day we will plant a new one every hour. If the current growth rate remains, and I believe by God's grace it will accelerate, we will reach our goal of transforming 100,000 communities through the planting of local churches by 2030.

From the beginning, our intention has been not just to plant churches, but also to create an authentic church-planting movement modeled on the book of Acts. This is now happening. As an example, we had no work in the Lucknow region of Uttar Pradesh until 2004; in 2016 we have over 2,670 churches along with nine training centers and nine children's homes. The same is true in other regions.

These local church planting movements are not centrally controlled or governed. We don't take a hierarchical or denominational approach. Instead, we use a regional structure based on relationship for accountability and biblical integrity. Church planters are organized in small groups of twenty to twenty-five and are overseen by a coordinator. Every month, they meet together to learn, share, pray, plan and celebrate what God is doing. Our coordinators are overseen by a regional director who, in turn, is

> INVEST IN YOUNG LEADERS. ONE OF THE GREATEST RETURNS
> YOU WILL GET ON YOUR INVESTMENT HAPPENS WHEN YOU
> INVEST IN THE TRAINING AND ESTABLISHMENT OF YOUNG
> LEADERS; IT IS LIKE PLANTING AN APPLE TREE—ITS LIFE
> WILL CONTINUE TO PRODUCE GREAT FRUIT AND MULTIPLY
> LONG AFTER YOU'VE GONE.

supervised by Empart's national ministry team. Our overarching goal is to provide a network of encouragement and accountability while protecting the freedom of each local church; we want them to do what is appropriate in their cultural context, rather than be dictated to by strangers in some far-off headquarters.

Church planter group numbers are deliberately kept small, so that they are practically manageable and replicable. Doing so enables the development of deep and meaningful relationships. These relationships establish vulnerability, which creates growing trust among the trainees and at the same time minimizes organizational risk.

Without structures and accountability, a movement will fail; ironically, too much structure and control will also kill a movement. It is critical that you have an internal structure if you want to build a movement; otherwise external and controlling structures will not allow it to develop. We seek to find the fine balance between them. Jesus compares his church to a body, each member working in relation to the other, not because of hierarchy or contracts. Jesus and Paul knew the power of relational accountability, and they have set the example for us to follow.

The life of a church planter in Asia is not easy. Many struggle to feed their families or send their children to school. The full Bible may not be available in their mother tongue. Resources like books, CDs, magazines or DVDs are non-existent. They have no cars, phones, faxes or email. Frequently, there is nowhere for believers to meet other than their own one-room homes. They face blatant persecution.

It is impossible to reach the unreached without external support. This is why partnership of Christians in the West is invaluable. Empart has developed many practical ways to partner with the work in Asia: Praying, Giving, Going and Advocating.

Praying. These young leaders and churches are under significant attack. Only prayer can help them. If you sign up with Empart, we will send you their ongoing and specific prayer needs.

Giving. Church planters also need financial and practical help. One way to partner with them is by providing "church planting kits." Upon graduation, each trainee receives a kit which consists of a bicycle, mat, Indian drum, tambourine, Bibles and gospel tracts.

Empart has also developed a financial support structure for our church planters. Our support of these workers is only for a maximum of seven years. We try to balance the pioneering needs of church planting with the goal of growing self-supporting churches. For the first three years (beginning with training), each church planter receives 100% support. Then over the next four years support is progressively scaled down to zero. This gives the church planter time to disciple his people so they accept ownership of the church and responsibility for their pastor's welfare, but it is also short enough to avoid fostering long-term dependency. In that first seven years, your help can make all the difference to a new pastor.

I believe that one of the greatest returns you will ever get on your investment happens when you invest in the training and establishment of young leaders; it is like planting an apple tree, its life will continue to produce great fruit and multiply long after you've gone. We invite partners to adopt a specific region and focus your prayer and giving in that region.

Going. While Empart provides necessary reports and ongoing information, partners are also invited to come to India and see the full impact of their partnership. We organize regular conferences for pastors, lay leaders, children, youth, men and women where partners and leaders from the West can continue to encourage and inspire them.

Advocating. Actually, we're looking for more than advocates. We're looking for champions—those who will be the face and voice in the West of all the magnificent indigenous workers who can't be here to represent themselves.

When people, in whatever capacity, big or small, speak to others and raise resources in their families, churches, small groups, schools, workplaces, clubs or elsewhere, it can throw open massive doors. Seven years ago, a man who had been on an Empart trip visiting North Indian villages shared in a small church in Europe how we were caring for children. Only about fifty people were there—but one of them happened to be a businessman who ever since has made large contributions to Empart every year. You never know who is listening.

As necessary as money is to live, however, it is not what our church planters rely on. Instead, they have an extraordinary trust in God, a trust that characterizes every aspect of their lives.

These pioneers of God's Kingdom come in various shapes and sizes. They are not eloquent or highly educated. They have never written a book or recorded a CD. Like the early disciples, it would be easy to ridicule them as "unschooled, ordinary men" (Acts 4:13). What can they possibly do?

But for the sake of the Cross, they take risks everyday. As they step out in faith, they themselves are not looking at what they can do. They are looking upwards at what God can do.

CHAPTER 13 LEADERSHIP LESSONS

+ Vision and risk go together. In most cases, if your vision is big, your risk will be too; if your vision is small the risk will be as well. Your reward will match. If you are not willing to die for your vision, it is not worth living for. If you are not willing to live for your vision, it is not worth dying for.

+ Risk with passionate wisdom. Risk dwells with passion on a precipice called wisdom. Without risk, your vision can't be fulfilled. Passion can fuel the growth of your risk-taking capacity, but temper your risks with wisdom.

+ Balance your structure. Without structure and accountability a movement will fail; ironically, too much structure and control will also kill a movement.

+ Invest in young leaders. One of the greatest returns you will get on your investment happens when you invest in the training and establishment of young leaders; it is like planting an apple tree—its life will continue to produce great fruit and multiply long after you've gone.

CHAPTER 13 REFLECTION QUESTIONS

1 If we define passion as your "willingness to sacrifice in order to see your vision realized," how passionate are you about what you are doing? How would you rate yourself (on a scale of 1-Low to 10-High)? What are you not willing to sacrifice for your vision?

2 Review the structures you have in place. Do they encourage exponential growth or strangle momentum?

3 How are you investing your time and talents to raise up young leaders? What can you do to intensify this in positive ways?

LIBERATING THE LOST

It is early morning in February, the end of winter. Dressed in a bright purple sari, Sudha hurries past puddles of oily water and men wrapped in scarves towards a narrow, shuttered shop. She unlocks the metal roller shutter and raises it to reveal a small window display of ornaments and a wooden door. As the door swings open, an Indian beauty queen smiles enigmatically from a poster on the inside panel.

Sudha removes her slip-on sandals and steps inside the Blue Heaven Beauty Parlor.

In 1999, she accepted Christ after experiencing a miraculous healing. Since then, Sudha has become one of the hidden dynamos of God's Kingdom. She has planted three churches and two mission stations among gypsies and hardened criminals on the outskirts of India's national capital. Despite illness and opposition from her Hindu in-laws, she also cares for eighteen young children in her rented one-bedroom house. On top of all that, Sudha runs three tailoring centers where women trapped in poverty can learn the skills to become seamstresses—and in the process she shares the good news of Jesus.

When Sudha isn't sharing God's love as she gives beauty treatments to her customers, she uses the space of The Blue Heaven Beauty Parlor for one of those tailoring centers. Most of the women who attend the tailoring classes are in tough personal circumstances; many have husbands who are alcoholic, abusive or imprisoned. The training these women receive gives them a second chance at life; their new abilities help them to forge a path out of poverty. And when they give their lives to the Lord, they experience transforming forgiveness, deliverance and healing.

Regarding how we treat the poor, the Bible is crystal clear. The prophet Isaiah thundered, "Learn to do good; seek justice, rescue the oppressed, defend the orphan, plead for the widow" (Isaiah 1:17, NRSV). Jesus' example in Mark 6, where he both taught and fed the lost, reinforced by his words in Matthew 25:40: "Whatever you did for the least of these, you did also for me."

God wants to liberate people in every aspect of their lives—spiritual, personal and social. Jesus asks us to be the light and salt, changing the world wherever we go. In the Great Commission, he makes it clear to us about the need to preach the gospel and make disciples. But then in the Good Commandment, he tells us to love our neighbors, to be good Samaritans. These mandates, to share Jesus and to do good, cannot be ignored by any follower of Jesus. Fulfilling one mandate will never bring sustainable transformation. Obeyed together they can bring transformation—right now and also for eternity. In line with this, at Empart we want to plant churches that understand the gospel in all its holistic dimensions.

The two most disadvantaged groups in India's population are women and children (see facts on pg 173). Domestic violence, gender selective abortion, female infanticide and child labor are rife. Without help, there is little hope for these segments of the population.

In 2000, the year we established our first church planter training center, we also began experimenting with ways to respond to these needs. Since then we have tried many ideas, from instruction in typing to running medical clinics, and we dreamed of many more. We are always on the lookout for strategies that can be initiated and managed by local church planters within their communities. Some ideas have been successful, some not, but two in particular have been pure gold: children's homes and tailoring centers.

Ever since my encounter with Raju, the plight of abandoned and needy children had weighed heavily on my heart. But what could Empart do about it? Asia already had hundreds, probably thousands, of institutional orphanages. Should we simply add to the number?

WOMEN & CHILDREN AMONG INDIA'S POOR

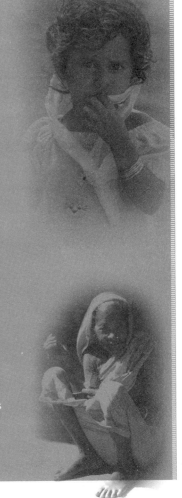

- India has a population of approximately 1.3 billion people
- Every year approximately 20 million people are added to the 1.3 billion population
- 1 out of 2 children in India is malnourished
- Fewer than half of India's children between 6-14 attend school
- An estimated 60 million children under age six live in abject poverty
- In 2014, United Nations declared India the most dangerous place on the globe for a woman to grow up because of these conditions:
    › The Indian population is missing an estimated 25 million girls because of gender selected abortion *(more than 1 million/year)*
    › Female infanticide. A South Indian study of Dalit women reported 60% of Dalit had killed a born daughter
    › Under five-year-old morbidity rate is twice as high as boys
    › Approximately 50% of women are illiterate. This perpetuates a cycle of poverty
    › Every year 50,000 women die in childbirth
    › Girls who give birth before age 15 are five times more likely to die in childbirth. Early marriage means early pregnancy and a heightened likelihood of early death from complications in childbirth

I was not convinced. As a child, I had seen mission-run orphanages in South India. I knew the life-long stigma that could haunt those who grew up in them. The fact that children were cared for was good; but the lack of exposure to the wider world that came from living in a mission compound meant they developed few of the life skills needed to survive as adults in the cutthroat world outside the gates.

Even more seriously, children raised in institutions were ignorant of how a normal family operated. With no role models, boys had little idea of how to be a husband and father. Girls didn't know how to be a wife and mother.

Too many children from institutions ended up producing dysfunctional families of their own.

With the high costs of setting up and maintaining an orphanage for, say, 300 children—buying land, erecting buildings, paying staff and so on—the economics were also questionable. And such institutions would be very difficult to multiply. The case against them seemed compelling.

We proposed a different model: what if we got one of our church planters and his wife to take ten or fifteen children into their family?

From a Western viewpoint, the idea was absurd. But in India such large families do not stand out as unusual. In such an arrangement, the children would live in a home in the local community and attend the local school. They would play with the local kids and be involved with the local church. The pastor and his wife would have the opportunity to raise them in godly ways.

And I could see one further potential benefit: we would be raising future servants of God. A significant number of our future church planters, evangelists and pastors could come from such homes.

A young pastor who joined us from South India caught the vision. Pastor Mark had been raised in a children's home himself, and early in 2000 he and his wife Sarah opened their hearts to take in ten girls. Their Punjabi village house was too small so we rented a bigger building for them. This doubled as a meeting place for their church on Sundays.

Over the next four years, we gradually refined the concept, opening a handful of other homes as we went along. The idea proved to be exceptionally good. Culturally, it fit perfectly in the Indian context of extended family and community living. Spiritually, the children were brought up according to biblical principles. Economically, it was a great value for the money, we could support the children directly rather than sinking money into expensive infrastructure. And strategically, it had the benefit of earning a pastor considerable respect and credibility in the community.

This last point was dramatically demonstrated after our second children's home was started by Pastor Daniel, a church planter in Orissa. Militant Hindus from outside the village, determined to disrupt his work, constantly harassed Daniel. One evening a party of men descended on his house, shouting abuse and demanding that he leave for good.

Pastor Daniel immediately rounded up all the children and brought them into the street. The villagers, attracted by the commotion, surrounded them in a big circle. He lined the children up and turned to the Hindu radicals.

"All right, I'll move from here, but on one condition," he said. "You must take care of these children. From now on you will be fully responsible for them. You must pay for their food, their education and their health care. And you must teach them the principles of life I would have taught them: forgiveness and mercy, grace and compassion, reconciliation and harmony."

Murmurs rippled through the crowd. One of the community's elders stepped forward.

"The young man is right. If you people want him to leave this village, you need to do everything he is prepared to do. If you're not willing to accept this responsibility, get out of this village and don't come back."

The militants glared at the elder and then turned and walked away. Pastor Daniel had no more trouble from them.

In certain areas this strategic value is even more pronounced. Some villages refuse to let Christians set foot on their land because the villagers believe the Christians will bring it under a curse. This makes even entering some villages impossible. But our church planters discovered an exception: by adopting a child from a village they could come and go freely in that village. If a church planter adopts children from, say, five villages, he has free access in those five villages to preach the gospel.

Some of our children's homes are for boys and some are for girls. The perception in the West is that girls are often unwanted in India because the dowry system makes them a liability, and this is often true. However, in some tribal cultures it is the boy's family that supplies the dowry, so it is boys who are not wanted. In these areas, the need for boys' homes is greater.

In early 2005, we started to multiply the children's homes in earnest. By the end of that year, around fifteen were operating, some in villages, some in tribal areas, and some in cities. Children came from the communities nearby; they were orphaned, abandoned or handed over by families too poor to care for them. Today, we have thirty-eight children's homes and have modified our strategy to include safe homes, hostels and schools. All told, Empart is presently caring for and educating 4,506 children. And we continue to watch for strategic new ways to care for children through our churches.

Another way to care for needy children came to us through an official government request. Would we assist with a government program where children are rescued from abuse such as trafficking, prostitution rackets, drug mafia, body parts trade, child labor and begging syndicates? The police were busting these illegal operations but they had limited places to shelter the children other than in jail!

We agreed, received the necessary approvals and licenses, and became one of the few Christian agencies the government entrusted with these children. Their stories are heartbreaking: as young as five years old, these boys and girls may be sold by desperate family members or simply snatched from their homes by unscrupulous opportunists. By no fault of their own, they end up on the streets and ensnared in a web of terror and abuse.

We took a similar approach to the children's homes but have adapted it to meet government compliance standards. Several of these "Safe Homes" are now operating, providing a safe and loving environment where the Lord is using our team to bring healing and restoration to these broken little lives.

We saw another opportunity to care for poor children whose families cannot afford school fees. These kids are left to roam the slum or village streets where they are vulnerable prey for traffickers. How could we care for them and help them achieve in life?

While our leadership team grappled with this challenge, God was already at work. The highly esteemed Director of Education for one of the North Indian states had recently chosen to follow Jesus. He entered an intense time of re-evaluation and prayer. Without naming it as such, this gentleman was aligning his new faith with his "second half purpose." As Bob Buford says, this process can be "more like archaeology than architecture." And so it was for Vivek—the clues to his future of impact and adventure were found in his past.

Vivek quickly determined that he wanted to use his skills and experience to serve the Lord. With his leadership, and some miraculous God-connections, we were able to start several high quality English medium schools. Middle class, fee-paying students enable us to provide

NON-NEGOTIABLES. THE MANDATES OF JESUS, TO MAKE DISCIPLES AND TO DO GOOD, CANNOT BE IGNORED BY ANYONE WHO CLAIMS TO FOLLOW HIM.

quality, free education for children living in poverty. External support is required to set up these schools, but they are then able to continue as self-supporting projects.

As the ministry continued to grow and mature, we discovered another purpose for these schools. Our single, energetic church planters, many who lived sacrificially in very remote regions, were now married and had their own energetic children. Very few had access to good quality schools. Some had no access to any type of school. They had to make the difficult decision to either leave the area God had called them to or forgo a good education for their children. To me, neither was a good solution.

After much modeling and experimentation, we decided to add residential capacity to our existing schools. Here we can provide quality accommodation, education and holistic care for the children of our church planters. Again we took a business approach: by incorporating fee-paying students, we could provide free accommodation and education for the children of our workers.

As with the children, the impetus to help women came from understanding their plight. Untold millions of Indian women are chained to a cycle of poverty. If a poor family has, say, two boys and two girls, it will almost invariably be the boys who are educated. The reason is simple: in a country without insurance programs, retirement plans or nursing homes, boys are their parents' "retirement plan." Girls, after all, will only marry and join their husbands' families.

This neglect, however, creates a problem. A girl with little or no education, skill or money will find it hard to attract a husband. If she does, generally, it will be someone below her station. That being the case, illiterate, unskilled girls marry illiterate, unskilled men. Being unable to do anything to raise either themselves or their children from poverty, they simply perpetuate the cycle, attributing their destitution to karma.

Empart church planters could not ignore this situation; they asked what we could do to empower women like these. Out of our discussion grew the concept of a program to help poor women learn skills like sewing. As usual, these programs would be initiated by our church planters and offered through our local churches.

This led to the first of our tailoring centers in 2000. Once again, we experimented for a couple of years and then began to multiply rapidly. Our model later expanded into other skill development programs such as making soap, shampoo, detergent, candles, various paper products, greeting cards, bags and jewelry. Today, thousands of women are being trained and empowered across North India.

Soniea is typical of those who attend the tailoring centers. Coming from a poor village background, she was in an even more desperate situation because her father had died when she was young. Thus she had little in the way of dowry to attract a husband. When she graduated from the course, she set up a small business making clothes for her village. One day when I was visiting the area, she came to a meeting and handed me a wedding invitation. I was naturally delighted for her.

"So who are you marrying?" I asked.

"Oh, a businessman."

"A businessman! Why does he want to marry you?"

"Because he wanted to marry a businesswoman," she grinned proudly.

Along with her sewing skills, the young seamstress had gained dignity, self-respect and the courage to believe in a life of possibility. The future for her and her children would be very different from the one they would have faced had she never learned to pedal a sewing machine.

I realized the incredible importance of this one day when I attended a village tailoring center graduation. The father of a young graduate bent down and grabbed my legs, shaking and choking with emotion. "Thank you for doing something that I could never do for my daughter," he said. "I could never give her an education." Deeply moved, I picked him up, hugged him and prayed for him. Training his daughter had cost us no more than $150 (USD), but it was a gift beyond his wildest dreams.

Another woman, Sushila, was one of the first students in Sudha's tailoring center in New Delhi. A young, unmarried Hindu woman, she was eager to learn a vocational skill, but the six-month diploma course gave her much more. Each morning she listened carefully as Sudha shared the word of God while she taught sewing. After being healed of a bout of appendicitis, Sushila accepted Jesus and joined Sudha's church.

This highlights the wonderful opportunities created by the tailoring centers. Because they are located in a pastor's home or a local church's building, the women both learn a skill and hear the gospel in a loving, encouraging community. In the process, many share their problems, whether it be the pain of singleness with few prospects or the harsh suffering that so many married Indian women endure in domestic violence. Counseling and prayer takes place, and sometimes the restoration of relationships.

Through this, the pastor and the sewing instructors—local Christian women like Sudha—establish relationships with the women's families. If someone's daughter is attending your tailoring center, then you can visit them, not as a pastor, but as their daughter's teacher. And if you are doing something for someone's daughter that they could never do, in Indian culture that earns you great respect.

Attending a tailoring center is not conditional on the women becoming Christians, but we have found that around 40% of participants become baptized disciples of Jesus Christ.

An average of fifteen women attend each six-month course, with separate courses often being run both morning and afternoon. A typical rural tailoring center will service five or six villages, representing perhaps 10,000 people. In a city like Delhi, it will be many more. Participants range from young teenagers to sixty-year-old widowed grandmothers. They learn to sew traditional local styles so their products will sell readily.

When a woman graduates, she receives a diploma and a robust new cast-iron sewing machine. Made in India and carrying a lifetime warranty, these machines are operated either by foot pedal or hand crank, so no electricity is needed and they are very easy to service.

People sometimes ask me, "Why are you doing something like this for women and not for men?" Sadly, our experience and research have taught us that, in India, women are far more responsible. Many men fall into gambling, smoking, alcohol and drugs, wasting their money and leaving women to pick up the pieces. Women, on the other hand, usually make their children their priority. Focusing on them brings long-lasting fruit.

Unlike the children's homes, most of the tailoring centers are not intended to be long-term, especially in villages. A center will normally operate for two or three years and then it will be moved to a new location. (We don't want to saturate an area with seamstresses!) Nonetheless, our goal and prayer is that eventually tens of thousands of centers will be operating; another glowing thread in the garment God is weaving among those who need to hear the good news.

One of the most rewarding things about being involved with what God is doing in Asia is that everything we do feeds into the one central goal: bringing lost sheep to the great Shepherd. An example occurs in women's ministry: Alongside the tailoring centers, which empower women to reach their potential in practical terms, Empart holds "Sister, You Are Special" conferences that aim to teach pastors' wives and other women of influence the spiritual truth about their incredible value in

God's eyes. Women in India are told in a million ways that they are worthless, so the teaching that they are actually special daughters of the King can be revolutionary.

In the same way, Empart organizes health education camps. Most rural Indians have little knowledge about basic hygiene (washing hands, keeping things clean, bathing, brushing teeth). We are educating church planters on these issues through the training centers, as well as children in the children's homes and believers in the churches. We also hold broader public health education programs and medical camps, including showing health videos as part of our itinerant film ministry.

The film ministry itself illustrates how Empart's various strategies all feed into one overarching purpose. People in the land of Bollywood are crazy about movies, so alongside health education material we often show a film called *The Merciful One*, the story of Jesus set in India and played by Indian actors. This film brilliantly overcomes the misconception that Jesus was the blonde-haired, blue-eyed founder of a Western religion. It has become one of our most powerful evangelistic tools.

Running a children's home, tailoring center or other social program is not something that church planters can achieve alone. This is another area where partnership with Christians in the West is central to what God is doing. Such partnership provides resources that empower workers on the ground.

One kind of support is prayer. Another is for Western believers to visit Asia as part of a short-term team: Empart coordinates dozens of teams from different parts of the world every year. Sometimes these bring together people with particular skills, such as medical training or pastoral leadership. Whoever they are, though, teams mostly share a common desire to be a blessing to the church in Asia and to learn from what God is doing there.

Of course, much of the needed support must necessarily be financial. It is surprisingly cheap in Western terms to provide a woman with a sewing machine and training or to provide effective support for children. Putting resources into the hands of transformational leaders like Sudha always achieves great returns on your investment—it can change a family, a community, even a whole nation. And it can certainly change life for the broken individuals who are branded by society as the least of the least.

CHAPTER 14 LEADERSHIP LESSONS

+ Cohesive strategy. All good ideas and initiatives must feed into the central goal and flow out of the same vision. If not, you will end up with mission drift and dilute the core vision and become ineffective. But when they are interconnected, the core vision is strengthened and propelled to new heights.

+ Test first. Don't allow good ideas to be set in concrete without testing them first. Set up a systematic process through which all your good ideas can be tested and proven to be great ideas (or not!). Once you know they work and produce the desired results, you can expand and multiply. This risk management strategy will save you money, embarrassment and potential loss of credibility as a leader!

+ Non-negotiables. The mandates of Jesus, to make disciples and to do good, cannot be ignored by anyone who claims to follow him.

+ Invest wisely. Investing in transformational leaders has the best return on investment—here and in eternity.

CHAPTER 14 REFLECTION QUESTIONS

1 In your context, are there activities that have been added which are not feeding into your central vision and goal? Set a time to review ALL your activities against your vision. And remember that strategy alignment often requires difficult decisions.

2 Write down the good activities that you are involved in that may not be producing the desired outcomes? Take time to establish an annual audit and review all activities that are going on, measure to see if they are achieving the desired results.

3 What activities are you not engaged in that could deepen the expression of your vision? Again, set a time to explore this with your team.

4 How are Jesus' Good Commandment and Great Commission integrated into your strategy? What changes are required?

15 LOVING THE LEAST

Pastor Paul expertly wove his motorbike through the busy suburban street. The relentless midday heat had done nothing to calm the frenetic activity on the road. Cows, dogs, beggars, pedestrians, bicycles, rickshaws, cars and buses all vied for space. Salesmen bartered beside their mobile carts, selling sun-scorched Hindu devotional books and parched-looking fruits. Nothing seemed to be spared from the charring heat wave.

Paul was used to this organized chaos. He and his wife Rachel lived here on the outskirts of Lucknow, where they led a growing church. But today, Paul was on autopilot as he drove home. He had a strong sense that there was something more that God wanted him to do—but what was it?

That morning Paul had led a fasting prayer time. They examined the story of the Good Samaritan and prayed for healing of a young lady who was either demon possessed or mentally unstable. She was okay for now but Paul knew from experience that her battle was far from over.

A car beside Paul swerved towards him, narrowly missing his motorbike. He slowed down just in time as the car slammed on its brakes. Horns blaring, the traffic around him ground to a halt. Frustrated drivers yelled abuse as the traffic slowly diverted itself around the offending blockage. Everyone started to move again—everyone except Paul.

The blockage was a package of barely-recognizable humanity. Draped in rags, the package lay motionless in the middle of the road. Paul jerked his motorbike kickstand out, swinging himself off his bike. The package moaned as Paul leant over. Judging by the amount of dirty, unkempt facial hair, it was a man. A filthy shell of a man. Blood coagulated quickly around his wounds, mixing with dirt and drying in the heat. Flies clung to his body, at home in the grime.

Beggars and homeless people are a common sight on India's roads. But today was different. Whether it was the story of the Good Samaritan or the girl he had just prayed for, Paul knew in that instant that he could no longer walk past these broken people. Refusing to help because of the man's state, passersby watched as Paul gently lifted the man from the road, paid a friend to take his motorbike home, hailed an auto rickshaw and left the scene with the package stowed safely beside him.

As a nurse, Paul's wife took this all in her stride. She bathed the man, Paul cut his hair and they took him to the local hospital. The medical bill was well above their own means so they contacted our Empart leaders who were able to help them with assistance from our partners.

When John was discharged from the hospital, Paul and Rachel refused to let him go back to the streets, instead persuading him to come and live with them so they could continue caring for him.

During this time a pastor from Indonesia came to speak at our pastors' conference. He shared a story about a mentally ill person in their community who was healed and restored. For Paul, this was a confirmation. My own father's mental illness had already given me a deep compassion for these people and their families. So it was decided: we would start a special ministry for these people. Our first Mercy Home was a trial. Mentally ill people who were living homeless in the streets now had a home there. They were bathed, clothed, fed and cared in every way by our church planters.

Mental illness in India still carries a terrible stigma. When treatment fails, families have been known to abandon their sick loved one in a megacity rather than face the shame this will bring on the family name. The Hindu disregard for the misfortune of others means these people are off the humanitarian radar—lost and homeless, sometimes for life.

Paul and Rachel tell of finding people lapping like dogs at dirty puddles. Or running naked through the train station, clawing wildly at themselves. Women who are sexually abused, babbling incoherently at anyone they see or men who go into violent rampages, dangerous and threatening. The list of horrors goes on.

Through prayer, love, medical treatment and counseling we have seen many of these broken people healed, delivered and restored with dignity. John, that unrecognizable package on the road, is now a church planter. Janitha had been raped on the streets before she was brought to the Mercy Home by police. She received love and care, and gave birth to a beautiful baby boy. Months later, she was able to recall the contact details for her family. When we contacted them, we discovered she was from a wealthy, high-caste family, married to an accountant! Two years on, fully healed, she was finally restored to her family. As a family, they now follow Jesus.

Word about the Mercy Home began to spread. There was no way we could accommodate every person brought to us, so we designed a Mercy Bus. The back of the bus is equipped with a bathroom where we can wash and clean people and the front area is like a lounge where they can get food, prayer and counseling. The police continue to bring people from all over the cities to us for care.

We now have a number of these homes and are expanding this ministry to other major cities. Mentally ill homeless people might seem like the least of the least, but for Pastor Paul they are the "something more" that he felt God wanted him to do!

I celebrate with Paul—finding your "something more" in life leads to great fulfillment and satisfaction. As a leader, my job is to create an atmosphere where good ideas can flourish. As those ideas develop, I need to empower my people to take the necessary risks to move them from ideas into reality. The more Pauls I can release to find their "something more," the more impact we will have as a team.

Another vulnerable group of people we are privileged to serve is widows who have been neglected by their family. A widow in India is often blamed for her husband's death and widowhood is described as a state of social

CREATE THE RIGHT ATMOSPHERE. LEADERS MUST BE THERMOSTATS, NOT JUST THERMOMETERS. WE MUST GAUGE THE SITUATION, THEN CREATIVELY MOVE IT FROM WHERE IT IS TO WHERE IT SHOULD BE, GENERATING OPPORTUNITY FOR OUR PEOPLE TO MOVE FROM WHERE THEY ARE TO WHERE THEY NEED TO BE.

death. Although widows today are not forced to die in ritual sati (burning themselves on their husband's funeral pyre), they are still expected to mourn until their own death. Traditions, neglect and abuse culminate in an average mortality rate that is 85% higher for widows than for married women.

After experimenting with several ideas, we now care for these widows as part of our children's homes. Rather than putting them all together in a home where they have no purpose, these women are now caring for the children and have a renewed zest for life. The children and the widows all seem to thrive on this new opportunity.

In India, trafficking and prostitution are like two halves of the same cage. An estimated 90% of women in prostitution want to leave but are unable to for reasons of poverty, discrimination or violence. When some of our church planters were approached by women who were trapped in prostitution in a major city, they stepped in to help. In the process, they quickly realized that the problems of trafficking and prostitution were being fed by a flow of women who were released from jail but had nowhere to go.

India's shame culture makes families reluctant to help newly released family members, preferring to leave the person to fend for themselves rather than bring dishonor to the family. Trafficking predators and pimps are quick to offer help. Promise of a job and a place to stay lures these women into a vicious cycle of drugs and prostitution.

Our team decided to work at the source to stop this flow. We now have a ministry in the women's jail and the nearby red light district. The women are supported in jail and on release, teaching them new skills, helping them set up small businesses, arranging marriages where possible and generally re-establishing in the community and in a church.

As a leader there is a very real tension in maintaining the balance between being focused on the vision and yet not ignoring needs that arrive unexpectedly on your door step. For Empart, it is the whole balance of fulfilling the Good Commandment and the Great Commission. Where exactly is the crossover between doing good and making disciples?

It is interesting to look at Stephen in the New Testament (Acts 6 and 7). Stephen was chosen by the disciples to serve as a social worker, negotiating between the church factions and waiting on tables. Yet he was then martyred as a preacher of the gospel! It seems that he wasn't following his job description very well!

Clearly, right from the early church, there was an intertwining of both doing good and making disciples. This encourages me that we are on the right track. Yes, we must not allow mission drift to take us away from the core, but nor should we neglect these unplanned opportunities to represent Jesus. While holding that tension may not be easy, it is essential—and it is Christ honoring.

Our Empart leaders continue to effectively address social issues like the mentally ill homeless people, widows and prostitution. As we developed a reputation for these good works, the government invited us to partner with them in solving some significant challenges like water and sanitation.

Getting access to safe, clean drinking water is a problem for millions of people in India. With the cooperation and partnership of various authorities, we started to dig deep core bore wells. Drought and caste discrimination are both problems. These wells are constructed in communities where there is already an Empart worker and they are always accessible for people of all religion and caste.

At least 636 million Indians lack toilets, according to the latest census data. Open defecation has dramatic consequences on human health, dignity and security, the environment, and social and economic development. It is considered one of the clearest manifestations of extreme poverty. The lack of improved sanitation impacts vulnerable populations such as persons with disabilities and women, who are more exposed to sexual violence. Lack of private toilets in schools is a major reason why girls do not continue their education once they enter puberty. This is a crisis that contributes to disease, childhood malnutrition, loss of economic output and violence against women.

With the help of local government and partnership from the West, we have developed an effective toilet design, approved nationally and internationally, that is eco-friendly, socio-culturally acceptable, and economically affordable. The toilet can be easily constructed using local materials and skills, and are being built in urban slums and rural villages.

Another opportunity to make a difference started with local clean-up campaigns. This led to developing a Volunteer Network which, by 2015, had more than 16,000 young people. They are from different faiths and castes but are united in the vision for a cleaner India. We train them in principles of servant leadership, values of volunteering, practical skills in organizing, mobilizing people, values of cleanliness and good character.

We also have started a lay leaders' movement in our churches. We provide relevant training to raise up the lay leadership potential in the pews. A mentoring program has also started. We now have 52,000 people involved in the lay leaders and mentoring programs.

We realize that our vision of transforming lives and communities can't be fulfilled through the church planters alone. It requires massive people power. We are doing all that we can to equip and mobilize ordinary people to do what they can, where they can, with what they have. Unless and until we activate the dormant power and potential of the ordinary masses, we will never see national transformation.

The challenge is huge—but what an opportunity to make a significant impact on whole communities, and even entire castes!

CHAPTER 15 LEADERSHIP LESSONS

+ Balance your activities. As a leader there is a very real tension in maintaining the balance between being focused on the vision and yet not ignoring needs and opportunities that arrive unexpectedly on your door step.

+ Seize unplanned opportunities. While we must not allow mission drift to take us away from the core, nor should we neglect unplanned opportunities. Holding that tension may not be easy, but it is essential. These unplanned opportunities often hold the key to the next level of your vision.

+ Recognize and activate dormant potential in your people. You already know you can't do everything yourself, but you need to have a plan in place for activating the dormant power and potential of your people.

+ Create the right atmosphere. Leaders must be thermostats, not just thermometers. We must gauge the situation, then creatively move it from where it is to where it should be, generating opportunity for our people to move from where they are to where they need to be.

CHAPTER 15 REFLECTION QUESTIONS

1 How is your balance of activities? Look back at your list of core activities from chapter 14 and see if they are weighted too heavily in one direction. What do you need to do to create the right balance?

2 What are your strategies to activate the dormant potential in your people? Are they working? What changes do you need to make?

3 How is the atmosphere in your organization? What do you need to do to become a better thermostat?

4 On a scale of 1-10, how inspiring and empowering are you as a leader? What do you need to do to be become better at it?

16 SHEPHERDS AND SNAKE CHARMERS

Sunil was dissatisfied and restless—he had been searching for truth and meaning for years. One night, Jesus appeared to him in a dream and spoke to him. Shortly afterwards I met him and I gave him a Bible and encouraged him to read it as this is God's word. He was so happy and grateful.

That evening he rang me back. "This is the most incredible book I've ever read," he said.

"Wait a minute," I replied. "You couldn't have read the whole Bible in that time."

"No, no—just the first few pages."

"Well, you can't say that it is the most incredible book by reading the first few pages. Read the whole Bible and then tell me what you think."

"I don't need to. This really is the most incredible book in the world." I asked him why and his answer was like a thunderclap. "Because I've read many holy books, and this is the only one that tells me I am created in the image and likeness of God."

Sunil enthusiastically explained further. "You don't understand what that means. All my life, I have been told I'm worth less than a snake, an elephant, a rat or a cow. My caste has less dignity than those animals. So for me to read in a sacred book that I am created in the image of God—you don't appreciate the power of that. I don't need to read the rest of the book to know how wonderful and precious it is."

Over the following months, Sunil continued to explore the Christian faith. God met him in more dreams. He began to write poetry to communicate the new message of Jesus to his people in a contemporary, culturally relevant way. He went on to create a seven-point strategy to take this message to his whole caste.

"The government wants us to be better educated and to advance economically," he told me. "But how can we become enterprising if we don't know who we are? If we believe we are less than animals, how can we aspire to become more than that? What we need, first and foremost, is to renew our minds. Will you help me help my people to renew their minds so they can believe who they are?"

Who could refuse a request like that? He was handing us an incredible opportunity to take the gospel to a whole new group of people. We started working with this caste group, teaching from God's word, especially focusing on their worth and value, that God has a plan and purpose for each one. At the same time we commenced some practical and social initiatives.

Sunil's experience reminds me of God's desire to reveal himself to people and the power of his Word to transform perspectives and paradigms. Sometimes Western Christians ask me why we need to preach the gospel: shouldn't we concentrate first on meeting people's socio-economic needs? My answer is always the same: socio-economic needs are important, but it is the power of the gospel that brings dignity, value, worth and respect—not just in eternity, but here and now.

Caste remains a massively contentious issue in India. Government policy reserves a percentage of positions (in politics, public service and education) for those from the lower castes. This policy fuels communal riots and ongoing tensions between caste groups. Over thousands of years the system has vested social and political power in the hands of a privileged few and kept untold multitudes in poverty and suffering. These people long for the recognition as human beings they have always been denied.

As I continued to develop relationships with various politicians, I was introduced to other caste leaders too. My interactions with these leaders deepened my understanding of caste struggles. Having grown up in India I thought I understood the caste system, but I hadn't fully grasped the extent of its destructive evil. I met the leaders of various sub-castes whose members swept streets, collected garbage, emptied toilets, disposed of dead bodies or washed clothes. They explained to me that the only thing their people could do—the only thing they could ever dream of doing—was what they had been born into. Trapped by centuries of social and religious conditioning, they lived in a psychological and emotional prison under the sign: "This is what you are; you can never be anything else."

Hindus are taught that a person's karma is directly linked to their commitment to religious obligations and doing their caste-appointed job well. Failure to do so incurs bad karma. The way to freedom is to be diligent in your job all your life so that in the next life you can become somebody better. If you resist, you will be worse off in your next life.

Millions are held in this modern-day slavery, subject to grinding discrimination and abuse. Most are simple, illiterate folk, yet they are beautiful and have wonderful hearts. They are forced to work twelve or fourteen hours a day, six days a week, for thirty to fifty cents a day—about the cost of a bottle of water. In some cases they can't even expect a wage; they must just take what is given to them.

India is a nuclear power, a world leader in fields such as information and communications technology, yet under the stronghold of the caste system, vast numbers of its people—more than half the population—still live as they did 2,000 years ago. This includes the so-called "Scheduled Castes" (Dalits or Untouchables), "Scheduled Tribes" and "Other Backward Classes." These three categories are further divided into thousands of sub castes, creating yet another hierarchy just within these castes. As caste system is a part of the Hindu creation story, it is very difficult to remove from the society. But God is at work.

While still seeking answers to the complex caste system and structure, I met the leaders from the shepherd caste. Fifteen years before, one of these men had questioned, "Why should we be trapped in this untouchable caste system? We should invent a new identity for our people."

They started searching for their identity, studying Islam, Buddhism, Sikhism, Christianity. When they came to the twenty-third Psalm—"The Lord is my shepherd"—they were electrified. Never before had they encountered a god who was a shepherd. They kept reading and reached the New Testament, where they read Jesus' words: "I am the good shepherd... My sheep hear my voice...I lay down my life for the sheep." Once they understood the connection between Jesus and the Shepherd of Psalm 23, the pieces fell into place. "We are the shepherd caste but Jesus is our shepherd," they said. They found their identity in Jesus and in following

ENGAGE IN ALL SPHERES. ENGAGE WITH LEADERS FROM SPHERES BEYOND YOUR OWN. FOR EXAMPLE, IF YOU ARE A CHURCH LEADER, CONNECT WITH BUSINESS AND POLITICAL LEADERS TOO. IT MAY NOT BE COMFORTABLE BUT YOU WILL BE STRETCHED AND GROW.

him. They are now actively working on a strategy to take this Jesus to their entire caste and spread him all over India.

A similar transformation is underway in one of the most unlikely groups: snake charmers. These outcasts are so far below the caste system they are considered to be lower than the untouchables. Traditionally they make their living by training snakes to dance to flute music and wandering from town to town performing in the streets. They live in dreadful poverty. Only the men are able to work. None of the children go to school. Their lives are even more precarious because the hunting and keeping of snakes has been illegal in India since 1972.

One day, a newly graduated Empart church planter, eighteen-year-old Ajit, was walking and praying in the streets of Agra, near the Taj Mahal. He came upon a small crowd watching a snake charmer. The performance ended and the crowd dispersed, but Ajit offered to buy the young man a drink. Later, Ajit asked if he could accompany him back to his home village. There he found an entire community of snake charmers and their families living in slum-like conditions. In the surrounding area were thirteen similar snake charmer villages, all extremely poor.

Ajit's new friend introduced him to his fellow villagers. Moved with the compassion of Christ, Ajit began to pray and ask Empart leaders what he could do to help these people. While seeking for an effective strategy he kept returning to his new friends and building a deeper relationship. He asked the people to identify their most pressing need and they answered quickly, "Education for our children." So with the help of Empart partners, he started a literacy program for their children under a tree on the side of the road. Once this was underway, he added an adult literacy program.

Amazed that an outsider would serve them in this way, the people began to listen when he shared the gospel with them. Eventually the villagers opened their hearts to God.

The transformation this brought didn't go unnoticed. Over time, all thirteen of the neighboring snake charmer communities joined in. The literacy program has now grown to an English medium school, where hundreds of children are being educated. A tailoring center has been set up where women learn sewing. We have dug water wells for them, built toilets and trained them in basic health and hygiene. Four of the young men have been trained as church planters and have returned to work among their people. Today, you will see the same instruments used to make the snakes dance now being played to worship Jesus.

The challenges facing this group are gigantic. Consequences of generational illiteracy and poverty can't be changed overnight. They need long-term reskilling, so we are trialling projects such as soap-making and candle-making with the hope of setting up micro-enterprises. We have a responsibility as brothers and sisters in the kingdom to continue walking the journey with them until the image of God is fully restored in their lives.

We grappled with what this new caste involvement meant for us. Was it enough to help individual caste groups, or should we do more? As we and our Indian leaders wrestled with this question, a startling new vision emerged. We called it the Caste Reconciliation Movement.

The objective was simply to eradicate caste discrimination and restore dignity, worth and value to all human beings. Achieving this is not straightforward. Many people are reluctant to acknowledge that these people have been abused and mistreated—by the higher castes, by European colonizers, by Arabs and other Muslim invaders, by Christian missionaries and by modern democratic politicians. All of these groups have done little or nothing to release these people from their bondage.

So in launching the Caste Reconciliation we decided to create opportunities where people of all castes could meet together. We would invite political leaders, Westerners, Brahmins and other high caste people, Christian and other religious leaders—anyone who was willing to share in this grander vision for the nation. This would simply provide a chance to say, "We're sorry for the way the lower castes have been treated for thousands of years." Westerners could apologize for the way people were neglected and mistreated by the British, French, Dutch and Portuguese. Muslims could say sorry for how the lower castes were not helped under Mughal colonization. Christians could apologize for the lack of efforts by the church to fight for their cause. Politicians could apologize for not upholding the Indian Constitution, which guarantees equality and freedom.

As well as asking forgiveness, we would affirm their value as people made in the image of God. We would encourage them to pursue a brighter future, if not for themselves then for their children. We would advise them to raise their families with that mindset. And then the Christian leaders, and anyone else who was willing to participate, would do something unheard of in the caste system: wash the feet of the lower caste participants.

The intention would not be to convert people, but to reach out to them with a message uncompromisingly based on the biblical teachings of creation and the way Jesus treated others. We would simply try to help people understand their worth—and then see what God would do.

For the untouchables to experience having their feet washed by members of the higher castes was a watershed moment. It was deeply moving to see these men, women and children weeping as they realized, not just through words but also through actions, how worthy they really were.

We encourage all Empart church planters and churches to champion this cause and take action to practice total brotherhood and oneness. Of course, individual events like these, no matter how powerful, are not enough to bring lasting change by themselves. They must be followed by education, both for those wanting a better life and those who must accept and encourage them. Lower caste people must learn to see themselves differently; others must learn to see them as precious, not as dirt.

This fight will not be won overnight. It needs a long-term strategy pursued over the long term. We are exploring possibilities and continue experimenting with various strategies, encouraging governments from other countries, NGOs, the United Nations and others to take an interest in this cause.

It is a big challenge with big potential results. And it is going to take a huge commitment from all our team.

CHAPTER 16 LEADERSHIP LESSONS

+ The power of the gospel. Socio-economic needs are important, but it is the power of the gospel that brings dignity, value, worth and respect—not just in eternity, but here and now.

+ Network and partner with other leaders. It sounds so basic but many leaders fail to do this effectively. Continue to sharpen your networking skills. Develop strategies to leverage those relationships towards greater outcomes and results.

+ Engage in all spheres. Engage with leaders from spheres beyond your own. For example, if you are a church leader, connect with business and political leaders too. It may not be comfortable but you will be stretched and grow.

CHAPTER 16 REFLECTION QUESTIONS

1 What does "the power of the gospel" mean to you? Do you need to draw on this more? Personally? For your business or church? How will you do this?

2 Consider the network of leaders you connect with. Do you need to increase the number of connections? Or deepen some existing connections? Or broaden into spheres beyond your own? How do you plan to make the necessary changes?

3 How well do you leverage your network for achieving good and great outcomes that are beyond your reach?

17 COMMITMENT THAT WON'T FLINCH

I stood at the front of the meeting room in our Chandigarh training center while twenty-six men shuffled to get comfortable, sitting on the floor. We were approaching the climax of a graduation service filled with passionate prayer and fervent singing. Now my job was to encourage these new church planters as they launched on the missions God had given them.

I turned to Joshua chapter 1. Comparing the graduates to Joshua being told to take the Promised Land, I pointed out that the time had come for each of them to walk into the unknown with God. The Lord told Joshua, "I will give you every place where you set your foot," and in a similar way God had something special to give each of them. They needed to receive it in faith and confidence. Just as Joshua was told to "be strong and courageous" in order to face what lay ahead, so they needed to summon their courage.

"Just because the Lord is going to give it does not mean things are going to be easy," I said. "Sometimes it will mean tests, trials and battles before you will have what he is giving you. Many of you will face persecution and some of you may lose belongings, loved ones or even your own life. But the Lord wants to encourage you to be strong and courageous as you move to take hold of what he has prepared for you."

I paused for a moment to let my listeners absorb these words. Then I gave them the final charge: "Who is willing to pay the ultimate price to take possession of the Promised Land?"

An ear-splitting silence filled the room. Then one man stood, followed by another. Soon all were standing, holding their Bibles above their heads and shouting, "We are willing to give our lives for the sake of the gospel!" These men knew that the possibility of suffering and death was real. When you invade the devil's territory, the devil fights back. But they were setting themselves to "take the land" with a commitment that wouldn't flinch.

"Have I not commanded you? Be strong and courageous. Do not be afraid; do not be discouraged, for the Lord your God will be with you wherever you go." (Joshua 1:9)

Any picture of how the Kingdom of God is advancing in India would be incomplete without understanding the obstacles that stand in the way. Massive obstacles. Reaching the unreached is tough, especially in the era of Hindutva, the radical ideology that advocates India becoming a "Hindu nation." Many Indian states have already passed anti-conversion laws. Although not all of these have yet been implemented, they are already being used as a pretext for persecuting Christians. So, while the silent majority of Hindus and Muslims are peaceful people, the minority radicals are taking advantage of every opportunity to oppress, persecute and silence the followers of Jesus.

It would be wrong to think it is just church planters and their families who suffer the torment of persecution (although they often bear the brunt). Anyone who dares to call Christ their Lord and Savior is vulnerable.

This became crystal clear in the eastern state of Orissa during 2008 when anti-Christian violence surged to such an extent, it is labeled as "the largest attack on the Christian community in the history of democratic India."

Orissa has long been a difficult region. The Australian missionary Graham Staines and his two sons were murdered there in 1999. A largely tribal state, it is a fertile breeding ground for religious fundamentalism. On December 24 and 25, 2007, supporters of the VHP, a radical Hindu organization, armed with guns, knives, trishuls (three-pronged spears) and other weapons, launched a series of attacks on Christians in Kandhamal District in central Orissa. Over ninety churches and seven hundred Christian homes were burned, Christians were beaten and killed as they were fleeing into the jungle for safety.

This was just a foretaste of things to come. On the evening of August 23, 2008, an outspoken VHP leader, Swami Laxmanananda Sarawati, and four others were murdered in Sarawati's ashram. Responsibility for the assassination was claimed by the Naxalites, a group of Maoist rebels, but VHP supporters blamed Christians. The following day mobs unleashed a wave of violence on the villages of Kandhamal.

With the goal of "cleansing" the region of Christians, they systematically went from village to village, house to house, demanding that believers renounce their faith and become Hindus. Those who refused were assaulted, raped and worse. Reconversion to Hinduism was the price to stay in their homes, so thousands fled. The persecution continued for days, with similar outbreaks in other parts of Orissa. All together an estimated 4,400 homes were destroyed, hundreds of church buildings and many orphanages razed, 18,000 people injured and over 60,000 left homeless. At least half of these, including up to 15,000 children, were forced to hide in the jungle, without food and shelter, in monsoonal weather. As relief camps were set up, radicals attacked these too, even poisoning water supplies.

Hundreds of Christians lost their lives (exact numbers are not known as many bodies were never found). An Empart church planter described to me how one of his church elders was shot dead and his body chopped into small pieces which were taken in buckets to various church members' houses. "The same thing will happen to you if you don't deny Jesus," the rioters threatened. Then, as they left, they scattered the buckets' contents around the homes. The believers had to collect all the body parts and put them in a box for burial.

Another church planter told me through tears how he was made to watch his wife being raped. "If you become a Hindu now," the perpetrators shouted, "we will stop." The psychological and emotional pressure was unbelievable.

Over seventy Empart churches were directly affected by this. Three hundred and fifty of our own families lost everything. Three of our workers died and five children's homes were completely destroyed.

I visited our people in Orissa three times in the immediate aftermath of these events. I went to try to encourage them, but I came away profoundly challenged. They had lost homes, belongings, everything because they refused to deny Jesus. I still don't know what I would do in a similar situation. These brothers and sisters had demonstrated extraordinary commitment to their Savior. Some publicly said, "You can take everything, even our lives, but you can never take Jesus away from us."

Were they fearful and worried because they had lost family members or didn't know whether they were alive or dead? Of course. But beneath their surface anxiety I detected something else. Not one person asked me, "Where is God, and why did he allow this to happen to us?" Instead, I met an extraordinary confidence that said, "Yes, this is extremely bad, but we know that God is going to bring something good out of it. We don't know how and we don't know when, but it's going to happen."

I was amazed at the price people were willing to pay. I asked one believer about his loss and he responded, "But I didn't lose anything."

"What do you mean?" I said. "You lost your farm, your home, your church building—"

"No, no," he interrupted. "I actually didn't lose those things because I never owned them in the first place." Then he quoted 1 Corinthians 6:20, "You are not your own; you were bought at a price." "I'm not my own anymore. Jesus owns me. He owns everything."

As I write this, even now many displaced Christians have never returned to their villages because of threats and fear. Some have moved to more welcoming towns; others have been forced to try to make a new life in the jungle where they fled. More positively, the Orissa government has taken proactive steps to manage community tensions, and major Christian relief activities during natural calamities—cyclones, typhoons and floods—have publicly demonstrated that followers of Jesus are generous, loving people who refuse to hold resentment for the past.

We are at a key moment in India's religious history. Within India there is a strong sentiment that to be an Indian is to be Hindu. This right wing militant ideology propagates three core beliefs: Hindustan is the land of Hindus; Hindi is the language of Hindus; Hindutva is the lifestyle of Hindus. If you want to be accepted as an Indian, according to this perspective, these are the things you must champion. To them, faiths that are born in India such as Buddhism, Sikhism, Jainism and New Age movements are tolerable, but religions brought from outside, especially Christianity and Islam, must be stopped. People who want to become Christians are seen as betraying their country and selling their birthright, especially in North India.

Indian believers, of course, protest that this is not the case. We love our country. We pray and work hard for it—in fact, Christians in India punch far above their weight in fields such as education, health and social development.

203

> DEVELOP A CAPACITY FOR PAIN. A PERSON'S LEADERSHIP
> CAPACITY IS DETERMINED BY THEIR CAPACITY TO BEAR PAIN.

Despite our protests, there are powerful militant groups lobbying the Indian government to bring in tough federal legislation based on five policies:

1 All foreign missionaries to leave India.
2 All foreign money used for missionary activities to be stopped.
3 All Christian activities to be monitored and investigated by a special commission in an ongoing way.
4 All literature that speaks against Hinduism to be seized and destroyed.
5 All conversion activities to be prohibited.

This is an extremely serious threat. With 80% of the population being Hindu, Christians can't block such developments through political means. We need to pray. Only God's intervention will keep the doors open for the spread of the gospel.

I first learned how far grassroots anti-Christian sentiment could go in the early days of our ministry. We were supporting a church planter named John pioneering a church on the Orissa–Andhra Pradesh border. He regularly held prayer meetings in two different villages and rode between them on his bicycle.

Though John had encountered some hostility to his work, he had never felt really threatened. Then one evening around 10 p.m., he was cycling home after a prayer meeting. The night was pitch black and the only light came from his bicycle headlamp. Somewhere along that narrow dirt road someone ambushed him, and his body was found the next morning. It was riddled with stab wounds.

John's death shocked me deeply. I felt a great weight of responsibility to make life as safe as possible for these brave men and their families. When I met John's wife, however, I got another shock. She was neither angry nor bitter. Instead, she was absolutely determined to carry on with her husband's vision. I began to understand that for these church planters suffering was not a problem, but an honor.

I strongly believe that a person's leadership capacity is determined by their capacity to bear pain. In places throughout Northern India and Nepal, their courageous commitment to spread the gospel is unhindered. Given their clarity of vision, courageous commitment and this capacity to bear pain, I salute our church planters as some of the finest leaders I have been privileged to meet.

The power of God to protect and his ability to bring good out of suffering are the twin anchors that hold these faithful brothers and sisters firm. This is demonstrated by the story of Shanker.

Shanker was a young Nepali who originally came to India to work as a laborer. Along the way, he met some Christians and opened his heart to Jesus. One day he felt God calling him to become a church planter and decided to attend one of our training centers. The Lord made it clear he should work in a particular village on the Haryana–Punjab border, so when he graduated he rented a house there and moved in.

He faced considerable opposition at first, but knuckled down to the task. Then one day Empart's office phone rang. "Your man, Shanker, was bashed early this morning, outside the village," the caller said. "No one knows who did it. He's badly injured. You'd better come and pick him up."

When the leaders arrived, they found Shanker with cuts and bruises all over his body. One of his eyes had been severely damaged.

They took Shanker from the village and put him with another pastor and his family. He needed time to heal and to regain his shattered confidence. After about six months, he decided to try again, this time in a different village. Things went reasonably well there.

Then, one morning he woke up with a sense that God wanted him to go back to visit the old village. Shanker was filled with fear. He didn't want to go. But the sense of God's direction was so compelling that he climbed on his bicycle and set out, praying desperately all the way.

As he rode into the village, God spoke to him again: "Go over to that house and knock on the door." He looked at the hut; there was nothing distinctive about it. But he obeyed, and a man and woman came to the door.

Suddenly Shanker knew what God wanted him to do. He introduced himself and said, "I'm here to pray for you to have a child."

For a second, the couple looked at him in astonishment. Then they burst into tears. "We've been trying to have children for seven years," the husband explained. "We've gone to doctors and made many pilgrimages to holy places. Nothing works. We can't have children."

"Well, I'm going to pray to Jesus, the true God," Shanker said, "and he is going to give you a child."

Shanker prayed, and while he was speaking he had the distinct impression the couple would have a son. He told them this, reassured them that Jesus would answer their prayer, then got back on his bike and pedaled home.

Shanker didn't think any more about the incident, but some time later the couple sought out another Empart worker in a different village. An ultrasound had just confirmed that the wife was pregnant with a son. Through that miracle they became Christians, and their testimony became a powerful witness to their village. This second pastor started a prayer meeting and Bible study in their home, and within a few months about twenty people had been baptized.

Sometimes when a person is beaten up and thrown out of a village, it is easy to think that is the end of the story. But the Bible says God will bring good out of every circumstance. We just need to continue being obedient. If Shanker had been unwilling to confront his fear and go back, that new church would not have been planted.

We as a family have also tasted a little of what our leaders often face. In 2005, Jenni arrived in Delhi with Jasmine, our five-month-old baby, only to be arrested and detained at gunpoint. I was thousands of miles away in Australia, unaware of what was happening. Hours after her flight landed, our leaders who were waiting outside the airport to receive her, called me to see if I knew where she was. Many hours, many prayers and many phone calls later, I finally established that she had been detained because she was blacklisted as "a threat to national security." Jenni was later deported with a warning never to return to India.

As a foreigner and "terrorist," Jenni had no access to the legal systems to fight to clear her name. Only the federal parliament and intelligence services had the power to help us. Up until then, we had largely focused on the villages, slums and poor people, so we had no contacts in the nation's high places. God did though, and he began to connect me with the people who could help us. Finally, after many trips and many meetings, her name was cleared and she was allowed back in to the country that we both love and serve.

Through this situation, God gave me the opportunity to become friends with many people in positions of power and influence. As I got to know these rich and powerful people I began to see that their world was just like the one Raju had taken me into—socially the complete opposite, perhaps, but equally filled with desperate people in need of love and healing. In a way, the power brokers were worse off than the poor because they were trapped by their privilege behind barriers they couldn't pass to seek help. No one felt sympathy for them. No one knew their need.

God used Jenni's deportation and its aftermath to give me a heart for these people. It was as though He was saying: "Here's another group my Son died for that you are ignoring. I don't want them to perish either, I want you to let them know how much I love and care for them."

Since then I've built relationships with many parliamentarians, bureaucrats and others in influential places. A number have become followers of Jesus. We've been able to organize various functions to reach them with the love of Jesus. We give Bibles and other helpful books to them, like Rick Warren's *The Purpose Driven Life*. They crave genuine love, relationship and friendship; we visit them in their homes to encourage and pray for them.

Through this experience, I've also gained a fresh appreciation of the influence these people have. Politicians, bureaucrats and business leaders together shape society. They make up just one or two per cent of the population, but they wield ninety-nine per cent of the power. If Christian leaders don't have relationships with them and become their friends and influence them, how is a nation going to be transformed?

Much of the opposition that Christians face is not physical. Curses and other spiritual attacks release demonic forces that bring debilitating spiritual oppression. False accusations, threats, complaints to police and negative depictions in the media are daily trials. New Christians in a village can be punished for their faith by being denied access to community properties like wells and roads. Homes used for Christian gatherings can be singled-out by neighbors claiming noise violations. Church planters must tread with great care—even apparently genuine enquirers may be people sent to gather information about their activities.

The harassment of their wives and children creates great pain for our church planters. Children of Christian families are bullied and discriminated against at school. Christian women shopping alone are intimidated. This is particularly distressing in an Asian culture where the man is the protector. All our church planters report the same feeling: "We don't mind getting insulted or beaten up ourselves, but to hear that our children and wives have been attacked is unbearable."

I personally feel a strong protective impulse towards these workers. As I watch them being persecuted heavily and even martyred—and their wives and children left with nothing—my heart breaks. Believing that the Body of Christ has a moral and spiritual obligation towards them, Empart changed our earlier policy and began to take out both life insurance for church planters and emergency medical insurance for them and their families. It is limited but something they can fall back on. The church planters themselves did not ask for this, but to me it is the least we can do to stand with them in their extraordinary surrender to Christ.

In addition, we established a Martyrs' Fund through which brothers and sisters in the West can contribute to help the persecuted and oppressed. I am praying that God will bring a deep conviction among Western Christians that we have an obligation to care for these people, pray for them, share with them and love them as we do our own. After all, if we call God our Father, then these are our brothers and sisters, and they are serving the same Jesus that we love and serve.

Persecution from outside is only one of Satan's weapons in his unabated war on the Kingdom. Sometimes we face "friendly fire" from other Christians. Early on, it was questioning of our motives and criticism for expressing Christianity in North Indian cultural forms. However, one of the biggest challenges we have faced has come from other Christian organizations trying to poach the workers we have trained.

They do this by offering them more money, better working conditions, motorbikes, cars, cell phones, and even houses.

Some organizations, often funded from Western countries, seem more intent on building their own brands than the Kingdom of God. One organization adopted a goal of having a thousand full-time workers in India within five years, but it devised no strategy to train them. Instead it enlisted agents to find and recruit existing workers. These agents operated on incentives and commissions. It was no different from selling insurance.

Within Empart, we have no contracts with our workers. The link with them is purely relational, a faith commitment to train them and help establish them in church planting. We believe this way of operating serves people while leaving them free. But it also makes us vulnerable.

I don't believe we should be possessive of our workers. We don't own anybody. Whatever we do should be founded on our common love for Jesus and the shared vision for the lost and needy world. My concern is more with the pain and damage this process causes: pain for those who have loved and invested in the workers who leave, and damage to the workers themselves. Their innocence is lost. Their passion is compromised. They become materialistic, and often they only stay with the new organization until someone else comes along and offers them an even better deal. Finally, if these organizations stop giving support, many of these workers leave ministry and go into secular jobs because their small village churches are unable to help them maintain the high lifestyle they now prefer.

I believe we need more organizations and ministries to reach all the unreached people of the world. However, it is important that organizations have not only a vision, but also comprehensive training and sustainable support strategies to go with it. To me, it's like having children. If you set yourself a goal of having twenty children, fantastic! But don't steal other people's children to reach your goal.

Though we may not want to hear it, the commitment to make disciples is not about convenience. Reaching the unreached doesn't work like that. Like marriage, it requires commitment that won't flinch, commitment "for better or worse, in sickness and in health." True commitment perseveres no matter what. This kind of commitment praises the Lord if miracles and quick results happen, but it is not based on these. Instead, it is moved by Jesus' mandate and a God-given vision. Whatever happens or doesn't happen, it keeps going. It stays on course until everyone has had the opportunity to hear the good news at least once in their life.

Jesus told a parable about a shepherd who left ninety-nine sheep in the fold to go out and look for the one that was lost. Too many Christian ministries would rather stay where there are plenty of sheep; then when someone asks, "How many have you got?" they have ninety-nine to show. The man who goes out is different.

"How many have you got?" someone asks.

"One" he replies. "I just picked him up."

It might not seem an impressive answer, but how does Jesus see it?

CHAPTER 17 LEADERSHIP LESSONS

+ Develop a capacity for pain. A person's leadership capacity is determined by their capacity to bear pain.

+ Build commitment that won't flinch. Know your challenges and understand the reality of possible persecution and suffering, but set yourself to "take the land" with a commitment that will not flinch.

+ Measure success. A vision that can't be measured can't be held accountable. An effective leader must create the right KPI's (Kingdom Performance Indicators) and regularly measure the progress. Success is only achieved if we measure the right things.

CHAPTER 17 REFLECTION QUESTIONS

1 How do you view suffering and persecution? Are you comfortable with it?

2 On a scale of 1-10, rate your own commitment to the vision. Now do it for your core team members. Initiate any discussions that you might need to from this exercise.

3 How do you measure your success? Are you measuring the right things? If not, why not?

18 GREAT CHALLENGES

Apart from persecution and this frustrating rivalry among Christian groups, other challenges to reaching the unreached have become clear to me since Empart began. I sat down one day with a pen and paper and made a list.

1. Unsympathetic government authorities.

In some areas, God has given us favor with significant politicians. But elsewhere, political leaders are indifferent, even antagonistic. Among the unreached, Christians (if there are any) form a tiny minority and have no influence. No politician will speak up for them.

The support of politicians is important because they make laws and are very influential. The legal situation can make preaching the gospel very difficult. To convert a person in some regions, a pastor must apply for permission to a court, which orders a police investigation. Based on the report, a judge will decide if that person can become a Christian or not. This is a drawn-out process, and approval is seldom given because most of the police and judges are Hindus.

Unfavorable regulations often make something as simple as holding an outdoor meeting with a sound system a bureaucratic nightmare. Church planters must get permission from a range of entities: the governor's office, the police department, the state government and the local village elders, as well as bodies with names like "Pollution Control Council," all of which can be very obstructive. Often most of these things are only required of Christians.

Having the civil authorities on your side is important for another reason: when harassment or persecution strikes, they are the protectors. Unfortunately, in many cases the complaints of Christians are completely ignored or even turned back against them.

2. Puzzling cultural practices.

When our church planters move into unreached territory, they must come to grips with the culture of that place. Many cultures in India are undocumented, consisting of practices passed down orally from generation to generation. It can take a long time to understand the intricacies.

In one people group in Orissa, for example, hosts serve food to their guests with their bare hands. To use a spoon is an insult, like treating the guest as an untouchable. In some villages, people even share the same cup with guests as a sign of acceptance. With low hygiene levels being the norm, this is a challenge to any outsider.

Other issues are more significant, such as marriage customs. In one tribal area, when a boy identifies a girl in another village he wants to marry, he organizes a posse of men from his village to abduct her. The boy and girl then go into hiding while her family and fellow villagers hunt for them. If the couple is found, the girl must return home; but if at the end of three months they have avoided capture, she becomes his wife. A ceremony is held in the boy's village and a bride price negotiated with the girl's family.

How do we make disciples of such people? Are their customs wrong? Once they become Christians, how should they be married? We now have a number of pastors working with us who were married like this.

3. The legacy of "Christian" colonialism.

So-called "Christian" countries once colonized most of the countries that have unreached people groups. This has given them bad memories of Christianity. "Look at what these Christians did to us," they say. "They took possession of our country, drained our resources and dumped us."

We may protest that the colonial powers weren't really Christian,

> INVESTIGATE BEFORE INVESTING. ALWAYS DO DUE DILIGENCE BEFORE YOU INVEST. PEOPLE AND PROGRAMS MAY SOUND GREAT BUT TAKE TIME TO VISIT, INVESTIGATE AND VERIFY BEFORE INVESTING YOUR TIME, TALENTS AND TREASURES.

but most Indians don't understand the distinction. To them, Western civilization is Christian civilization. This is a big barrier for anyone preaching the gospel in India.

A related legacy is that of traditional mission work. Colonial-era missionaries built big mission compounds. Outside the walls, people lived in poverty, but inside was a beautiful campus where the missionaries lived in comparative luxury. Even today, Christians in former colonial countries often understand missions in this light: the bigger your campus, the more successful your mission. But the average lost person sees this as arrogance and an ostentatious display of wealth.

Generally these missionaries are good people whose lifestyle is not opulent by Western standards. But in local terms, they are very rich.

4. What it means to say "yes" to the gospel.

Another hangover of colonialism is a mindset of inferiority. Indians have been told for 200 years that white people are superior, so if a white person asks anything, they will say "yes" even if they mean "no." So if a white missionary asks, "Do you want to be a Christian?" they will agree. However, it won't necessarily come from the heart.

One advantage of national church planters is that other Indians treat them as equals. This allows more dialogue and discussion, leading to clearer and more sincere outcomes.

For this reason, we emphasize baptism as a significant turning point. In the Indian context it is a strong public declaration to family and friends that says, "Every other god is gone and I'm only going to follow Jesus."

5. Confusion sown by New Age teachings and cults.

Religious confusion in India is rife and one source is the New Age movement. New Age teachings mix ideas from everywhere, a bit of Hinduism, a bit of Buddhism, a bit of Jesus and the Bible. Someone influenced by New Age thinking will often tell a church planter that they already know about Jesus. It takes time to help them understand the difference between what they "know" and the true gospel.

Western cults like the Mormons and Jehovah's Witnesses are also active everywhere, which adds further to people's confusion. Who is telling the truth?

Traditional crusade evangelism has not always helped here. Church planters sometimes encounter people who have attended a crusade somewhere, and when the church planter tries to share the gospel, they say, "No, no, we're already Christians. We went to that crusade and heard a man preach and put our hands up." They were told their names were now written in the Book of Life and they would go to heaven when they died. So they returned home confident that they had done the ritual necessary to get to heaven, and continued to practice all their old beliefs.

This kind of confusion is one reason Empart only does evangelism through the local church. Local Christians can put in the consistent, long-term work to help people become true disciples of Jesus.

6. Lack of resources.

Most of the people groups we are trying to reach don't even have the Bible in their heart language, let alone other resources. India has almost 3,000 languages and dialects, with more languages without Scripture than any other country in the world.

> INVEST IN PEOPLE NOT PROJECTS. IT IS EASY TO BECOME TOO INVESTED IN A PROJECT CLOSE TO YOUR HEART. INSTEAD, INVEST IN THE PEOPLE LEADING THE PROJECTS.

Christian books, tapes, CDs and DVDs are virtually non-existent. These disciple-making tools, taken for granted in the West, are simply not available, and no Christian publisher will produce them for such small markets. Somehow we need to develop strategies to create them.

Finding people resources is also a challenge. Significant Christian leaders with gifts and talents tend to be attracted to established organizations that can guarantee salaries, promotion and retirement benefits. Most of these are based in heavily Christianized regions. People are reluctant to work among the unreached because pioneering brings no such guarantees. It involves risk all the way.

These, then, are some of the challenges within Asia itself. I also listed the challenges Empart faced outside Asia, particularly in building partnerships with Western Christians to support the ministry.

1. Lack of understanding about the unreached.

Many Western Christians have little or no understanding of whom the unreached are or how resources can be channeled strategically to reach them.

One Australian church, for example, got very excited about the idea of working among India's unreached and set up a ministry through some contacts. When the pastor told me about it, I realized it was just twenty-five miles from where I was born, in a region already 30-40% Christian. Lack of strategic understanding meant that that church was not focusing its resources effectively.

How can we help well-meaning Western Christians understand the true nature of the challenge to reach the unreached?

2. Lack of media attention.

Most unreached peoples live in remote, hard-to-access areas. Apart from natural disasters like tsunamis or earthquakes, news from these regions is rare, both in Christian and mainstream media. This lack of information keeps the average person in the dark. Without this exposure, awareness and education, it is difficult to prioritize our praying and giving.

I first became aware of this difficulty in the late 1990s. In just one year, fifty pastors in the Gujarat and Rajasthan regions were killed and their churches burned down, but nobody heard about it. In contrast, when

Australian missionary Graham Staines and his two sons were murdered in Orissa in 1999, the international coverage was extensive and very powerful. Without denigrating their sacrifice in any way, I have to wonder whether we place the same value on a Western and a non-Western life.

I believe the Christian media needs to spend much more time educating people about the unfinished Great Commission. One of my heart's desires is to be able to create high-quality documentaries that educate people about the unreached and what non-Western workers are doing to reach them.

3. Western Christianity's focus on numbers.

To many Western churches and mission organizations, numbers equal success. They want to be connected with something big that gives them credibility and significance.

In our early years I approached many substantial Christians leaders about visiting India to help mentor our inexperienced young leaders. Few would go because our numbers were so small. They wanted to speak to 5,000 pastors at a conference, not five! If they were going to take a week off and spend $4,000 in travel, it seemed they wanted value for their money.

Similarly, South Indian mission leaders have told me, "Jossy, if we come to the north, we won't get the same level of support from the West. Western leaders want to see big numbers and big events."

This is very hurtful. When you're trying to reach the unreached, there are no numbers to begin with. There are no pastors—you have to train and raise them up, which takes time and money.

Working among the unreached is like cultivating a tree. After you plant it, it won't bear fruit immediately. You have to keep watering it and fertilizing it. One day it will be a giant, but for a long while it may seem quite small.

In the West, we have a "we want it now" mentality that doesn't like delay. Our culture of instant gratification gives us a button for everything, one press and it happens, and if it doesn't, throw the button away and find another one. Making disciples among unreached people groups requires perseverance and patience.

4. The under-allocation of financial resources.

Globally, Christians spend 98% of their resources on people who are already evangelized and only 2% on the unreached. Never have I met a Christian who disagrees with me on the need to make the unreached our number one priority. "Why should anyone hear the gospel twice before everyone has heard it once?" asked J. Oswald Sanders. But somehow the allocation of our finances, time and people doesn't reflect that.

Most of the time we are not strategic in our giving. We give in response to emotional appeals or out of guilt. Our money goes to the cause that presents the saddest, most pitiful, most heart-wrenching story rather than to where it is most strategically needed from God's perspective. This must change if we are to see the Great Commission fulfilled. We should give out of love for the Lord who loves a lost world, not guilt. Before you give next time, I challenge you to ask these questions:

Why am I giving?

How will this fulfill the Great Commission?

"Commitment" is an uncomfortable word to most Westerners, but that is what reaching the unreached requires: long-term commitment. Like raising children, making disciples takes time, lots of time. We need Western partners who will look long-term and take a fifteen-twenty-thirty-year view. Admittedly, this requires more of us than giving to something once and then not thinking about it again. To accomplish the inherent goals of the Great Commission, this attitude has to change.

5. Western Christians' mistrust of national workers.

Western Christians are often suspicious of Indian Christians. Some of this is understandable, where bad experiences and broken promises by national leaders have caused hurt and mistrust. While this is very sad and wrong, I want to encourage those who have been hurt by such actions to learn from them: build better systems and processes to avoid the same things happening again; instead of withdrawing from the front line of missions, take time to investigate before you invest. Visit the work on the ground; don't just rely on glossy reports and emotional stories; talk to those who are already involved and supporting the work. Using independent, third-party organizations like Excellence in Giving (www.excellenceingiving.com) to investigate and verify organizations can avoid pain and heartache in the long run.

Sometimes people say, "You're working with young converts. How can you trust them?"

My response: How long had people been believers in Thessalonica or Philippi before Paul trusted them? He was in some places only three or four months before he appointed elders and deacons and moved on. How long was it before Jesus trusted the disciples and handed over the destiny of the church to them?

Some fear that young pastors might be involved in Empart's mission for the money. But the support we give is equivalent to the average local wage in the church planter's area, and it is scaled over seven years to zero. Materially speaking, this kind of church planting is not an attractive proposition compared with the sacrifices and potential persecution involved.

For any relationship to work, whether a marriage or a mission partnership, there has to be trust, along with an alignment of vision and values. The reluctance I find in the broader mission community to accept national workers as valid servants of God reflects an outmoded perception that missionaries need to be of Western origin or have white skin. National workers must be embraced as equal co-laborers in the harvest. There are a growing number of regions in the world where Westerners cannot go. So, if the future of the Great Commission only rests in the hands of Westerners, then it is doomed to failure. We must learn to pray, love, encourage and support national workers as our own. Like Jesus, we must be prepared to say, "These are my brothers and sisters."

For a long time I was grateful I wasn't white because it meant I didn't have to be a missionary! That was what I was taught and believed, until I began to see the Great Commission and the plan of God through different eyes.

6. The lack of support for home staff.

Empart is a new kind of mission organization. Our workers in Western countries don't go as missionaries, but work to support national workers. This puzzles many in the broader Christian community who struggle to see the role of home staff as vital and worthy of support.

Again the culprit is traditional thinking. If a person were to pack their bags and move to India as a missionary, many churches would happily

> BE AGILE. WHILE THE VISION AND MISSION SHOULD NEVER
> CHANGE, YOUR STRATEGIES NEED TO BE AGILE CONTINUALLY
> ADAPTING TO MEET THE CULTURE, CONTEXT AND TIMES. A
> LEADER WHO IS BOUND TO SPECIFIC STRATEGIES WILL DIE
> WITH HIS OR HER VISION, WHILE AGILE LEADERS WILL ENJOY
> WATCHING THEIR VISION THRIVE BEYOND THEIR LIFETIME.

support them, even though it costs $120,000 (USD) or more a year to sustain a missionary family on the field. On the other hand, it might cost only $60,000 (USD) to support a home staff member who by their contribution can enable scores of national church planters. Unfortunately, people struggle to see such staff members as missionaries and give them the same support and encouragement.

Empart staff members often make enormous sacrifices, giving up high-paid secular jobs to use their skills in fulfilling the Great Commission. My prayer is that more and more churches and Christian businesses will understand this and get behind those who are willing to lay down their lives in this way for the cause of Christ.

7. Lack of support for infrastructure projects.

In general, people are happy to support individual projects that produce tangible results. However, they are often reluctant to give to build the infrastructure needed to sustain a movement.

I don't believe in infrastructure for its own sake. There's nothing ultimate about buildings or equipment. But the fact is that we need things like buildings, computers, tables and chairs. We can't impact the lives of a billion-plus people without such tools.

Local churches can't function without some level of infrastructure. Now, multiply that across a region of millions and calculate what we need to plant 100,000 churches!

Buildings, equipment and technology are just a means to an end. That end is reaching the unreached. The value of infrastructure lies in the purpose for which it exists.

My heart is to find people who will partner with us in the overall vision, not just in individual projects. Supporters who will specifically help us to build and maintain first-class infrastructure are absolutely essential. This is not a glamorous type of giving, but I believe Christian businesses and larger churches understand this need and can have a particular role here.

Surveying this list of obstacles, it would be easy to think the task is too difficult, except that we're doing it! The obstacles we face are more like hurdles, and we are jumping over them. We just need more partners who choose to prioritize the Great Commission, just like our workers in Asia do each day.

CHAPTER 18 LEADERSHIP LESSONS

+ Clarify your challenges. You not only need to be clear about your vision, but also about the challenges and obstacles. Being clear about your challenges will enable you to address them more effectively.

+ Investigate before investing. Always do due diligence before you invest. People and programs may sound great, but take time to visit, investigate and verify before investing your time, talents and treasures.

+ Invest in people not projects. It is easy to become too invested in a project close to your heart. Instead, invest in the people leading the projects.

+ Forge transformational partnerships. A partnership of mutuality allows both parties to use their strengths and enables both parties to celebrate wins they would never achieve by themselves. Without good relationships, it is very difficult to build transformational partnerships. Focus on the quality of your relationships not just on the results.

CHAPTER 18 REFLECTION QUESTIONS

1 What are your greatest challenges at present? List them. Now number the list in order that you need to address them.

2 How do your partnerships reflect an attitude of mutuality?

3 Review your giving habits and strategies. Ask yourself these questions: Why am I giving? Am I giving because of guilt and manipulation or because it is strategic? How is my giving connected to the mission of Jesus?

4 Take time to review all your partnerships and relationships. How do these relate to the results you are achieving (or not achieving)?

19 GREAT COMMISSIONARIES

I began this book by describing my childhood spent in the lush hills of Kerala. I learned many things on our family farm that still illuminate my life. Watching my grandfather manage his various properties and enterprises was God's way of training me for what was to come.

I particularly remember the hustle and bustle of harvest time. No one could slack off. We had people out in the fields gathering the crop, people transporting it, people organizing its storage, people preparing food for the workers, people keeping records. If my grandfather had employed fifty workers but neglected to feed or pay them, would the job have gotten done? No. For an effective harvesting process, people were needed at many levels, and everyone was vital.

Jesus said, "The harvest is plentiful but the workers are few" (Matthew 9:37). We often assume he was talking about those out in the fields gathering the harvest—the evangelists, the church planters. But "workers" means everyone needed to bring in a successful crop, whether they are laboring in the field or in the office. Everyone involved in the process is a worker, not just the ones in the paddock.

In my travels I've found that while some want to be out in the fields as missionaries, many others have concluded, "God hasn't called me to be a missionary." Until this mindset changes we are not going to fulfill the Great Commission. I believe that the responsibility of the Great Commission either rests with all followers of Jesus, or none of them.

What we actually need are "Great Commissionaries," people from every walk in life, from every nation on earth, who all prioritize the Great Commission.

Great Commissionaries understand it's not *what* you do that matters, but *why* you do it. It is not about your geographical location or the color of your skin. It is about making the most strategic use of your time, treasure and talents for the maximum impact of the Kingdom. Cleaning a toilet in our Empart office is mission work. Administration, typing, accounting, writing letters, operating computers, making videos, building websites, raising money—all these are part of fulfilling the Great Commission. You can use your skills in the marketplace to enrich yourself, or you can use them to expand the Kingdom. You can build a great company, become a billionaire and be a Great Commissionary if you connect the mission of Jesus as the purpose of that money.

Great Commissionaries see the big picture, the picture from heaven. When we get to heaven no one is going to be wearing a badge listing who preached to them or who baptized them. The particular role each of us played will have disappeared. It is of no consequence. The only thing that matters will be whether you had any role in enabling others into eternity.

Great Commissionaries are people who have decided that Jesus' command to do good and make disciples of all nations is going to be their top priority, whether that means planting a church on the front line, praying and giving to resource the task, or becoming an advocate or ambassador.

The devil, of course, doesn't want people to be Great Commissionaries. He constantly throws up obstacles. I've identified four pervasive attitudes that stop people from becoming Great Commissionaries, robbing them of the joy of partnering with God in the deepest mission of His heart.

1. It is all about me.

The first big problem is that a great deal of what we do is self-focused. This is even true of our spiritual activities. Why do people go to church on Sundays? For many, it's to get pumped up for another week so they can go out and do their own thing. Is this our purpose as Christians, to come together once a week for a lovely time of prayer and worship and teaching? We attend conferences and accumulate books, then go to our graves with

BE A GREAT COMMISSIONARY. FIND PARTNERSHIPS WITH
MINISTRIES WHERE YOUR TIME, TALENTS AND TREASURE
CAN BE USED MOST STRATEGICALLY FOR KINGDOM
TRANSFORMATION.

all these teachings in our heads. But what have we done to fulfill the Great Commission? How many will be in heaven because of our time on earth?

The Bible says that our names are already written in the Book of Life. What more do we want? Do we think that God puts a tick beside our names whenever we understand some new mystery? Does God get excited: "Ooh, Jossy's got that revelation now"? No, I don't see that. Luke 15 clearly tells us that it's when the lost are reached that there is great joy in heaven.

As Christians, everything we do must help fulfill the Great Commission. If you have a great worship time that fires you up to fulfill the Great Commission, then your worship has purpose. If the teaching you receive trains and empowers you to fulfill the Great Commission, then the teaching has meaning. Paul was the greatest Christian teacher who ever lived, yet all his teaching had one goal: to somehow, anyhow, win people to Christ (1 Corinthians 9:22).

Satan keeps us ineffective by constantly dragging our gaze back to our needs, our wants and our feelings. This is a constant battle, and everything, from consumer society to our own family and friends, is fighting us. My family and I face these challenges and temptations daily. But this is a battle we must win or we'll never see the Great Commission fulfilled.

Following Jesus involves some uncomfortable truths: carrying our cross, denying self, crucifying self, dying to self—until we can truly say, "It is no longer I who live, but Christ lives in me" (Galatians 2:20, NKJV). If it's no longer me that lives, how can my life be all about me?

When Jesus said, "Follow me," he meant it. In our apathy and laziness, we Christians in the West often forget that. Like the people of his time, we try to avoid the full impact of his call with self-centered pleas: "Lord, first let me go and bury my father;" or "I will follow you Lord, but first let me go back and say good-bye to my family." Jesus didn't accept excuses then and he doesn't accept them now. With him, it's all or nothing.

2. I know what I like.

When I invite people to travel with me to India, I often hear responses like, "Oh no! It's too hot and I don't like curry!" Or when I ask someone why they want to go to Asia, they reply, "Well, I love Asian music, and the children are so beautiful. And the shopping…" In other words, we base what we do on what we like or don't like, rather than on God's command.

To me, this is deeply flawed. My likes and dislikes have nothing to do with the mandate of the gospel. I can't say, "I'm sorry, God, I didn't fulfill your mission because I didn't like the smell and taste of the food of that people."

This attitude reared its head in the early church as well. A lot of believers in Jerusalem didn't like Gentiles at all. They certainly didn't like what they ate, even Peter (Acts 10:14; Galatians 2:11–14). But Paul had a different revelation. It wasn't that he always loved the places he went— he repeatedly got sick and was beaten and thrown in prison. But he knew it wasn't about his likes and dislikes. It was about God wanting the gospel presented to everyone.

Western civilization has evolved to be more feelings-based than values-based. And Christians are not immune. When it comes to the mission of Jesus, we support something according to whether or not it makes us feel good. And therein lies a massive problem.

Too often we're blown around by the winds of changing trends and sophisticated marketing. One day, I received a call from a church whose support over many years had helped train more than 300 indigenous church planters who had planted over 700 churches. But now the church wanted to reallocate the money towards helping trafficked children. Their reason shocked me: "Our people go to conferences and see these kinds of projects promoted, and they feel we as a church should be involved in them. But we don't have the money to do that as well as what we're already doing, so we want to change."

Now don't get me wrong, these are good things to do. Empart runs children's homes and rescues trafficked children. But when believers want to redirect money from training and releasing preachers of the gospel because the trend is to something else, something is very wrong.

In any area of our lives, the important thing isn't how we feel or what we like, but what the Scriptures say. I don't necessarily feel saved all the time, but the Bible says I am, so I believe it. And it's the same with the

Great Commission. If it is God's will that none should perish, then any effort I am engaged in to rescue perishing people is God's will. It's not about my emotional gratification, but about what God says.

Paul wrote, "It has always been my ambition to preach the gospel where Christ was not known" (Romans 15:20). What is our ambition? For many of us, our ambition is to go where we like, do what we enjoy and be involved in things that bring us satisfaction. I challenge that. Why are you giving where you are giving? Why are you going where you are going? Why are you staying where you are staying? Is it based on your likes and dislikes? Or is it based on the deep foundations of God's word?

3. Poverty versus lostness.

The Western world believes materialism is the answer to all the world's problems. Consequently, it sees poverty and injustice as the biggest challenges, and improving people's physical well-being as the most important response. Even in missions, our first tendency is to provide people with "things."

In line with this, there is a trend in the Western church to make issues of poverty and social justice our primary focus. Resources from the Great Commission are being diverted to the poverty/social justice space. Our emphasis is more and more on poverty rather than on lostness.

I ask the people who champion such ideas, "So if we make the whole world like America, so what? America has money, but does that mean America has no problems? Depression? Suicide? Loneliness?" When we solve the poverty problem all we are doing is creating a new set of problems. Until and unless the root cause of all human problems and misery is addressed, we will not see total transformation. That root problem is sin and the only solution is Jesus.

Jesus certainly fed the hungry and helped the needy, but not all the time. Rather, he "went through all the towns and villages, teaching in their synagogues, proclaiming the good news of the kingdom" (Matthew 9:35). Even when he fed the five thousand, it was only after he had taught them in response to the compassion he felt because they were lost, like "sheep without a shepherd."

I understand the pain people experience when they see the plight of the poor. My own heart has been broken many, many times. I know what people feel when they travel to Asia or Africa and their heart burns with compassion for people in their suffering. Jesus felt this too. But primarily he felt compassion for people because they were alienated from God.

Jesus was crystal clear about his mission: "I have come to seek and save the lost" (see Luke 19:10). "It is not the healthy who need a doctor, but the sick. I have not come to call the righteous, but sinners" (Mark 2:17). "I have come that they may have life, and that they may have it more abundantly" (John 10:10, NKJV). Yes, these statements have practical, earthly implications, but for Jesus "abundant life" referred primarily to eternal life.

He also said, "As the Father has sent me, I am sending you" (John 20:21). Why do you do what you do, give where you give, go where you go? Is it in line with the mission and priorities of Jesus?

My observation is that people often confuse the Great Commission and the Good Commandment (to love your neighbor as yourself). "What are you doing about the Great Commission?" I ask, and they reply, "We're digging wells in India and providing education for kids in Africa." But that's not the Great Commission! If we think that by helping the poor we are fulfilling the Great Commission, we are fooling ourselves—or the devil is fooling us.

Let's go back to Matthew 28 and read what it actually says: "Go and make disciples of all nations, baptising them . . . and teaching them to obey everything I have commanded you." Make disciples, baptise, teach to obey. It's doing those things—not just one by itself, but all of them together —that fulfills the Great Commission.

Poverty and injustice are dreadful and we are right to fight them. Empart is deeply involved in almost every sphere of social service: caring for orphans and widows, rescuing the mentally ill, providing education, teaching livelihood skills, facilitating caste reconciliation, building

BUILD STRONG PARTNERSHIPS. NONE OF US CAN DO EVERYTHING BY OURSELVES, BUT PARTNERSHIP WILL ENABLE US TO DO WHAT WE OTHERWISE CANNOT DO AND GO WHERE WE CANNOT GO ALONE.

toilets, even planting trees and helping set up solar plants. We must love and care for our neighbor. But don't allow those good things to make you feel you have done the Great Commission. We must not overlay the Great Commission with the Good Commandment. Doing one does not automatically fulfill the other—both are imperative commands of Jesus to be obeyed.

4. Vanity versus eternity.

King Solomon was by far the wisest man of his time. In Ecclesiastes 2, he describes an experiment he conducted to discover the meaning of life. After trying pure hedonism and being thoroughly disillusioned, he organizes a big building program, sets up huge gardens, plantations and reservoirs, and amasses stupendous wealth: an army of slaves, vast herds and flocks, uncountable reserves of gold and treasure, choirs of singers and a harem of beautiful women. But it all came to nothing.

After all this experimenting, involving virtually every kind of accomplishment and indulgence known to man, his conclusion is chilling: "All was vanity and grasping for the wind" (Ecclesiastes 2:11, NKJV). According to Solomon, trying to find the meaning of life in mere material things is foolish and futile.

The early Christians didn't make that mistake. They lived with an incredible vision of eternity. There was an excitement, an urgency about their life. Jesus was coming back! The kingdom was coming! Eternity was at the forefront of everything. Over two thousand years that vision seems to have slipped away from us.

As we strive to help Western Christians understand the wonder and excitement of being a Great Commissionary, inspirational stories continue to flow into Empart offices from the frontier villages of North India.

Pastor Chitra prays persistently for Been, the mentally ill daughter of a Brahmin family, until her mind is restored and her family accepts Jesus.

Pastor Naval, falsely accused of murder and imprisoned, brings thirty prisoners to faith in four months before being acquitted and released.

In a village of tree worshippers, a youth named Binod, bedridden with back pain, walks again after Pastor Bijay prays, then goes on to attend a training center.

Palwinder, an eighteen-year-old girl whose family accepted Jesus when her father was healed, breaks her caste's restrictions on women and establishes a church in her village.

And the stories keep coming: Rama, a nineteen-year-old man possessed by an evil spirit, is instantly delivered after his mother knocks on Pastor Gutamajki's door at midnight. A formerly paralysed woman named Sheema leaves no stone unturned in sharing the name of the Jesus who healed her. After three days of fruitless digging, a new bore suddenly starts gushing water as Pastor Sikander and the believers of a drought-stricken village are worshipping. Two men opposed to the ministry of Pastor Bandhu threaten his life, but after the church prays they are sitting in the front row the next week, wanting to learn about Jesus.

These are everyday occurrences in the ripe fields of Asia. The harvest is there, and the laborers are there as well.

Yet every year we have to turn away hundreds of young people who want to be church planters and key women because we don't have the capacity to train them. If they had the opportunity, within five years most would have planted more than three churches. In fact, if we had the resources to start 250 training centers tomorrow, I believe we could fill every one of them, because God is doing something.

What these unbelievably passionate laborers need are equally passionate Great Commissionaries prepared to partner with them and equip them. The Bible says that God has put eternity in everyone's heart (Ecclesiastes 3:11)—we mustn't let the allure of materialism and Western ideology rob us of the joy and satisfaction of being people who prioritize the Great Commission.

CHAPTER 19 LEADERSHIP LESSONS

+ Be a Great Commissionary. Find partnerships with ministries where your time, talents and treasure can be used most strategically for Kingdom transformation.

+ Keep following Jesus. The quality of your leadership will be a reflection of your followership of Jesus.

+ Build strong partnerships. None of us can do everything by ourselves, but partnership will enable us to do what we otherwise cannot do and go where we cannot go alone.

CHAPTER 19 REFLECTION QUESTIONS

1 How well are you following Jesus? What excuses have you been using?

2 What is the basis of your decision making? Is it your personal preferences or the foundation of God's word?

3 Do your likes and dislikes get in the way of you fulfilling the Great Commission? If yes, which preferences are causing the problem? Confess it to the Lord now and ask for his help as you realign.

ETERNITY IN OUR EYES

In 2003, one of our church planters asked me, "Does the Great Commission apply to us in North India too?" The sad reality is that most Christians in Asia believe, as I did—that you have to be white and wealthy to be a missionary. So this small question opened a gigantic door. As I began to teach them, our Indian leaders became convinced that the Lord didn't want them just to plant churches in North India. He wanted them to ignite church-planting movements in neighboring countries as well.

They asked me if Empart would facilitate this new vision. With a leap of excitement I said yes, and then stopped short as I realized the implications.

Throughout my life God has often taken me by surprise. I have found again and again that he has been ahead of me, directing my steps in paths he has already laid out. In Empart we always try to make decisions with much prayer, fasting, discussion and godly counsel, yet I have to say that the Lord repeatedly surpasses our efforts and expectations. With this new direction, he was doing it again.

I now saw that the vision of planting 100,000 churches was only the beginning. As our church planters began planting churches with a proper evangelistic mind-set, it was obvious they would want to reach the unreached everywhere. Billions more unreached people were waiting outside India. God was calling us to be part of something much bigger.

It wasn't so much a new vision as an expanded one. To me vision is progressive. It grows as your capacity to comprehend it grows. God opens one curtain and you go through it; then when he sees you're ready, he opens another one, and then another. The direction is the same, but the horizon keeps getting bigger.

Our focus on North India remains absolutely central. We are continuing to multiply our training centers, children's homes, tailoring centers and other projects. But we've become clearer than ever that these Indian churches need to become mission-minded as well, entering into partnership with believers in countries like Nepal, Tibet, Bhutan, Burma and Bangladesh to foster church planting movements there. Many of these countries are closed to Western missionaries, but Indians can travel freely, often without visas. Their culture is more Asian and they are free from a negative colonialist past. Half of the world's population, including 90% of its unreached people, lives virtually on India's doorstep.

I knew this flame had been lit when some of our Indian leaders came to me in late 2004. "We want to plant churches in Nepal," they said. I was over the moon! Before long, one of our church planters had married a Nepalese girl in anticipation of moving into the country. Brothers from Nepal came to study in one of our training centers, and Indian leaders started to make short-term visits to train Nepalese workers. By 2016, 1,104 churches had been planted in the Himalayan kingdom and five training centers had been established, with other projects and programs in full swing.

As these global contacts grow, the partnership is becoming more and more dynamic. Western Christians, Indian Christians, Nepalese Christians are working together in a network of powerful relational connections. This is our dream, not some kind of ecclesiastical empire, but church planting movements ignited by passion for the lost and interconnected by the Holy Spirit.

I can't tell you how satisfying this is for me. It's like bringing up children. You spend all your time and energy raising them, and then one day they in turn have children. You realize: This is fantastic! My genes won't finish with my children, but will be passed onto new generations. Knowing we are igniting a church planting movement that has the DNA to ignite other church planting movements makes me the happiest man in the world.

My dream is to see a new generation of mission-hearted men and women raised up. They will have the Great Commission at their heart. But their skin color won't be white—it will be brown or black or caramel. They won't speak English—they will speak Hindi or Punjabi or Nepalese. And they will be able, I believe, to unleash an incredible church planting spirit and momentum into the whole region.

I see a great global web of relational links, spreading out among people who share a burning passion to see churches planted among unreached people. I'm not interested in setting up new churches to compete with existing ones—the world isn't a supermarket where we can tout different religious products at competitive prices. My focus is on unreached people, and my desire is to empower and partner with both national and Western Christians to see the Great Commission fulfilled.

For the last 250 years, the Western church has largely carried mission responsibilities. While many great things have been done this way in the past, the new world in which we live requires a significant change. We need a strategic change in our thinking. It's time to step alongside our Asian brothers and sisters and empower them to do the good and the great works of Jesus. In the end, it doesn't matter who fulfills the Great Commission, whether they have white or brown skin, whether they speak English or Hindi. If they can be more effective than I can, let them do the job. I'm prepared to play the supporting role.

The Western church has played the lead role for so long that to accept a supporting role will be a huge challenge. Colonial thinking still colors our mindset; feelings of superiority and inferiority exist even amongst Christians. All this needs to change, and I'm excited to be part of the movement to change it.

When we capture this big picture vision, we realize there is a place for everyone in reaching the unreached. I often break what we need into three kinds of resources: people, finances and infrastructure.

+ *People* are the biggest need. Ephesians 4 says God has provided apostles, prophets, pastors, teachers and evangelists to equip the church, so people with those giftings are essential. Romans 12 and 1 Corinthians 12 name other gifts. We also need administrators, entrepreneurs, financial experts and media people. We need churches, pastors and denominational leaders to get excited about the privilege of reaching the unreached. We need passionate business people to plug their resources into the dream of seeing extraordinary things happen among unreached people. How many people and what kind of skill will we need to plant 100,000 churches? What sorts of resources are required to reach over a billion unreached people?

Finding these people resources is our biggest challenge and need for prayer.

+ *Finances.* The reality is that working among unreached people is very expensive. It takes time to make disciples, and in that process, at least in the early pioneering stages, we need to be prepared to financially resource the work. Paul found this to be true in his day. As he reached out to the Gentiles on his missionary journeys, he often depended on partnership. Eventually the churches he planted were able to support themselves, but to do the pioneering ministry he needed churches like the Philippians and individuals like Timothy to partner with him.

It's going to take hundreds of millions of dollars to achieve this vision. I love to see individuals, churches, denominations, businesses and corporations embracing the mission of Jesus as their reason for existence.

+ *Infrastructure.* Without infrastructure and the right tools, reaching the unreached will remain only a dream. It's going to take buildings, equipment, tools and technology. I believe God is giving us technologies in these last days to accelerate the spread of the gospel, so we need both smart people to use them and generous people to pay for them to see the Kingdom advance.

Where are all these resources going to come from? From Great Commissionaries, normal people who are committed partners in the Great Commission.

I get excited when I think about the emerging partnerships between Eastern and Western Christians. We have so much to learn from one another and so much to teach each other. The days when Western churches can assume they have all the answers are over. We in the West have a lot to give, but we have a lot to learn as well. The partnership is two-way, a stream flowing in both directions.

Christians in different countries have different strengths and weaknesses. The Western church, for example, is very good on leadership, structure and strategy, planning and organizing. I think the Asian church can learn from that. On the other hand, the Asian church has strengths in flexibility and faith, in sacrifice and commitment and passion. If we put the two together, we have the church of Jesus Christ operating beautifully.

If your piece of wood doesn't have fire, the best thing to do is to move it closer to one that is already alight. What the Western church lacks in first

VISION IS PROGRESSIVE. VISION GROWS AS YOUR CAPACITY TO COMPREHEND IT GROWS. THE DIRECTION IS THE SAME, BUT THE HORIZON KEEPS GETTING BIGGER.

love and passion for Jesus can be reignited as it relates more closely with the church in Asia.

My passion is not just for the church in Asia, but also for the whole church. So many churches here in the West are dying because they have lost the vision of the Kingdom. Their life is inward-focused. As they rediscover an outward vision to fulfill the Great Commission among the unreached, they are revitalized and energized. We are already seeing old dying churches turning around because their leaders have been visiting Asia and seen the fire of God burning among people who are utterly sold out to Jesus.

In the contemporary business world, most smart businesses are connecting to Asia because they recognize that's where the future lies. Similarly, one of the best things the Western church can do is to connect itself to the Asian church. It is like connecting to a church in the book of Acts. When people who go on short-term trips return, they bring life back to the home base.

My dream is a dynamic two-way partnership between the church in Asia and the church in the West. I know it won't be easy to start with—there are many dangers and pitfalls, cultural and communication gaps. This is where organizations like Empart can help.

Such a vision requires that Western Christians be willing to learn. A good partnership involves both giving and receiving. Paul commended the Philippian church for the fact it was willing to do both (Philippians 4:15).

But Paul didn't stop there. He told the Philippians that the help they gave to him would actually be credited to their account (verse 17). Similarly, Jesus urged his disciples, "Store up for yourselves treasure in heaven" (Matthew 6:20). By investing in someone else's ministry I am actually investing in my treasures in heaven! Jesus also said, "Anyone who receives a prophet . . . will receive a prophet's reward" (Matthew 10:41). I don't have to be a prophet to receive a prophet's reward; I just need to be willing to receive and partner with a prophet. Likewise, I don't have to be an apostle or an evangelist or a church planter. If I'm willing to partner with such people, I will get the same reward.

This is the incredible power of partnership. It's not just the church planter baptizing five hundred people who gets all the rewards. No! Anyone who prays for him, financially supports him, supplies him with a Bible or literature or a bicycle—in fact, anyone who is part of the whole team that makes his work possible—will share equal reward. So when we say "Support church planters," we're also saying, "Share in their reward and store up treasure for yourself in heaven."

With our culture's individualistic perspective, we often don't understand the power of partnership. It goes way beyond praying and giving money, as vital as these things are. Partnership lies at the core of how God wants his church to operate in the world. God didn't make a mistake when he compared the church to a body with many members. Wherever His work is happening, anywhere around the globe, the different members of the body can be connected in that work, with Jesus as the Head. There are no inferior or superior members—we're all brothers and sisters with one Father.

All of this is why I believe profoundly in Western Christians visiting Asia. It's one part of partnership. Empart's short-term teams are rapidly growing—we now have the capacity to send hundreds of participants each year and we actively encourage our partners to come and visit. I know some people question the value of short-term trips and the money spent on them, and certainly the strategy has its challenges. Done properly, however, with good preparation, well-organized programs and the right field support in place, short-term teams can be life changing.

I'm convinced that every Western Christian should go on a trip to an unreached people group region somewhere in the world at least once. Before they go a second time, however, they should stop and ask, "What will be the strategic value of my going?" If such trips don't benefit the Kingdom of God strategically; it is just another self-indulgent act.

Like partnership as a whole, such a trip is a two-edged sword. Western Christians think they are going to help the "poor Asians," and certainly the Asian believers are blessed. But the visitors' own lives are often transformed. I sometimes offer people a money back guarantee: "If you go to India with Empart and return feeling it was a waste of time, I will gladly refund your money, no questions asked." Thankfully no one has ever claimed it! The impact of meeting these fantastic brothers and sisters and seeing how God is using them is life changing.

The benefits for Asian Christians are significant too, especially for leaders. On average, our workers have been Christians for just five years. They have the passion and the heart, the willingness to sacrifice and to die, but they need mentoring. They are hungry to glean from others' experience.

One of the most exciting things for me is the growing number of experienced church leaders willing to go to Asia and share their personal journey with these eager young leaders. We ask them to teach universal biblical principles, leaving the local believers to work out the practice in their context. By going personally, these leaders also impart their spirit and heart. It is discipleship by interaction and impartation, not just information. I'm convinced that when believers from different places share their life and experience, a spiritual transfer takes place that we in the West probably don't adequately understand.

As Empart heads towards its third decade, it is full steam ahead. We are stunned by the speed with which God is working and we are running flat out to keep up. What He has done in just seventeen years is phenomenal.

What amazing and wonderful things lie in the future?

Our challenge on the field in Asia is to keep pace with God as He inspires a new generation of Kingdom heroes. But our challenge in the West is to help Christians in Western countries become the Great Commissionaries they need to be, to help them wake up and embrace Jesus' call to help the poor and make disciples of all nations as their number one priority.

This means nothing less than embracing God as He really is. The God I know is like the father of the prodigal son (Luke 15). He is waiting for His lost son, longing to have His family whole again. As soon as He sees the prodigal in the distance, He runs to welcome him home. In exactly the same way, God lost fellowship with human beings when they sinned. The whole story of the Bible, from Genesis to Revelation, is about God trying to get His family back together again.

He is still in love with a lost and needy world. John 3:16 is as true today as ever.

If we are not playing an active role in this process, we are simply not in the will of God. We may be doing many good religious things, but if they are not directly linked to bringing the lost sheep back to the pen, we've missed the point.

All around the world I meet Christians who are waiting for the will of God. Many have done some training, but now they're just waiting. As far as I'm concerned, God's will is very clear: "He is patient with you, not wanting anyone to perish, but everyone to come to repentance" (2 Peter 3:9). What more do we need to hear?

Some people go on waiting for years while millions die without ever hearing the name of Jesus even once. If you don't know what God's will is, just get involved in any efforts to share the love of Jesus with the perishing people. Just jump in and get going. If you become involved in a program to reach the unreached, help the poor and needy, is God going to be angry with you?

Too often our perspective is more on this world than on the world to come. Jesus said "Lay up treasures in heaven" but many of us are too busy laying up treasures here and now. How much time do we spend thinking and planning strategically about investing in eternity as opposed to planning for our holidays or retirement?

The Bible is very clear: God's desire is that none should perish. How much time do we give to that desire? We give so much time to our desires, time to eat, time to drink, time to buy clothes, time to relax. Jesus says in Matthew 6 that only pagans worry about these things; we should trust our Father in heaven to look after us. This means we ought to spend less time praying about our needs and more time praying for the lost. What really matters in the end?

I had to face this question in my own life. Although I was a committed Christian, I was very materialistic, very driven to make money. Then God stepped in. After my encounters with Raju and Rakesh, I prayed, "Lord, put eternity in my eyes so that I will see everything in that light." I believe God has answered that prayer.

What would it mean if we gave equal time and energy to investing eternally as we do to investing in life now? How you spend your talent, your time and your treasure in this life is pretty telling. Scrutinizing your life in these areas will tell you a lot about where you place your security. So, let me give you this challenge: for one day, put on the glasses of eternity and look at everything through them: your car, your house, your job, your family, your food, everything. I guarantee it will change your perspective.

Imagine if every Christian prayed every day, "Lord, help me see everything in the light of eternity." The whole world, every tribe and every nation, would be for the taking – for his glory!

CHAPTER 20 LEADERSHIP LESSONS

+ Invest time in eternity. As a leader, spend time strategically thinking and planning about your investment in eternity.

+ Maintain a teachable spirit. Admitting you need help to grow doesn't show you are broken—it shows you are teachable. True maturity is staying teachable, regardless of how much you already know. There are so many things in life to keep learning: mindsets to challenge, habits to retrain, alternative methods and fresh strategies. Maintain a teachable spirit.

+ Vision is progressive. Vision grows as your capacity to comprehend it grows. The direction is the same, but the horizon keeps getting bigger.

CHAPTER 20 REFLECTION QUESTIONS

1 How much time do you spend thinking and planning strategically about investing in eternity?

2 What would these look like through the glasses of eternity: your vision, your ministry/business, your priorities, yourself?

3 Maintaining a teachable spirit can be hard when you need to be a confident leader. It is often hard to evaluate ourselves in this area so ask your mentors and core team members to rate your teachability and give you feedback. What do you need to do to become more teachable?

4 How has your vision progressed over time? Is it still progressing? What do you need to do to see the next horizon?

PS EVERY TRIBE, EVERY NATION

Not many years ago, an elderly Indian man named Arun sat on a stool outside his hut in a tribal village in Rajasthan. He looked down at a book and a small pamphlet in his hands. He didn't know the visitor to the village who had given them to him or what they contained. But at eighty-nine years of age, he had little else to do, so Arun opened the book and began to read.

In all his long life he had never come across anything like the stories in this book. They told about a guru, a teacher, named Jesus who was the incarnation of the One True God. Old Arun didn't understand everything he read, but something about the stories penetrated his heart. Over the next few days he read and reread them until he was convinced that Jesus was the true way to God.

He also read in the book that those who wanted to be a shishya, a disciple, of this man should be baptized. He wasn't sure how to arrange this. It seemed obvious, however, that he needed to find someone to do it. He began to search.

For the next three months, old Arun wandered around the villages in his region looking for a Christian. No one could help him, but he persevered. Finally he came to a village where someone suggested he inquire at a particular house. With rising hope he knocked on the door.

A young man answered. Arun explained he was looking for a Christian and the man invited him inside.

The man's name was Jos and he was an Empart church planter. He listened carefully to Arun's story. Arun could tell the pastor was nervous. *Perhaps he's afraid I'm here to get information and trap him for the RSS,* he thought. Arun spoke quickly to allay any suspicions. Eventually Pastor Jos seemed to accept his story, and much to Arun's excitement agreed to teach him further.

They met regularly for a month before Pastor Jos baptized Arun in water. Then something extraordinary happened. Arun went home and started to tell people about Christ. Because of his age and good standing in the community, other people started to believe in Jesus too. After three months, 170 of his fellow villagers had been baptized. The numbers kept growing, and in less than a year almost 400 people had been baptized and all their idols had been destroyed. A powerful new church had begun.

Among the converts were two of Arun's own sons. They subsequently committed their lives to serve the Lord and trained in an Empart training center so they could go back and lead the church.

To me this story encapsulates the miracle of what God is doing in Asia today. This is what Empart is about. Because we were able to train and support Pastor Jos, he was there for an eighty-nine-year-old man whom God wanted to use in opening a village to the gospel. If Jos hadn't been there, the whole harvest may have been wasted.

When we tell the gospel to one person, they will tell someone else, who in turn will tell someone else. I was once asked, "How many people do you think you can reach?" I replied, "How many apples are in an apple seed?"

Right now, God is spreading thousands of seeds, not only among individuals but in countless villages and towns and even in entire caste communities. Whenever I go to Asia I see opportunities exploding on every side. People are hungry for the gospel. Literal multitudes are ready to embrace the Christian faith. But that mind-boggling opportunity also brings a mind-boggling challenge. How on earth do you disciple all those people? What resources are required? Where will the Bibles come from? We don't need a hundred or a thousand. We need millions.

This is the challenge facing us in the Western churches. We need to rise up to this level of opportunity and take advantage of it. The Scriptures say, "While it is day, let us work because the night is coming" (see John 9:4). If the harvest is not reaped in time, it will become a lost harvest.

Ever since my encounter with Rao, the father who offered his own blood in the quest for forgiveness, I've understood that the greatest injustice in the world is not economic deprivation or political oppression. Terrible as such things are, they only have earthly consequences. The greatest injustice has eternal consequences. It is this: that you and I can hear the gospel over and over again, twenty-four hours a day, seven days a week if we choose to, yet people like Rao, Raju and Rakesh have never heard it even once. They can't hear it even if they want to—yet their eternity depends on it.

When those who have received God's forgiveness have the opportunity to give the message to millions, but don't—that's injustice.

I believe God has already given the church everything necessary to fulfill the Great Commission. But it is tied up in other things. Someone has estimated that around 96% of all money given by Western Christians is spent on the Western church itself. We are like hosts putting on a party where some people are fed entrées, mains, dessert and coffee (with refills) while others haven't even had the entrée.

This inequality is my greatest frustration. On one side, Christians live with so much abundance; on the other, people are so desperate and hungry.

We've forgotten what it means to be lost. Think about what happened on 9/11—some 3,000 innocent people were killed in minutes. Or think about HIV/AIDS, which kills over 6,000 every day. Hunger-related deaths account for another 25,000. All these are appalling tragedies. But consider this statistic: it is estimated that 63,000 people die every day without having heard the gospel even once in their entire life. Two billion people living right now do not have access to the gospel. If 9/11 was a tragedy because so many died, if HIV and hunger are tragedies because they kill thousands, how much greater a tragedy is it that so many people are plunging into eternity without the opportunity to hear about Jesus?

Why don't we see this as a crisis? Why don't we see it as an urgent priority?

Picture a boat carrying one hundred people. It runs onto rocks and starts to sink. Unfortunately, only two of the passengers can swim, but they manage to rescue two others. After they get them safely to shore, the swimmers head back into the water to save more. But the two who have been rescued call out, "Come back! We're wet and cold and hungry—don't leave us!" So the two swimmers decide to stay.

I feel that's what the Western church has done. We've been rescued, but we think that now we're safe we need to be warmed, clothed and fed. All we can see is what we need. We've totally forgotten the ninety-six other people still drowning out there.

In the story of the prodigal son (Luke 15:11–31), the older son asks, "Father, I have been with you all these years but what have you done for me?" Not only did he refuse to contribute to the homecoming party for his lost brother, he could not even rejoice with his father because he was so full of himself. All he could think about was his needs, his wants, his desires. It seems that little has changed after 2,000 years.

It's time for this greatest of all injustices to be overthrown. If God sent his only Son to die for the world, wouldn't he want the world to know? And if so, shouldn't our resources be prioritized for that purpose before we consume other things?

The apostle Paul said, "Faith comes by hearing, and hearing by the word of God" (Romans 10:17, NKJV). He also asked, "But how will they hear unless someone preaches to them? And how will they preach unless someone sends them?" (verses 14–15). That's the key. Someone must go. Right now, God is raising up a new breed of indigenous leaders who are willing to go and preach the gospel. All it takes from us is a seven-year commitment to help them. The effect is transformational.

Stories like Arun's give me hope that we can complete the Great Commission and see Matthew 24:14 fulfilled. When I first heard about Arun, all I could think of was the magnificent scene in Revelation where a vast sea of people is spread out before God's throne:

After this I looked and there before me was a great multitude that no one could count, from every nation, tribe, people and language, standing before the throne and in front of the Lamb. They were wearing white robes and were holding palm branches in their hands. And they cried out in a loud voice: "Salvation belongs to our God, who sits on the throne, and to the Lamb." (Revelation 7:9–10)

If God has a vision statement, this is it! Close your eyes and picture it. Try to see people of every race, culture and language standing before the throne of God, shouting with the loudest roar: "Salvation belongs to our God!" Every nation is represented, every tribe, every people—every single one! And a tribal community from Rajasthan is there, too.

This is God's dream. This is the incredible vision He is waiting to see fulfilled.

How is it going to become reality? God could send an army of angels and make it happen in days or hours. But He has chosen another way. In His sovereign will, He has chosen you and me to achieve His dream. Why? So that when we get to heaven, we will feel a deep ownership of what God and we have done together. The power will have been God's, but we will have played a part. Then our joy will truly be full.

This is what I live for. Whenever I think of this vision in Revelation, I ask myself: *How many people will be there because of me? How many tribes and nations will be there because of my efforts?* I know that nothing will ever compare with the joy of knowing that my efforts have meant one more people group will be standing before God's throne.

I challenge you to ask yourself the same question. How many people will be there because of you?

Imagine that great scene before God's throne again. Look at the old Indian man in the corner, standing and shouting, "Salvation belongs to our God!" He is there because someone prayed, someone trained a church planter, someone sent him out and someone supported him. Will you do it?

In eternity you'll be so glad you did!

ENJOYED *MADNESS* ? LOOK OUT FOR JOSSY CHACKO'S NEXT BOOK COMING SOON.

Think you're an unlikely leader? You're in good company—God is developing an army of unlikely leaders who are part of a leadership revolution.

Not excited by the leadership potential you see around you? Don't fret —God has a habit of using people that would be overlooked by a judicious selection committee.

People like Pascal, a blind man from Paris, who heard Jossy speak at a conference in Switzerland. Pascal was curious, so he went to India to investigate. What he heard and learned from Jossy and the Indian leaders has inspired him to plant a dynamic and transformational church in the heart of Paris. In less than 2 years, he has seen more than 140 people make Jesus their Lord. Their Sunday gathering is over 200 people. Pascal has built a team and is in the process of handing the church over to them so that he can plant his second church in Paris, a great melting pot of spiritual disinterest!

Absorb powerful principles for your own leadership development. Learn how to spot potential and identify leadership talent. Understand how to empower and release unlikely leaders.

John is from Penguin in Tasmania, Australia—a little town on a little island, at the bottom of the world. This hard-nosed Dutch businessman was more interested in building the family trucking business than in following Jesus. His wife Louisa needled tenaciously until John agreed to visit India with Jossy. He was so impacted that he returned a few months later with his entire family, keen for them to share his experience. John and Louisa encountered young churches that resembled the church in the book of Acts. Young churches led by unlikely leaders. If they can do it, why shouldn't we? So they set about planting a vibrant church in their home town. Within three years, more than 10% of the population attended the church—statistics that are unheard of in Australia.

John's dream used to be to make enough money to live a comfortable life. Then he discovered that God had greater plans. God gave him ideas about expanding the business, of new business opportunities. Still leading the church with Louisa, John has grown the trucking business into a dynamic shipping and transportation solution company that is many times larger than before.

Jossy recently met with Abhik, an Empart church planter who has started 47 churches in places where there has never been a church. Abhik has raised up 24 full-time leaders to oversee these churches and started a school with over 300 children—all in just 7 years! This leader seemed all the more unlikely when Jossy learned that he is illiterate. How can someone who can't read and write become a leader of leaders?

Be inspired and challenged as you read these and other stories. Engage with their lives and imbibe powerful principles that are producing this leadership revolution.

READY TO TAKE THE NEXT STEPS TOWARD
BECOMING A WORLD-CHANGER
THROUGH EMPART?

VISIT WWW.EMPART.ORG TODAY:

- Find out more about how you can transform communities in Asia
- Get regular updates from Jossy
- Order copies of *Madness!* for friends & family

- Partner with national Church Planters
- Invite an Empart speaker to speak at your church or event
- Make a one-time or monthly donation to see more lives transformed

Modeled after Jesus' ministry, Empart's vision is to reach the unreached—physically and spiritually—by impacting men, women and children through vocational training, children's homes, schools, spiritual equipping and caste reconciliation. In order to reach the unreached, we are restoring, releasing and resourcing indigenous leaders to fulfill the Great Commission through partnership with the global body of Christ. With a successful track record already, Empart's goal is train 35,000 leaders to reach the unreached people groups in Asia by 2030.

THIS IS ACHIEVED THROUGH:

Abolishing Spiritual Poverty \\ Evangelism, Church Planting, Biblical Training and Leadership Development

Defending Dignity \\ Homes for children, elderly, widows and the mentally ill

Transforming Communities \\ Deep-water wells, constructing toilets, health education and medical work, vocational skill training, aid and relief

YOU can get involved with Empart in reaching unreached people too through prayer, giving and participating in a partner development tour to Asia. By partnering with Empart, YOU will help us change Northern India one unreached people group at a time.

Empart USA
empartusa.org
info@empartusa.org
(888) 863-6727

HOW EMPART WORKS

Transformation Centers //
25 men or 25 women live with a pastor's family for a year and learn biblical and practical skills, along with character development

Church Planting //
Transformation Center graduates are equipped to plant churches throughout their regions

Meeting Needs //
The local churches are enabled to meet the social and spiritual needs of the communities through schools for children, hostels for orphans, homes for widows and mentally ill, and vocational training

100,000
CHURCHES

&

35,000
LEADERS

BY 2030

EMPART ENDORSEMENTS

"Empart has a clear strategy and a history of meeting ministry goals. Founder Jossy Chacko has structured the organization to maintain accountability at the local level without creating a hierarchical institution… Empart has many more strengths than weaknesses. Their accountability structure, policies to prevent financial dependency, commitment to training indigenous leaders to reach their own people and track record of continuous improvement make Empart one of the top-performing ministries in North India."
– Excellence in Giving – www.excellenceingiving.com

"I have traveled to India a number of times over the last 25 years to do field audits for organizations… so I am familiar with many of the accounting and reporting issues they face.

Based on … the review of Field finances I believe that Empart has developed adequate processes and procedures to account for the funds that they receive in India, to provide adequate controls over the funds they expend for ministry and to report on the results of the ministry each year."
– C.E. Crouse, Co-Founder Capin Crouse – www.capincrouse.com

EMPART'S TRANSFORMATION CYCLE

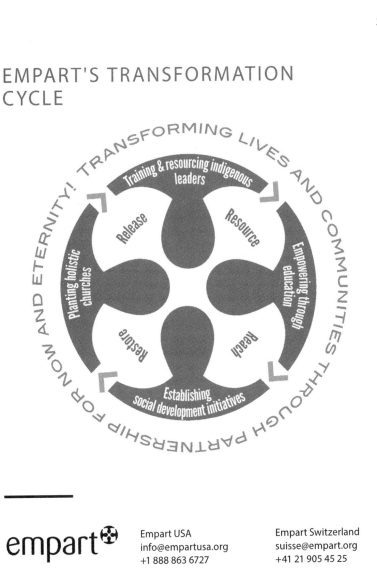

Empart USA
info@empartusa.org
+1 888 863 6727

Empart Australia
info@empart.org
+61 3 9723 9989

Empart Canada
canada@empart.org
+1 416 487 1051

Empart UK
uk@empart.org
+44 78 49 44 678

Empart Switzerland
suisse@empart.org
+41 21 905 45 25

Empart Germany
deutschland@empart.org
+49 421 37 83 083

Empart France
france@empart.org
+33 685 208 288